HLK

Mr Unbelievable

Chris Kamara

Fighting Like Beavers on the Front Line of Football

Mr Unbelievable!

HarperSport

An Imprint of HarperCollins*Publishers*

First published in 2010 by
HarperSport
an imprint of HarperCollins*Publishers*
77–85 Fulham Palace Road,
Hammersmith, London W6 8JB

www.harpercollins.co.uk

1 3 5 7 9 10 8 6 4 2

A catalogue record of this book is
available from the British Library

ISBN 978-0-00-736058-1

Printed and bound in Great Britain by
Clays Ltd, St Ives plc

Mixed Sources
Product group from well-managed
forests and other controlled sources
www.fsc.org Cert no. SW-COC-001806
© 1996 Forest Stewardship Council

FSC is a non-profit international organisation established to promote the
responsible management of the world's forests. Products carrying the FSC
label are independently certified to assure consumers that they come
from forests that are managed to meet the social, economic and
ecological needs of present or future generations.

Find out more about HarperCollins and the environment at
www.harpercollins.co.uk/green

This book is dedicated to the memory of
my parents Irene and Albert

Contents

SECOND HALF

Acknowledgements

When Colin Young and I conjured up the idea of my autobiography way back in 2005, I knew I had a host of stories to tell. As my TV and media career extended it became more and more difficult to choose which tales should be included and which should be left out. I will leave it to you the reader to decide if I made the right choices. My apologies to those people involved in stories I have left out, and maybe to those who have been included too!

The final work would not have appeared at all but for a small army of people who have in some way or another supported me throughout my life and my career, from a very young man to the old fogey I am today.

So ... to my wife Anne, a thousand more grovels than usual for helping me put my life stories together, and immeasurable praise for standing by me throughout the years. My two sons, Ben and Jack, make life worth living every day and have been my inspiration to work as hard as I can for the future of our family. So much appreciation goes to lifelong pals and supporters of my career over the years, which includes many people but particularly Peter Conley, Bernie Wilkinson, Steve Gibson and Mike Jeans. And to my in-laws Roy and Sylv, for tirelessly tuning in to my TV appearances and keeping the newspaper cuttings for the scrapbook.

A big thanks to my colleagues and bosses at Sky. Without the patience and support of Vic Wakeling, Andy Melvin, Barney Francis and co I would not be working for Sky.

So many people have contributed to the path my life has taken, and also to bringing this book to fruition. I am not always easy to work with as Colin, during his many months of piecing my tales together, will know, and as Matt Allen, in the final stages of this book, was to discover. Massive thanks to them both – we got there in the end!

A special mention must go to good friend Richard Digance for his help and wit, and for allowing me to run by him the many drafts of this book for his approval.

And finally, thanks to you for reading my life story so far – I hope you enjoy reading about it as much as I have enjoyed taking part.

A Note to Reader

Like an afternoon in front of *Soccer Saturday*, *Mr Unbelievable* is a game of two halves, complete with some big-match punditry from your host Jeff Stelling and plenty of shouting, giggling and nonsensical babbling from your author. Get the kettle on, put your feet up and watch the fun kick off. Enjoy the show ...

Kammy
A Premiership touchline near you, 2010

Team Sheet

MR UNBELIEVABLE!
**TIME: MONDAY NIGHT, KICK-OFF 8.00 P.M.
WHERE: FRATTON PARK, VALLEY PARADE,
ELLAND ROAD, WEMBLEY AND MANY, MANY
MORE ...**

HEROES

Kammy ...	Himself
Anne ...	Mrs Kammy
Ben, Jack ...	The Kammettes
Albert Kamara ...	Dad
Irene Kamara ...	Mam
George ...	Brother
Maria ...	Sister
Jeff Stelling ...	Mr *Soccer Saturday*
Le Tiss, Thommo, Merse, etc. ...	The *Soccer Saturday* panel
Johnny Giles, Eric McMordie ...	Boyhood heroes

Team Sheet

Sir Alex Ferguson ...   The Best
Vic Wakeling ...   Sky impresario
Steve Gibson ...   Boro chairman, schoolpal
Harry Redknapp ...   Top, top bloke
José Mourinho ...   The Special One
Sven-Goran Eriksson ...   Dinner date

SUPPORTING CAST

Howard Wilkinson ...   Visionary
Ian St John, Frank Burrows ...   Pompey managers
Stan Bowles ...   Gambler
Terry Hurlock ...   Hard man
Vinnie Jones ...   Actor
Gordon Strachan,   Leeds team-mates
    Lee Chapman, etc. ...

Danny Williams,   Swindon managers
    Bobby Smith, etc. ...

Lou Macari ...   Disciplinarian
Frank McLintock ...   Brentford manager
Gazza ...   Genius
Mick Mills ...   Stoke manager
Alan Ball ...   World Cup winner
Neil Warnock ...   Loose cannon
Papa Bouba Diop ...   The Man Mountain

VILLAINS

Jim Melrose ...	Opponent
Bobby McGuiness ...	Dodgy car salesman
Geoffrey Richmond ...	Bradford City chairman
John Hollins's backside ...	Goal thief, Arsenal
Radley Smith ...	Brain surgeon
Frank McAvennie ...	Injured playboy
Referees ...	Know-alls
Stephen Bywater ...	Pottymouth

Foreword

THE BIG-MATCH BUILD-UP

With your host, Jeff Stelling

Good morning/afternoon/evening (delete as applicable), dear reader, and welcome to your copy of *Mr Unbelievable*, one of the most anticipated literary fixtures of the season. Well, at least in the Royal Bank of Kammy, where shares have taken a slight tumble following collapses in the *Soccer Saturday* accumulator. According to our very own financial analyst (Paul Merson), Kammy has clocked up more negative numbers than a Manchester City financial report. Your shrewd investment will keep his *Goals on Sunday* shirts bright and pristine for the forthcoming season. You should feel very proud.

It's also money well spent, because *Mr Unbelievable* delivers far more than your average ex-footballer's autobiography. I've noticed that this work doesn't pull any punches when discussing former team-mates, managers and *Soccer Saturday* panellists.

Mr Unbelievable

Anyway, I'm honoured to be introducing such a literary masterpiece. As the suave, granny-magnet host of *Countdown*, I think I'm amply qualified for the task, but I have been pondering on how best to whet your appetites for the chapters ahead. Chances are you're already familiar with Kammy's role on *Soccer Saturday*, so I'll avoid detailing his greatest moments or blunders. The author does this very ably himself, somewhere around the front of the book.

You're probably also familiar with Kammy's day job. It won't come as a surprise to you that in Sky's lengthy contract, the details of his role include giggling like a schoolgirl, mispronouncing the names of Europe's football elite and shouting 'Unbelievable!' into my earpiece at Glastonbury Festival volumes. All of this is covered, too. Instead, I'll list five amazing, incredible and tantalising facts about his playing career which should prepare you for the excitement ahead.

1/ UNBELIEVABLE!

Kammy's had more death threats than George W. Bush. And not from viewers of *Soccer Saturday*. As one of the few black players in English football during the 1970s and early 1980s, Kammy was a target for racist organisations such as the National Front. He came through this horrible affair unscathed.

2/ UNBELIEVABLE!

He's played at Wembley. For a real football team. No kidding.

3/ UNBELIEVABLE!
He's managed a club to Wembley glory, too. I won't tell you which one. Giving it away would be like revealing the end of a J.K. Rowling novel, though some of you should know already.

4/ UNBELIEVABLE!
Eric Cantona was his replacement at Leeds. Seriously, I'm not drunk. Though Eric was hardly filling the boots of Cristiano Ronaldo, it has to be said.

5/ UNBELIEVABLE!
He played for England. Once. But not in the way that you'd think.

So with these tantalising nuggets delivered, it's time for you to enjoy the rest of the show. It's quite a performance. Just don't believe any of the scurrilous gossip featuring yours truly. I can assure you it's all lies.

Jeff Stelling
Winchester Service Station (northbound), 2010

Dictionary Corner

UNBELIEVABLE!

COLLINS DICTIONARY DEFINITION: Unbelievable *adj*
unable to be believed; incredible. **Unbelievability** *n*.
Unbelievably *adv*. **Unbeliever** *n* a person who does not
believe, esp. in religious matters.

UNBELIEVABLE!

SOCCER SATURDAY DEFINITION: Unbelievable *adj*
incredible; (loosely) Magic! 'Worldy!' (world class) Top
drawer! Out of this world! **Unbelievably** *adv*. **Unbeliever** *n* a
person who does not believe in the goal, tackle, fluffed pen
or refereeing decision that has taken place in front of his
very eyes; a habitually incredulous person; Kammy.

THE FIRST HALF

CHAPTER ONE
GROUND-HOPPING WITH KAMMY PT 1
(ON THE ROAD WITH *SOCCER SATURDAY*)

To the untrained eye of your girlfriend or granny, *Soccer Saturday* looks like a nuthouse in action. If you haven't seen it, here's the basic idea behind the show: four ex-professional footballers of varying repute – Phil Thompson (Liverpool fan club), Paul Merson (reformed gambler), Matt Le Tissier (saint) and Charlie Nicholas (playboy) – sit at a *News at Ten* style desk every Saturday afternoon and each watches one of four Premiership games on a row of tellies positioned in front them.

Over the course of 90 minutes, their job is to explain the action as it happens, usually through a series of shouts, groans and girly squeals. Meanwhile anchorman Jeff Stelling (or 'Stelling, Jeff Stelling', as he introduces himself to members of the opposite sex) delivers the news of every goal, booking and red card around the country via a vidiprinter that runs at the bottom of the screen. Even to the well-trained eye, *Soccer Saturday* looks like a loony bin.

My role in all of this is to act as a roving reporter. Every weekend, I'll be sent to some far-flung corner of the country to report on a game from a TV gantry, whatever the weather. It's a risky business. One day I'm standing in front of thousands of Pompey fans at Fratton Park in the pouring rain, the next I'm dangling under the roof at White Hart Lane. I bloody love it.

There are a lot of perks to being an intrepid touchline reporter with *Soccer Saturday*. For starters, I stay in some of the best hotels around the country and can eat as many motorway service station sarnies as I want. I also get a complimentary Sky Sports coat, which makes me look far more important than I am. When it comes to a Saturday afternoon, I watch some of the best footballers in the world strut their stuff, for free.

The biggest bonus as far as I'm concerned is that I've got the freedom of most of the stadiums in the Premiership. I can pop into the manager's office at White Hart Lane or wander into the dressing-rooms at Sunderland without any hassle. I've sat in the stands with Arsène Wenger at the Emirates and made reports from the dugouts at Craven Cottage. I've even had a heated discussion with Gérard Houllier on the touchline at Anfield, though I always draw the line at taking liberties at Old Trafford. The thought of getting a Sir Fergie 'hairdryer' scares me, although I have to say I get on well with him these days.

Generally, I get a greater access to the inner workings of a football club than most other football reporters would because people know me from the telly. If I'm at Goodison Park or Stamford Bridge, I rarely have to flash a pass and I can sometimes have a free run of the stadium, which is a bit like getting the keys to Disneyland. It also helps that I've built up a level of trust among the boys in the game. Most managers know that I won't take the mickey too much when I'm wandering around their ground with the cameras. Often they will tell me things over a cuppa that they wouldn't tell another reporter (but only if we're off air). They know I'm a football person and I'm not going to blab my mouth off for the viewers. Well, not all of the time.

Most of the Premier League managers and Football League managers look after me when I'm on the road. Harry Redknapp at Spurs is as good as gold. I'll visit him before a game when I'm reporting at White Hart Lane and we'll have a chinwag, usually about football and horses. We'll watch the early kick-off together, then around ten to three he'll kick me out: 'All right, Kammy, off you pop, I've got a spot of work to do.'

Most of the gaffers will invite me in for a drink with them after the game. Sam Allardyce is good for a beer in his office. Alex McLeish at Birmingham, Steve Bruce at Sunderland and another old-school manager, Roy Hodgson, will always tell me to come into their offices for a bevy. I used to have a small shot of brandy with my old mate Gary Megson when he was in charge at Bolton. Once or twice it was *before* the match. Who can blame him? The abuse some of the fans were chucking his way at that time was unreal. They didn't like the way Bolton were playing and would boo him, whatever the result. And I just needed it (hic!).

As a former manager myself, I know when I'm not wanted. If a mate's team has lost or even drawn, I'll always stay away from the office, unless I'm invited in. Losing is bad enough for a player, but I know from experience that losing as a gaffer is much, much worse. You feel a real pressure on your shoulders and Big Sam or Brucey wouldn't want me sitting at their desk, taking the mickey with a complimentary bottle of lager, especially if they had been hammered at home.

I always used to love seeing Bobby Robson whenever I travelled around the North-east, because he was such a great man. He was always hospitable at Newcastle and he would talk your ears off about this player or that player. Sometimes he wanted to chat about a game he had watched on the telly, and it was always a joy because he was so knowledgeable. It was hard to see him as he fought cancer at the end of his life and he was being pushed around in a wheelchair. Bobby wasn't the same person and it was heartbreaking.

It won't come as a great shock to learn that I still feel intimidated when I bump into Sir Alex Ferguson. He has an attitude which makes you feel like you're imposing on his time, wherever you are, but the little insights you get from him in interviews are always fascinating. In general, the managers from the likes of Arsenal, Liverpool and Chelsea have kept me at arm's length, so far. I'll always talk to Arsène Wenger when I'm at the Emirates, but I don't go into his office, and Rafa Benitez has never invited me into the famous Liverpool boot room either.

The exception to that rule was José Mourinho. He was great with me when he was in charge at Chelsea. Well, he was for a while. It eventually turned sour with Sky and The Special One after an incident involving Chelsea midfielder Michael Essien, but we'll come to that in a moment. We first met before a Carling Cup tie at Fulham and seemed to hit it off.

'I like you very much,' he said, shaking my hand. 'I like listening to you and Andy Gray. You educate the public on the game.'

It was really uplifting hearing it from a football man like him. I could hardly get the headphones on my swelling bonce afterwards. We struck up a great friendship immediately and he always made me feel at home whenever I visited Stamford Bridge. José loved *Soccer AM* and its silly humour and I remember we really took the mickey on the show while he was serving a European touchline ban after an ugly bust-up with referee Anders Frisk.

It happened during a Champions League game with Barcelona in 2005-06. José had been unhappy with the way the game had been handled and made some derogatory comments about Frisk. UEFA were not happy and banned José from the touchline for two games. They even called him an 'enemy of football'. The punishment also prevented him from having any contact with his players once they had arrived at the ground, which meant he effectively had to stay away from the game completely.

That didn't stop José from influencing the match. On the evening of Chelsea's next Champions League fixture, he sat at home (well, that's what we were told). On the bench, his coaching staff were wearing woolly hats; it was cold, but not that cold. I watched the game on the telly and noticed that Steve Clarke, José's assistant, was continually touching his ear and relaying information to the players immediately afterwards. I put two and two together and came up with a scam in which José was keeping touch with his staff via high-tech headsets. I wasn't the only one with the same theory. It was also just the sort of clever stunt that José would pull. He denied the rumours when they were floated in the press the next day, but it looked so obvious. It was even suggested that José had been smuggled into the ground in a skip, to get as close to the action as possible, without being visible to UEFA. Nothing was actually proven and the club have never admitted it.

By luck I was at Chelsea the following weekend with *Soccer AM*, the Saturday-morning show then presented by Tim Lovejoy and Helen Chamberlain. José had given us permission to use the dressing-rooms for filming, as he always did, but I had a surprise up my sleeve. Chelsea's kit man, Billy Blood, had given me an official woolly hat. I went into the home dugout to film a report, and the hat was pulled over my head but a mobile phone was stuck to the fabric with Sellotape, mimicking the antics from the week before. When our cameras went live, I could hardly stop laughing as I did an impression of Chelsea's backroom staff that night. I heard José took it in good spirits, too.

Sadly, our relationship changed when Sky's use of the action replay annoyed José. It happened during a Champions League game between Chelsea and Liverpool when Michael Essien clashed with Liverpool's Dietmar Hamann at Stamford Bridge. It was an ugly tackle and it was shown over and over again on *Sky Sports News*. Once it was out there, UEFA had to act, and Essien was banned retrospectively. Because it was the

Champions League, the incident was televised on different stations around the planet, but for some reason José personally blamed Sky for Essien's suspension. He cooled noticeably whenever our cameras were on him and his attitude towards me changed. He wasn't as friendly or welcoming as he had been in the past.

He was entitled to do whatever he wanted, of course, but the truth is, I was disappointed. José was a breath of fresh air when he first arrived from Porto and he was a joy to work with. I'll be honest, I thought the sun shone out of his backside. The Michael Essien incident put a big, grey cloud in the way, which was a real shame.

⚽ ⚽ ⚽ ⚽ ⚽ ⚽ ⚽ ⚽

A less imposing character was the former referee Paul Alcock. If that name rings bells it's because he was the Premiership ref who was infamously pushed over by the former Sheffield Wednesday and West Ham hothead (and brilliant striker, it has to be said), Paolo Di Canio. It was a fiery situation. Paolo had been sent off during a game between Wednesday and Arsenal and he reacted to the red card by pushing the ref over. Alcock had barely been touched, but judging by his tumble, you'd have thought he'd been thumped by Mike Tyson. The fall was so exaggerated it was hilarious.

Our paths crossed for the first time several years later when Alcock was the referee's assessor for an FA Cup tie between Southend and non-league Canvey Island. I was there as co-commentator for Sky Sports. It should have been a fairly run-of-the-mill evening, but trouble started as we waited for the teams to come out for the warm-up. I had spotted Alcock chatting to my colleague commentator Martin Tyler in the tunnel. When they'd finished I couldn't help myself and I gave Alcock a little playful shove. I thought it was really funny, but he was stunned. He lost it.

'You are a joke!' he screamed, in a funny high-pitched squeal. 'A chuffing disgrace' (only he didn't say 'chuffing').

Alcock then turned to John Smart, Sky's senior floor manager (the grey-haired bloke you'll always see at live games, sticking his thumb up on the touchline so the ref knows when to start a match). 'I want him reported because that's out of order,' he shouted, not seeing the funny side. Thankfully, John ignored him and Alcock shuffled off to the referees' room in a right strop. I turned to John, completely confused by the reaction.

'What the hell was all that about?' I asked. Before I could get an answer, the door to the referees' room reopened. A red-faced Alcock emerged and kicked off again.

'Four years ago that happened and I have been getting it in the neck ever since,' he yelled, clearly upset.

I raised my hands in apology. 'Paul, if it upset you, I'm sorry.'

'Apology accepted,' he said, sulking off to his room.

I couldn't believe it. If anything, Alcock should have been dining out on the Di Canio incident. I obviously touched a raw nerve that night, but I'll say one thing, he did well to stand on his feet in the Canvey tunnel because it was a fair push I gave him. Far harder than the one Di Canio dished out.

Paul Alcock wasn't the only person I annoyed that night. Stan Collymore was also in the ground because he was hoping to make a comeback as a player-manager at Southend. Stan had played for Villa and Liverpool and was one hell of a striker in his day, but word from Roots Hall suggested a successful return to the game was unlikely. I told Sky Sports the sad news.

'I'm not sure he is going to get the job,' I said. 'And it would be difficult for him to get back to being even half the player he was. Even then he looked bloated and overweight and I don't know what Southend would be letting themselves in for.'

Stan was really annoyed by my analysis. My mobile bleeped shortly afterwards.

'You're out of order about my weight,' read the text. 'Thanks for your support. Stan.'

I sent a reply, telling Stan that I always said it as I saw it and that I hoped there were no hard feelings.

⊕ ⊕ ⊕ ⊕ ⊕ ⊕ ⊕

Gérard Houllier, the Liverpool boss between 1998 and 2004, was somebody I shared a prickly relationship with. It all started during Sheffield United's memorable Worthington Cup run in 2003, when they were eventually tied with Liverpool in the semi-finals. In a lively first leg at Bramall Lane there was a spicy touchline spat with United gaffer Neil Warnock – a self-confessed trouble-starter – and Liverpool's assistant manager (and *Soccer Saturday* panellist) Phil Thompson. Somehow, I got caught in the crossfire.

A row between those two was always on the cards. Neil is the first to admit that he thrives in an argument. Thommo, meanwhile, is a one-man office of the Liverpool Supporters' Association (Sky Sports wing). Opposition fans used to sing 'Sit down, Pinnochio' whenever he raced out of the dugout, (a) because he liked to moan and (b) because he has a massive hooter.

My problems started when Gérard had given the details of the Liverpool line-up to Sky Sports commentator Ian Crocker in the build-up to the game. As I was the co-commentator for the game, Ian passed it on to me about four hours before the kick-off. This is common practice for companies who have the broadcasting rights for live matches. It's also helpful inside information. It gives the commentators and support staff some time to prepare themselves on the players and tactics for the match. Importantly, there is also an agreement that this is confidential information which should never be revealed to the opposition manager.

When I saw Gérard by the side of the pitch before kick-off, I asked if I could go through Liverpool's formation with him. He was as good as gold and willingly went through the team in detail. This is something I attempt to do with all the managers before a game. I want to be familiar with their systems, formations and teams. I don't pretend to be a smart Alec. I would rather know exactly what a manager is thinking before the match. It also allows me to analyse any tactical changes as the game unfolds.

Despite Liverpool being the better team that night, two late goals from Michael Tonge meant Sheffield United took the home leg 2–1. Just before the final whistle Gérard and Thommo had a massive touchline bust-up with Warnock. It was all handbags stuff. Something must have been said, but it soured the mood between the two camps.

At the time, I remember, results weren't good at Anfield. Gérard was being criticised for the team's performance and the media were raising eyebrows at his work in the transfer market. It didn't help that *Soccer Saturday* decided to put the boot in. The following weekend, the show ran an analytical piece on Liverpool, which basically asked the question, 'Where are Liverpool going wrong?'

During the inquest, Gérard Houllier's unsuccessful signings were listed on the screen (complete with transfer fees), and several angry fans were interviewed outside Anfield. To make matters worse, the programme was then watched by the Liverpool players and coaching staff as they ate their lunch before their evening game with Southampton.

Gérard was furious, but it was to get worse. I was then shown presenting Neil Warnock with the Scottish Mutual Performance of the Week Award in the United dressing-room immediately after the first-leg Worthington Cup win over Liverpool. The award was for their away win against Championship league leaders Portsmouth the week before. As the players celebrated their result over Liverpool, Neil and I were having a good laugh in front of the cameras. I was just doing my job and never considered for one minute this piece would cause me problems with anyone.

Gérard and Thommo didn't see the funny side. They were still smarting from the *Soccer Saturday* criticism, especially Thommo, who had previously been a panellist and took the analysis very personally. He didn't talk to Jeff for a while afterwards. They made up when he was invited back on to the show a year or so later, but at that point the Liverpool staff naturally put me and Neil Warnock together as mates.

Before the second leg at Anfield, Gérard refused to give details of the Liverpool team to Sky, and I heard I was getting the blame. Although I was advised against it, I went to look for him. I knew I'd find him by the side of the pitch, because that was always his pre-match ritual at Anfield. When I caught up with him I asked him what the problem was.

'You are very friendly with Warnock,' he said. 'You will tell him my team line-up.'

Bearing in mind Neil Warnock was going to get the team shortly anyway (they have to be in one hour before kick-off, and this was 90 minutes before), I couldn't really see the problem. Clearly he did.

'I am very friendly with a lot of managers, Gérard,' I said. 'But that doesn't mean I'll go running to them with team news or bits of gossip. I'm employed by Sky, not Sheffield United. If I got the sack from Sky tomorrow do you really think Neil Warnock would give me a job just because I've given him your line-up and formation?'

He mulled it over for a bit. 'I didn't think about it like that,' he said. He backed down and named his team for me, but it was a lesson. It emphasised how my role could be misinterpreted, or how my friendliness towards certain managers might be misconstrued. Without question, Gérard had overreacted. I was merely an innocent victim in the war of words between the two managers.

The good thing was that after winning the second leg and seeing off Sheffield United to reach the Worthington Cup final,

Gérard invited me into the Anfield boot room, where I sat with him, Thommo and Sammy Lee. We had a drink and a laugh. As far as he was concerned the whole thing was forgotten. If only Paul Alcock could have been as forgiving.

UNBELIEVABLE, JEFF!

Three weeks after my disagreement with Gérard Houllier, Neil Warnock actually did offer me a job – he asked me to become part of the Bramall Lane coaching staff. Sheffield United were still in the FA Cup and on course for the play-off final. He thought my experience would be a valuable addition. After careful consideration and a visit to the bigwigs at Sky, I turned it down. I knew I could do the coaching job part time, but it meant I would have to give up commentating on the Championship games. I had to be impartial at Sky and that would have been impossible if I was working for Sheffield United. A missed opportunity? Maybe, but thank goodness Gérard Houllier hadn't got wind of the job opportunity on offer. He really would have thought there was a conspiracy going on.

CHAPTER TWO

'HE COULDN'T HIT A BARN DOOR WITH A BANJO!'

PORTSMOUTH 7 READING 4
FRATTON PARK, 29 SEPTEMBER 2007

When people ask me just how exciting it can get when I commentate on *Soccer Saturday*, I'll tell them about the cracker between Pompey and Steve Coppell's Reading in 2007. Harry Redknapp was in charge at Fratton Park and had built quite an entertaining team. Meanwhile, Coppell's side played some tidy football, but nobody predicted the game was going to give us 11 goals.

Looking back, there probably could have been a goal with every attack. To watch it from the sidelines was great. To report on it was even better. I was screaming at producer Carly Bassett (daughter of the legendary manager Dave 'Harry' Bassett) in the studio, desperately trying to get back on air because so much was happening. The way the game was going, I could have talked for half the programme. It was the match I'd always dreamt of getting as a reporter.

'He Couldn't Hit a Barn Door with a Banjo!'

It's rare that I watch myself on the telly after a day on *Soccer Saturday*, but when my sons told me that the Sky reports - complete with me screaming into a microphone - were getting a lot of hits online at YouTube, I had to take a peek. It was weird to watch and I felt like a bit of a wally, in fact it made me side with those who reckon I can look a gibbering wreck at times, but if it has made for great TV viewing - unless you are a Reading fan, of course - then that's fine by me.

There was more action to come when Reading got stuffed by Spurs 6-3 later on that season. I was there to cover that for *Soccer Saturday* as well, and by that time I reckon Steve Coppell must have had me marked as a curse. But for those of you not from the Madejski Stadium, here's a re-run of the afternoon's action from Portsmouth, which you will find most entertaining, unless you are a Reading fan of course - then skip to the next page.

THE *SOCCER SATURDAY* TICKER TAPE ...

GOAL! 1-0
JEFF: 'Goal at Portsmouth, which way has it gone? Chris Kamara ...'

KAMMY: 'He couldn't hit the proverbial barn door last season, he didn't know where the goals were, but he certainly knows where they are now. It's Benjani for Portsmouth. It was so, so simple. Utaka took the ball down the left-hand side, looked up and saw Benjani in the middle and just put it on a plate for him inside the six-yard box. One-nil to Portsmouth.'

JEFF: 'I almost bought that when I was down in Portsmouth last season. Saw it advertised. One barn door, barely used.'

GOAL! 2-0

KAMMY: 'Unbelievable stuff here, Jeff, I'm telling you. I told you already last season, from a yard out, he couldn't hit a barn door with a banjo. Now he is absolutely on fire. He just picked up the ball in midfield, he ran past Shorey, he ran past Ingimarsson, he shifted the ball to the side of his right foot [I gave a drop of the shoulders for the benefit of the viewers at home] and then, bang! Away from Marcus Hahnemann, into the bottom corner. What an absolute beauty. Two-nil.'

GOAL! 2-1

KAMMY: 'It's amazing, Jeff. They've scored. They've scored! It's amazing really because it's their first decent attack. The assistant referee on this far side has given the goal. He is certain that the ball from Rosenior crossed the line. I am not as certain as he is. I'll have to see it again in the morning. Certainly Kitson and Hunt were trying to claim it and the assistant flagged when Rosenior shot. Two-one.'

GOAL! 2-2

KAMMY: 'That goal has given Reading renewed vigour. They have come out in the second half and they are a different team totally. But David James, hang your head in shame. What are you doing? He has come chasing out his box for a ball that's virtually in the right-back position, Jeff, and he doesn't get there. Kitson does, James leaves the goal gaping and Kitson has enough quality in that left foot of his to ping it and guide it into the bottom corner of the net. Two-two.'

GOAL! 3-2
JEFF: 'Fratton Park is not a place for people of a nervous disposition. Chris Kamara ...'

KAMMY: 'Jeff, unbelievable. I have to say, what a game this is. Magnificent. But who'd be a goalkeeper? Sylvain Distin goes down the left-hand side, crosses the ball into the box, Marcus Hahnemann comes out like Superman – only difference is, Superman gets the job done. Marcus Hahnemann doesn't get the job done [cue: laughter in the studio]. Hermann Hreidarsson gets to the ball before him and the net is gaping. It's in the back of the net off the top of his head. Three-two.'

MISSED PENALTY!
JEFF: 'Penalty at Fratton Park. Chris Kamara!'

KAMMY: 'Yeah! Thanks for coming to ... I've been screaming at you for five minutes. Papa Bouba Diop [the penalty kick is taken behind me. Pompey keeper David James saves] ... he's given away a penalty, Nick Shorey has just taken it and what a save from David James. He's made up for his error, he's dived to the left-hand side, he's grasped the ball, it's bounced off his hands after he got hold of it, it squirmed away and there was Hreidarsson to kick it away. Papa Bouba Diop should be going for a bath right now because it was a ridiculous penalty, he just handled the ball for no reason. Still three-two.'

Mr Unbelievable

GOAL! 4-2

JEFF: 'Only one word for it, Chris ...'

KAMMY: 'Well and truly buried the banjo. That's four words, innit? [well, actually, that's six]. Unbelievable, Jeff! One on one with Benjani and he just strolls past Marcus Hahnemann like he does it every week. There's the hat-trick, there's the ball in the bag and there's the game in the bag for Pompey. Four-two.'

GOAL! 5-2

KAMMY: 'They are absolutely running riot, Jeff! Reading have just thrown the towel in [I throw an imaginary towel to my left to emphasise the point. More laughter]. It's Niko Kranjcar. Portsmouth were showboating down the right, the cross came in from Sean Davis and Kranjcar had no right to get the ball, but he did. Five-two.'

GOAL! 5-3

KAMMY: 'Incredible. You have to admire their resilience because they have come back. It's James Harper this time with a volley from 16 yards. Bang! David James didn't see it. Five-three.'

GOAL! 6-3

JEFF: 'There has been an ... it is a rugby score now, isn't it? Chris Kamara.'

KAMMY: 'Unbelievable, Jeff. Ha Ha. It's amazing. It's raining goals, as they say. This time it's Sean Davis with a speculative shot from 30 yards which took a slight deflection and sent Marcus Hahnemann the wrong way. What a game. What a game! Six-three.'

PENALTY!
KAMMY: 'Benjani has gone off the pitch, he got a standing ovation. It is Sunny Muntari with the penalty ...'

GOAL! 7-3
KAMMY: 'And they have scored again, Portsmouth. There were five players fighting over the ball, Muntari got it first, Kranjcar was the player brought down. And I have lost the score, Jeff! What is it?'

GOAL! 7-4
JEFF: 'There has been another – I know you're going to find this hard to believe – there has been another goal at Fratton Park. Chris Kamara ...'

KAMMY: 'Jeff. Reading have scored, Nicky Shorey has just plundered one in from about 20 yards. It took a deflection off Sol Campbell. I can't believe it. I honestly can't believe it!'

JEFF: 'Kammy is the only person who hasn't scored. Referee Mark Halsey must have writer's cramp by now. Goodness me. Phew. What a game.'

⚽ ⚽ ⚽ ⚽ ⚽ ⚽ ⚽

Mr Unbelievable

Indeed, what a game it was, one of those rare games that make me realise I should have stopped gaping out of that school window at the football pitches back in Middlesbrough and worked on my maths. Number of goals, not a clue. Number of penalties, not a clue. Number of times he should have hit a barn door with a banjo, not a clue. I own up: adding up isn't my strong point and that game was the proof. As for hitting a barn door with a banjo, perhaps I should have studied a bit harder at English too, but hey, I've got the best job in the world and wouldn't have got a better one if I'd got a degree or two.

CHAPTER THREE

SMILE, YOU'RE ON KAMARACAM ...

I'll admit it, when I was first asked to take on the job as a touchline reporter in 1999, I was sceptical. Following my departure from managing Stoke City I flung myself into the media, working for anyone, anywhere who wanted to hire me. I loved my football and needed to be involved, and radio and TV was a good substitute for being on the touchline. Sky producer Jonty Whitehead invited me to work on a show called *Soccer Extra* with presenter Matt Lorenzo and journalist Brian Woolnough. I also became a regular guest on the Football League live games. I really enjoyed the media work and the lads at the studio seemed to think I was pretty good at it. One of the reporters at the time for *Soccer Saturday* was my good friend Rob McCaffrey, who convinced his producer Ian Condron to get me involved with *Soccer Saturday*.

At the time, the programme was finding its feet in terms of reputation and audience, and it was nothing like the cult phenomenon it is today. They also had a pretty heavyweight crew of pundits. The panel was a *Who's Who* of top-class footballers: George Best was one of the greatest players in the world in his time, Frank McLintock won the double with Arsenal in 1971, Clive Allen scored 49 goals in one season for Spurs in 1987, and Rodney Marsh was a flair player who excited fans of England, QPR and Manchester City. The fact that they had plenty of medals and top-class experience between them meant that they could criticise the best players and teams in the Premiership.

Meanwhile, I'd had a decent playing career, including an international call-up for Sierra Leone – if I remember rightly they reversed the charges – and I had managed Bradford and Stoke. I had a lot of experience for sure, but my medal haul didn't match the other guys. Condo had heard me on other programmes talking about the game and he just told me to go ahead and do more of the same for him. Things went really well. Besty was not just a legend but a really top bloke and Marshy kept you on your toes. I loved the odd Saturdays when I was with them, and I became a permanent fixture on the midweek shows which Jeff Stelling used to present in those days. After six months of me being a studio guest Condo decided he had a different role for me.

'Kammy, I want you to put a camera on you during games,' he said. 'As you know we are not allowed to show the action live from the grounds on a Saturday afternoon for contractual reasons, but we want to film you watching the game with the fans in the background.'

I was unconvinced. 'It won't work,' I told him. 'People are not going to be interested in me watching a game from the stadium.' Besides, I liked my stints in the studio. Working with

Besty and Rodney was a dream come true. Even so, I decided to have a stab at it because it was a new format and nobody had ever tried it before. To my amazement, Sky didn't help me out at all as regards how I should approach this new venture. I was thrown in at the deep end and shoved in front of a camera, which is generally how they operate. It's very sink or swim – if you're good at something, you survive. If you don't, you're out.

I know the Beeb sent Gary Lineker away for media training before he started hosting *Match of the Day*. He returned perfect and polished. There was none of that with me. Instead they just shoved me in front of a camera to see how it worked and, in the beginning, it didn't. In fact, it looked to a lot of people as if we were filming in a garage with a cardboard cut-out of the fans behind us. For some reason we kept getting our angles all wrong. I remember during the 1999–2000 season we did one practice show, but it took well over a month for us to get the look right.

Our first attempt took place at Cambridge, and thankfully it was not live. As I stood on the touchline, I was a nervous wreck. My shakes weren't helped by the fact that I had managed only three hours' sleep the night before because I'd been covering a match between Lazio and Chelsea in the Stadio Olympico for Radio 5 Live with Alan Green and Mike Ingham. I arrived back in London late and had to get up very early to make it to Cambridge. I soon discovered that this was an occupational hazard for a ground-hopping touchline reporter.

By the time I got to the post-match interviews, I was all over the place. My chat with Cambridge manager Roy McFarland was a complete disaster. He kept taking the mickey out of me because I had absolutely no idea what I was doing. 'You don't know what's going on, do you, Kammy?' he kept laughing as I faffed around with my microphone. I really wanted it to work as the recording was going to be shown the following weekend on *Soccer Saturday* and I knew people would all have opinions on how it went. So I ignored the wisecracks and ploughed on.

The following Saturday I sat in front of the TV to watch Jeff and the boys. I was devastated when it got to three o'clock and the piece had not got an airing. I thought, 'That's the end of that, then.' I had told everyone I knew, and a few thousand that I didn't know, that I was going to be on with this new format. I thought my TV career as a roving reporter was over. After a sleepless weekend I rang Condo, and he explained that Jeff and the boys had overrun with all their yakking and my piece would be shown the following week. Even better, it would become a regular fixture in the show.

After our second game I really did think that my Sky career was over for good. Oxford versus Walsall was my first live game. Before kick-off, because I was new to the job and unhappy with the camera angle we were giving back to Sky, I was driving rigger/cameraman Colin McDonald crazy! 'This looks like we are in a garden shed,' I grumbled. I can't tell you what he mumbled back under his breath, but I think he wanted me to go forth and multiply. The crowd just looked a hazy mess behind me. With contact made back to the studio through my new headphones (an essential piece of equipment I am never without!), Condo told me, 'You are going live in 30 seconds.' That was the cue for a rival cameraman to make himself busy. He had arrived late and hurriedly began setting up his own gear, regardless of me, the keen new reporter getting ready for my big moment. He reckoned I had taken his regular spot. 'I've been coming here for 20 years,' he ranted. 'I am here every week.' He was not a happy man and was not going to bow down to anyone that day. But it didn't matter to me – he was late, we were ready to roll and I was staying put. Still, I wasn't expecting him to make an attempt at settling our differences on air! As I went live, he walked across in front of me and the camera, momentarily blacking out the screen for the viewers at home and in the studio. Then, just to make his point, he tried to walk back again, but this time I was ready for him. I put out my left arm to keep him at bay as I spoke to the cameras, but there was clearly a struggle going on. God knows what the viewers at home must have thought. In the studio, Jeff looked pretty surprised, but I put his mind at rest.

'Don't worry, Jeff,' I said through gritted teeth, 'he won't be doing it again', and still holding my adversary at bay I continued with my pre-match report.

When the camera had stopped rolling, the pair of us went toe to toe. We were both braying at each other until Colin pulled us apart. I was furious with him, but moments later I was furious with myself for losing my rag live on air. I was convinced the boys at Sky would be thinking, 'Thanks, Kammy, but no thanks.'

Thankfully, with the help of Tim Lovejoy and Helen Chamberlain on *Soccer AM*, the producers saw the funny side. Tim and Helen showed the clip on their Saturday morning programme and absolutely loved it, laughing their heads off.

Mr Unbelievable

By the second viewing, even I was laughing. By that time, I knew that my job was safe and I was so surprised, it may have been the first time I used the term 'Unbelievable!'

⚽ ⚽ ⚽ ⚽ ⚽ ⚽ ⚽ ⚽

In those early days, in order to get things right for Kamaracam, myself and Colin the cameraman would often go to the stadiums a day early. We'd scope out the best places to stand and get the background shot just right. At first, I think that a lot of the people who watched the programme back then really believed it was all just a gimmick and we were producing the show in a studio with a blue screen behind us on which we then played crowd images. To shut them up we included more crowd scenes. Occasionally we'd even encourage the fans to jump up and down, just to prove we were really there.

It was important for me to work on my delivery too. My mate Rob McCaffrey – who would later go on to be my co-presenter on *Goals on Sunday* – spotted the Oxford United incident and called me shortly afterwards. He had found the whole thing hilarious, but said, 'That wasn't the Kammy I know, you are coming across like a TV news reporter on location. It was as if you were trying to be like Kate Adie, on the front line in the Falklands.'

He went on to explain that I should be myself in front of the cameras. He knew I could be a very excitable character and he reckoned I should make the most of it, no matter how much of a wally I looked. It was the best advice anyone had given me.

Smile, You're on Kamaracam ...

These days, I act as naturally as I can. It seems to be popular with quite a few people.

Sometimes it can be tough work, because for every four-all thriller, there can be a crap, goalless draw. Generally, though, there's always something to get excited about, whether it's a goal-line clearance, a controversial penalty decision or even a sending-off. I'll try to inject as much enthusiasm as I can into each incident, because I think that's what *Soccer Saturday* fans expect of me. They don't want me to be negative – they can get that from the guys on the other channel! It also comes naturally because I'm genuinely buzzing to be watching football for a living. I act like a fan when I'm reporting on any game of football: I'm so excited, and I just can't hide it. Hang on, perhaps I should have been a songwriter thinking up words like that!

Sometimes, it's very easy to get lost in the moment. I remember Heurelho Gomes dropped a clanger when Spurs lost to Fulham at Craven Cottage in 2009. The ball bounced in front of him and he flapped with his arms as the ball dropped into the net. It was the easiest catch to make, but Gomes blundered big-time. I patched through to the studio that a major incident had taken place and Jeff lined me up.

JEFF: 'Heurelho Gomes, the Tottenham goalkeeper, has his head in his hands at Craven Cottage. Let's find out why: Chris Kamara ...'

KAMMY: 'Ha, ha! And so he should have, Jeff! He is absolutely shocking. There's a shot from Simon Davies ... well, he could have thrown his cap on it. And it's bounced in front of him and, somehow, it's bounced off his chest and gone into the back of the net. It's laughable. Unless you're a Spurs fan ...'

I felt bad afterwards because I had got carried away. I was laughing my head off at him. It's not intentional, you just lose it when you're commentating. Thankfully, I'm able to say now what a fantastic player he is. A season later he played out of his skin for Spurs at Craven Cottage and kept a clean sheet. I was able to say, 'Look, this is a different fella. He's a class goal-keeper.'

Over the years, the mistakes made on the programme have given TV critics – the likes of Ally Ross in the *Sun* and Ian Hyland in the *News of the World* – plenty of material. I'm as likely as anyone to make a *faux pas*. I'm not precious. I love people taking the mickey out of it because what we do isn't rehearsed. It can't be. Most of it comes straight out, instinctively, and I've always been pretty good at saying it as I see it and retelling the action as accurately as I can.

⚽ ⚽ ⚽ ⚽ ⚽ ⚽ ⚽ ⚽

The official term is Kamaracam. Everyone who goes out on the road now – whether it's Ian Dowie, Scott Minto or John Solako – works under that title. It's even on the production sheet, and it used to confuse people at first. I'd have friends from Everton or Newcastle ringing me before games. They'd say, 'I see you're at our ground today – fancy a beer after?' I'd have to explain to them that I wasn't actually going to be there, it was another presenter working under the term Kamaracam.

I don't really have any preferences on where I do my reports. To be honest I love going to all the grounds. I've always said that you should never judge a book by its cover. In a football match you don't really know what's going to happen. I could be freezing my nuts off in front of Bolton versus Wolves, but then you might get a wonder goal out of the blue that could change the whole complexion of the game and indeed unfreeze my nuts. Stoke versus Wigan could be 5-0, but unpredictability is the beauty of football.

There's no class distinction either, because you're just as likely to get a flat game at Old Trafford or Stamford Bridge as you are at Goodison Park or the Stadium of Light. When it comes to choosing the games, I try to share it around as best I can. People also moan on about how often I go to the grounds of other teams. They say, 'You never come to the Emirates, you must hate Arsenal,' or 'What's your bloody problem with Liverpool? You're never there.' In truth, it all comes down to geography. I have to think about how easy it will be for me to get back to London that night to present *Goals on Sunday* the next day. Some grounds are harder than others – Hull is tricky to get back to London from; getting in and out of Birmingham is always a headache. Until I have a massive win at the Grand National, my private plane – Air Kammy – will remain grounded.

On Saturday mornings I'm up and running from the moment I awake, often with a sore head after a night out with Jeff Stelling and the gang in the hotel bar. The boys – Jeff plus

Charlie Nicholas, Phil Thompson and sometimes Matt Le Tissier – always meet up on Friday for a drink. It's a great night out and an essential part of the show. Jeff will usually hold court over several pints of Hoegaarden (I hear he's angling for a sponsorship deal), while I'll go to the steam room with Charlie Nicholas for a gossip. After that we'll go for a drink, usually into the early hours.

This might sound like a jolly boys' outing to most of you, but the truth is, the hotel bar plays an important role in the success of *Soccer Saturday*. What we talk about that night usually sets the tone of the show the next day. Jeff will go through all the hot football topics that week and gauge everybody's opinions. He'll also pick up rumours and news of what's been going on in the game from us, the stuff the papers might not have reported. I'm still involved on a day-to-day basis with players, agents and managers, as are Thommo and Charlie, so we can pass on plenty of info to Jeff. He would never categorically come out and reveal the gossip we have passed on, but he might float an idea or an opinion as a result of that confidence.

Different presenters have different methods of preparation. Jeff, for example, drives to a motorway service station in Winchester with a bag full of newspaper cuttings, magazines and an info pack from Sky on all the players, goals and stats. He'll memorise as much as he can. For me it's *Sky Sports News* from the moment I am awake. If I'm covering Stoke against Liverpool at the Britannia Stadium my preparation would be to watch the games of both teams from the previous weekend. I'll take a look at the teams and if there are any new faces in the side, I'll ring around and find out a bit more about them. If there's nothing new, then my work is done. I'm not there to deliver stats and facts on the teams, that's down to Jeff.

When Jeff comes to me on air, he wants to hear what's going on in the game, as do the viewers. They want the goals, the drama, the blunders and the controversy. It's no good me yelling, 'Unbelievable, Jeff! This is Everton's sixth win in 10 games! Tim Cahill has just delivered his eighth assist of the season!' The hard stats are Jeff's party piece and he works tirelessly on getting them right all week. I'm not going to tell anyone how to do their job, but some *Soccer Saturday* reporters try to cram their broadcasts with facts and trivia. That's wrong. You have to tell the studio what you're seeing, how both teams are playing and who has scored the goals or who has been booked, rightly or wrongly. In other words: 'Unbelievable, Jeff! Louis Saha couldn't hit a barn door with a banjo! Phil Jagielka is as useful as a fish up a tree today! Marouane Fellaini hasn't trimmed his beautiful haircut for nine weeks! One-nil!' I wouldn't dream of telling the viewers that I had the same hairstyle as Fellani when I was a player. The referees used to blow on my head like a dandelion to check the 90 minutes was up but I'd rather keep that a secret – whoops!

In the words of Roy Walker in *Catchphrase*, 'Just say what you see.'

Mr Unbelievable

From mid-morning, Kamaracam is up and running. I usually get to the ground as early as I can so I can catch up with the team news and have a chat with a few people at the ground, just to get some extra background on the game and what's going on at the club. At around 2.30, climbing into the commentary gantry can sometimes be an uncomfortable business. I remember our position at Portsmouth used to be particularly dangerous, until they eventually moved us. Nobody ever actually got injured, but that was a miracle really.

Once the game gets under way, Carly Bassett will communicate with me. She can see me on camera in the studio, but I can only hear her. The production guys also watch all the games, so as soon as someone scores in my game or an incident of note takes place, they can cut to me shortly after.

As the game progresses, Carly will tell me when I'm due to go live. 'We've got three waiting to come in and you're next.' It's a bit like air-traffic control at Heathrow, but without all the drunk pilots and near misses, though some people would argue that we suffer a lot of those as well. It can be a frustrating business. Sometimes there might be a penalty decision or goal and the studio can't get to me until minutes later. Other times they want me to give a report even though absolutely nothing has happened at all. That's when I have to say, 'Boring game, nothing has happened here.'

Sometimes, though, the action goes on behind me without me even knowing. The most famous instance of this – and I say famous because everyone who missed it on *Soccer Saturday* could watch it on the internet, and plenty have ! – happened when I was commentating on Fulham against

Middlesbrough at Craven Cottage. My monitor shows all the action so I can see in detail what's happening on the pitch when I have to turn my back on it to deliver my report. At one point that day the monitor decided to pack up. Typically this was the moment Fulham chose to score, as you can see from the action replay:

JEFF: 'Is there any way back for Fulham against Middlesbrough, I wonder? Chris Kamara ...'

KAMMY: 'Well they're trying, Jeff. Papa Bouba Diop, the man mountain himself, is playing as a striker and he's got [David] Healy on one side of him and Diamansi Kamara on the other side and ... it's Papa Bouba Diop with a header! AAAAGH! AH! It's a goal! It's a goal, Jeff! Is it David Healy? He's running away ... Andy D'Urso's playing on ... Sorry, my monitor's down again! [Turning around frantically] I'm looking over my shoulder ... What? I don't really know ... the assistant ... Has he given it? [Complete panic flashes across my face] Oh, the assistant hasn't given it, I don't think, Jeff. No! The referee hasn't given it either ... Don't really know what's happening, Jeff. Ha, ha! [cue: laughter from the studio panel] Could be, could be not ... Ha, ha, ha!'

JEFF: 'I tell you what, Kammy, it's not the first time you've not known what's happening, but I can tell you, well, the ball went in from close range, Schwarzer got both hands to it, it's over the line! There's no question the ball is over the line, but the referee has not given it. And Fulham, well, 2-1 behind,

Mr Unbelievable

Middlesbrough still lead, but that ball was a foot and a half over the line before Schwarzer managed to scramble it clear. They're still playing and there's going to be real controversy over that one.'

These little disasters have made the show an unbelievable success. *Soccer Saturday* has definitely revolutionised football coverage – other TV channels have tried to copy it, but they're still nowhere near as good as we are. It's also made a name for all the lads working on the show. Most of them had much greater success and fame during their playing careers than I did, and yet today my popularity as part of the Sky gang never fails to amaze me.

CHAPTER FOUR
KAMMY'S TV TWERP

OK, you've heard of *Harry Hill's TV Burps*, so now let me introduce you to Kammy's TV Twerps.

Over the years as *Soccer Saturday*'s roving reporter extraordinaire, I've made some bloopers and gaffes, usually at the rate of three an hour. Most of these are available for you to laugh at on the internet and, believe me, a lot of football fans have thrown them back at me over the years. But for those of you away from your computer at this moment, here's the transcript of the more calamitous moments. And please excuse my poor use of the English language in these following clips as I do tend on occasions to have trouble with my worms. Anyone who knows me will tell you that I can get very, very excited ... unless you ask my wife, of course – she'll tell you she doesn't remember the last time I got excited, but that's another story, even another three chapters.

These are the clips that change this particular roving reporter extraordinaire to roving reporter extraordinary.

ON ALEX McLEISH
'Alex McLeish has his hands in his head.'

IN THE BUILD-UP TO WIGAN v. WEST HAM
KAMMY: [Smirking] 'I've had a chat with both managers and obviously I can't tell you the teams, but Wigan are unchanged and Lucas Neill plays for West Ham.'

JEFF: [Sighing] 'OK, thanks very much for keeping that to yourself, Chris.'

ON A STRUGGLING NOTTINGHAM FOREST
'It's real end-to-end stuff, but unfortunately, it's all up Forest's end.'

ON AN ALAN SHEARER GOAL
'They've one man to thank for that goal: Alan Shearer. And they've also got to thank referee Alan Wilkie.'

ON JUNIOR LEWIS
'Not only has referee Graham Poll shown Junior Lewis the red card, but he's sent him off!'

ON BURNLEY
'For Burnley to win, they're going to have to score!'

ON CHELSEA 0 SCUNTHORPE 1
JEFF: 'It's not 0-0 at Stamford Bridge, the deadlock broken very early on, but it's Scunthorpe who've scored!'

Kammy's TV Twerp

KAMMY: [High-pitched laughter] 'Jeff, you're not going to believe this, it's incredible ... Can they believe it? I can't believe it! Ha, ha! They're winning one-nil!'

ON FULHAM
JEFF: 'Have Fulham got their just deserts?'

KAMMY: 'They have and they deserve it!'

ON A HUGO RODALLEGA INJURY
'Hugo Rodallega fell over the advertising hoardings as he was running in on goal.'

SOUTHAMPTON v. WEST BROM BUILD-UP
JEFF: 'Is West Brom a good game for them to have today, you know, in the sense that expectations might be slightly less than if they were playing another team who were struggling?'

KAMMY: 'Very much so, George. Oh, sorry ... I've just been speaking to ... er, George Burley, Fred ... I mean Jeff [cue: fits of unstoppable laughter]'

ON CARLOS TEVEZ
'They've got this man with a heart as big as ... as big as ... a plate.'

ON DARIUS VASSELL
'Darius Vassell has had a lot of weight on his shoulders but someone's just taken those shackles off his feet.'

Mr Unbelievable

ON THE BEAUTIFUL GAME

'That's the beauty of football. Sometimes it starts off crap, then it gets a bit better.'

So forgive me, Harry Hill, I don't know which is the biggest gaffe, Carlos Tevez's big heart or Fulham's just deserts. There's only one way to find out … FIGHT! Come on Carlos Tevez …

CHAPTER FIVE

UNBELIEVABLE, JEFF!
(HOW I CAUGHT A CATCHPHRASE)

Every great showman has to have a catchphrase. For some people it's a gimmick to grab the excitement of their audience. I remember that Bruce Forsyth used to open *The Generation Game* with the words, 'Nice to see you, to see you – nice!'; Dale Winton was forever saying 'Bring on the wall!' during Saturday night favourite *Hole in the Wall* (well, I loved it). Other TV entertainers have yelled something to raise a comic reaction. When Frank Spencer fell out of a window and clung on to the back of a double-decker bus (while attached to a pair of roller-skates, usually) the only words he could scream were 'Ooh, Betty!' It always got me giggling.

In truth, I've probably got more in common with Frank Spencer than Brucie. But instead of bus surfing or injuring myself in a calamitous fashion, every Saturday afternoon I watch footballers kicking lumps out of each other. Each goal, booking or Fergie tantrum is greeted by the word 'Unbelievable!', which is then boomed into the homes of millions of *Soccer Saturday* viewers. Often 'Unbelievable!'

arrives attached to the name 'Jeff!' as I relay the action to the show's anchorman and Smurf-in-chief, Jeff Stelling. It's become a bit of a cult phenomenon. For some reason, a lot of people seem to like me shouting into their living-rooms at jet-plane volumes.

When *Soccer Saturday* first started, I had no idea how much I said 'Unbelievable, Jeff!' on the telly. This sounds crazy, I know, because I must have used the adjective at least half a dozen times a weekend. I think I first got wind of my conversational tic (and it is an affliction, just ask Mrs Kammy) around six or seven years ago when the production team at Sky decided to run a Christmas special. This 30-minute programme showed all the gaffes and bloopers from the season. A lot of them were mine. Take a look online – it's all on youtube.com if you don't believe me. If you can't be bothered, here are the highlights:

'This is unbelievable, Jeff!'

'Unbelievable, Jeff!'

'Jeff, unbelievable!'

'Jeff, you're not going to believe this! Unbelievable!'

And so on. The day after the Christmas special, I covered a match between QPR and Manchester City at Loftus Road. Kevin Keegan, then the manager at City, came out of the tunnel as I was preparing to deliver a touchline report. Just as we were about to roll, he crept up behind me and shouted, 'Unbelievable, *Jeff!*' at the top of his voice. At that moment, I knew exactly how Jeff felt whenever I yelled into his ear piece. I also knew my big gob had been running on overdrive. My stock description of a dramatic incident in football as soon as I was linked to the studio was shouting the words 'Unbelievable, Jeff!', and everyone in the English game had known it. Everyone apart from me.

Kevin was laughing his head off. Apparently the whole City squad and coaching staff had seen the funnies that morning. 'It's all you ever say, Kammy,' he said. 'Let's go down to Kammy at Loftus Road [the home of QPR, where we were]. Unbelievable, Jeff ! Unbelievable, Jeff! Unbelievable, Jeff ...!'

I knew then that I had unintentionally created a monster. By all accounts, the boys in the studio had picked up on it months before, but the reason I wasn't conscious of saying 'Unbelievable Jeff !' was that I wasn't thinking about making a catchphrase for myself. I was just acting naturally. If I had deliberately tried to invent a saying, it wouldn't have worked and I would have looked wooden and awkward on air.

⚽ ⚽ ⚽ ⚽ ⚽ ⚽ ⚽

When it comes to *Soccer Saturday* fans, we all attract different 'types'. Jeff usually gets the grannies, mainly because of his work on *Countdown*, but also because he reminds them of a garden gnome and they want to pop him in their window boxes. Former Arsenal star and gambling disaster Paul 'Merse' Merson attracts Gunners fans and masochists looking for a no-hoper tip on the horses. I tend to get the lot – kids, OAPs, stattos and fanatics – because I do three shows on the telly, *Soccer AM, Soccer Saturday* and *Goals on Sunday*. There's never a day when somebody doesn't shout 'Unbelievable, Jeff!' at me. This morning it was the delivery guy with my supermarket goods.

I think the first time I really noticed the attention was when I went to Japan with Jeff and *Soccer Saturday* producer Ian Condron for the 2002 World Cup. From the minute we stepped off the plane, football fans were shouting 'Unbelievable, Jeff!' at us from across the street. Tourists were coming up, asking for photos and autographs. It was so weird. I loved it, but I think Jeff was quite taken aback.

'Bloody hell, Chris, it's like Kammymania out here!' he said. I think he ended up working the camera as a line of fans posed for a picture with me. I think it's fair to say that these days it would be me holding the camera for him – his popularity is immense.

The attention there in Japan was a bit of a pain in the nicest possible way. We were blocking walkways as crowds gathered around us. Traffic came to a standstill. At one point we had to duck down a side street like the Beatles in *A Hard Day's Night* and run for our lives. Or was that the night we jumped out of the taxi without paying? I can't remember, but it was upsetting at the time, because it was almost impossible to get a pint! The English fans were there in force, and so were the Irish. Between them, they had taken over pretty much every bar in the country. We were in double trouble. I signed so many autographs that writer's cramp had set in by the end of the trip and none of us could get to the bar without being recognised.

Unbelievable, Jeff!

It's my own fault. I'll chat to as many people as I can. I always remember a time when I was a kid and I approached Stuart Boam. He was the captain of Middlesbrough during the seventies and when I saw him in the street one day I asked for an autograph. Boam just brushed me aside. He might have been in a hurry, but it really stuck with me. Because of that, I always try to give attention to people if they want a photo or a signature. Besides, most people want to talk to you about their club, which is great because it sometimes gives me the inside track on what the fans think about various issues affecting them and I can use the info for *Soccer Saturday* or *Goals on Sunday*.

You might get one or two idiots who say, 'You hate our club and never say anything nice about us.' I only say what I see: if a club does well, I shout it from the rooftops; if it's not so good, then I say so. Thankfully those people are in the minority, but they're wrong. I don't hate any team. I don't support any particular one either, but they don't seem to take any notice when I tell them that. Leeds fans think I should be more like Jeff when he talks about Hartlepool, because I used to support Leeds as a kid. My old school-mate Steve Gibson, the Middlesbrough chairman, used to think when I was talking about Boro on the TV I was more against them than for them! Yes, they are my home-town club and he is my big pal, but I'm really 100 per cent unbiased. Unlike Matt Le Tissier, who wears Southampton socks under his *Soccer Saturday* desk when he's working.

When we returned from Japan, we were all aware of just how popular *Soccer Saturday* had become. It also dawned on me that my vocabulary was quite limited and I should have made more of my time at St Thomas's School in Middlesbrough. Still, I decided to play up to the 'Unbelievable, Jeff' saying from then on, as did Jeff. On New Year's Day during the 2003–04 season, I remember, I was commentating on the game between Manchester United and Wolves. Of course, I shouted 'Unbelievable, Jeff!' in my report. When the producers flipped back to the studio, Jeff looked into the camera, his face deadpan. 'There you have it,' he said. 'Chris Kamara, the first unbelievable of 2004.'

Each year it has become customary to film a *Soccer Saturday* Christmas Special, which is always light-hearted and great fun to record. A few years ago, we had an athletics challenge in the style of *Superstars*. If you're too young to remember the original, it was a programme made in the 1980s where sportsmen from various fields competed in a mini-Olympics competition. The events included running, swimming and cycling. I remember Kevin Keegan spectacularly left his bike during one heat and injured himself quite badly. Thank God he was wearing a helmet ... or maybe he wasn't – it could have been his hair. I think Bryan Robson had a bash too and came away unscathed: not bad for a bloke who could break his collarbone on *A Question of Sport* with ease.

Our competition was just as chaotic. When I jumped into the swimming pool, I was wearing children's luminous plastic armbands and splashed around pretending to be struggling. A concerned Alan McInally immediately dived in to help me to the side of the pool. Much to the lads' annoyance, when the race started for real I powered forward like Michael Phelps in top form, leaving Rodney Marsh, Charlie Nicholas, Jeff Stelling and Matt Le Tissier in my wake. McInally won the race, but I am sure he jumped the gun!

Much later, for the 2009 special, the programme was a cookery-themed competition called *Making a Meal of it*. We had pinched the format from *Ready, Steady, Cook* – the programme presented by Ainsley Harriot on the Beeb – and the producers threw Alan McInally, Matt Le Tissier, Phil Thompson and me into a fancy kitchen to see who could cook the best festive dish.

On the day we were working with superstar Italian cook Gino D'Acampo, who had recently finished first in *I'm A Celebrity … Get Me Out of Here*. Gino was on hand to taste the dishes as we cooked them. He had just spent two weeks eating rats, bugs and kangaroo's testicles in the Australian jungle, but even he couldn't stomach the delicacy I had to offer. Maybe my offering did taste worse than kangaroo's knackers, but to be honest I have no idea and no intention of finding out by comparing them.

It didn't help that we were nicknamed 'The Chef-chenkos' for the show. For those of you unfamiliar with cheap puns, the name came from Andriy Shevchenko, the former AC Milan and Chelsea striker, and it proved spot-on. When it came to our Italian cuisine, we were sharp, lethal and too hot to handle. Our English dishes were flat, cold and pretty wide of the mark.

I opted to make a turkey curry. I can tell you it's a traditional dish, passed through several generations of Kammys … So – if you're reading this, Delia Smith, I'm really, really sorry – come on, turkeys, let's be having you.

Sounds great so far, right? Well, Gino reckoned it was the worst thing he had ever tasted. Our judges for the day, A-list restaurant owner Aldo Zilli and Jeff, awarded me only one point, which was amazing because Jeff will eat just about anything, especially if he's had a glass of wine or three. The competition was eventually won by Alan McInally, who made a knockout fish supper with black pudding. He had really taken to the challenge, mainly because 'The Big Man' (as he's nick-named) had just scored himself a new girlfriend. He'd been seriously working on his culinary techniques as he wined and dined her. Judging by my work that day, the Kammy romancing skills clearly weren't up to scratch because people thought I was taking the mickey.

To be fair, I first cooked the dish at home with Mrs Kammy, and it was lovely. I thought I was on to a winner, but when we got to the studio kitchen, we were told that we only had 20 minutes in the kitchen each. I was worried. The Kammy Curry took over an hour to make. The producers said it would be fine, and our sous-chefs would do the work for us in advance. I was messing around, thinking that I already had the finished product in the bag and I only had to add the final ingredients.

'Sit back and relax, pal,' I said to Gino as I tightened my apron strings. 'You're going to learn something here.'

I don't think he could believe what he was hearing. He began shouting at me. 'What sort of stock are you cooking with?'

I shrugged my shoulders.

'What do you mean you don't know what stock it is?' said Gino in disbelief. 'Every chef worth his salt knows what stock he's using. What is it, Kammy?'

I couldn't help myself. 'Laughing stock.'

Unbelievable, Jeff!

He was impressed and giggled out loud. Gino wasn't wowed by my cooking, though. He took one taste of the Kammy Curry and pulled a face at the camera. 'I am not eating this,' he said. 'Oh my God, it tastes like sheet.'

This wasn't the first curry disaster I had caused either. When I was a young player at Pompey, my dad virtually lived off his home-made African curries at home. It wasn't unusual for him to make one and leave it in a pot for me to reheat when I got home. He lived in Middlesbrough with my mam, and when I got back from the south coast it was always a little taste of heaven.

One night during my first close-season break back in the Boro, an old school-mate Denis Alderson and I came back from a heavy night out in the town and put the pot of curry on the stove. We both fell asleep on the sofa. As we drifted in and out of consciousness, the pan caught fire and a small blaze started. Thankfully mam smelt the fumes and came down to rescue us. It was a close shave. Definitely the hottest curry Middlesbrough had ever known – so hot it nearly set fire to the street!

My stint as a 'Chef-chenko' was nowhere near as dangerous, though I have to say, Gino was right. The Kammy Curry – OK, the Kammy-kazi curry if you like – did taste like 'sheet'. I'm just pleased I didn't poison anyone! It would have left a bad taste in their mouths.

UNBELIEVABLE, JEFF!
This is probably as good a time as any to tell you about another famous phrase and explain the title of the book. When

Mr Unbelievable

I claimed that Spurs were 'fighting like beavers' in 2007, the jokes came flying in. It happened during a north London derby at White Hart Lane and I have no excuses at all. It was a total blunder. I distinctly remember it was the first half of the game, Spurs were a goal ahead, but Arsenal had them well pinned back in their penalty area. The studio cut to me for an update.

KAMMY: 'Their football, Arsenal, is on another level, but Spurs are fighting like beavers, defending for their lives. It's a terrific game. Still one-nil ...'

JEFF: [Laughing] 'Did I hear that correctly? Fighting like beavers? Ha, ha, ha! Not tigers or lions, but beavers, those ferocious little devils.'

I wanted to describe how hard Tottenham had been defending. The phrase I'd meant to use was 'working like beavers' (what do you mean you haven't heard of it?), but in the excitement, the words tumbled out all wrong. I tried to correct myself moments later but, by then, the damage had been done.

KAMMY: 'The game, as a spectacle, is magnificent. Spurs, *working* like beavers but the football from Arsenal is out of this world. It's sensational. They're carving them up as easy as ... as easy as ... well, as easy as anything, Jeff.'

JEFF: [Laughing] 'They're carving them up as ... as easy as ... beavers was the word you were looking for, Chris.'

Unbelievable, Jeff!

Jeff wasn't going to let it go; he was in floods of tears. I think he dined out on the story for weeks. In fact, it could have been months, judging by his waistline, but I couldn't help it. It was a spur-of-the-moment reaction and I've been unable to live it down ever since. But who cares? I want the viewer to know that I'm in the middle of an exciting game.

CHAPTER SIX

GROUND-HOPPING WITH KAMMY PT 2 (TAKING ONE FOR THE TEAM ON *SOCCER AM*)

If you think that messing around in front of the cameras for *Soccer Saturday* is a laugh, then you should see what I get up to on *Soccer AM*. For those of you unfamiliar with the show, or fans of *Saturday Morning Kitchen*, it starts at nine in the morning – that's three hours B.J. in Sky Sports terms (before Jeff). Any of you who can struggle out of bed would have seen me offending Premiership players, breaking into dressing-rooms and catching top-class managers on the hop. Over the years I've probably become an unbelievable pain in the backside, but I hope in the nicest possible way.

I got the job several seasons ago when presenter Tim Lovejoy asked me to walk the cameras around the dressing-room before a game. I would always be at a Premiership or Football League ground to cover a match for *Soccer Saturday* anyway, so it made perfect sense. It also gave me the opportunity to mess around, because there was a simple brief when it came to anything *Soccer AM* related: always take the mickey.

Ground-Hopping with Kammy Pt 2

The show made its debut in 1995, but at the time it was quite a serious programme. It was first presented by a guy called Russ Williams and the former Spurs and England defender Gary Stevens. But when Tim Lovejoy took over in 1996, the show changed completely. Suddenly football fans were laughing at 'The Nutmeg Files' (which shows players being nutmegged during the week) and ogling The Soccerettes. It was and still is a brilliant laugh.

My introduction, when the camera comes to me at each and every ground begins, 'Welcome to the Home of Football.' This is a segment of the *Soccer AM* show where the cameras go behind the scenes. I get pretty good access. Over the years I've rummaged through the boots at Sunderland, ruffled the shirts at Arsenal, Manchester United, Leicester and Fulham, and annoyed the stewards at pretty much all of the top-flight grounds. Typically, there's been a bit of controversy along the way.

Just before Gary Megson was sacked in 2009-10, I went up to Bolton to present a report for the show. The club had allowed me to go wherever I wanted, so, unannounced, I strolled into a meeting-room where the coaching staff had been going through the team analysis of Manchester City – Bolton's opponents that day. By the looks of things, 'Mega', as he's nicknamed, had been showing the squad a DVD of City's strengths and weaknesses. Clearly, he hadn't banked on me going in there. When I got to the TV, I noticed it was paused. On the screen somebody had written 'Manchester City's defence is disorganised'.

I couldn't believe my luck. I could hear howls of laughter in my headphones as I turned to the camera. Manchester City fans saw the offending words on the screen and went nuts. Loads of them texted in to complain. 'How the hell can he say that just before kick-off?' they wanted to know. Maybe it was tactless, but you couldn't fault the manager, because he was right. City later conceded three goals in the game. Then again, so did Bolton, so maybe he should have been a bit more careful himself.

My fooling around backfired quite painfully when I visited Sunderland during the same season. Steve Bruce is an old mate of mine and he gave me *carte blanche* to use the dressing-rooms. I had a good look around, as I liked to do, and although nobody was in there at the time, I noticed the giant striker Kenwyne Jones had left his boots out. They were enormous, probably a size 12 or 13. I held them up to the camera.

'Look at these, Helen,' I laughed. 'You know what they say about a man with big feet ...'

In the studio Helen's jaw dropped open. 'No, Kammy!' she screamed. 'You can't say that!'

I was laughing my head off. 'No, not that! I mean, he's got big toes!'

I left the dressing-room and wandered down the players' tunnel. Along the way, there were pictures of Sunderland's recent successes hanging from the walls. I pointed them out to the viewers.

'Look at the photos here,' I said. 'Some of them show the glory days from when they were promoted. There's [then manager] Mick McCarthy and there's an old friend of the show, [former Sunderland player] Liam Richardson, celebrating.'

It was a massive blunder. 'Liam Richardson' was, in fact, Liam Lawrence, who later moved to Stoke City. The moment I got off air, I turned on my mobile. A voicemail message flashed up. It was Liam.

'You pillock, Kammy,' he said, laughing. 'You got my bloody name wrong.'

He wasn't finished there, either. Liam was straight on to the studio to organise his revenge. 'Right,' he told Helen. 'He's taking one for the team.'

This meant trouble. Fans of the show will know that 'Taking One for the Team' is a punishment dished out to Soccer AM staff for making a major cock-up on air. It's bloody painful, because it involves a 20-foot high archery-style target, a chair and a hole where the bullseye should be. Victims of this torture have to park their backsides into the hole as a line of people – in this case the Stoke City team, including a chuffed Liam Richardson, or Liam Lawrence (now I'm even confusing myself) – lined up to take pot shots at me with footballs.

It must have looked hilarious. Peter Reid was starting his first day as assistant coach. Manager Tony Pulis was watching and was wetting himself laughing, although if I had been him, I'd have been furious. The boys were only shooting from a few yards out and none of them could hit the target! When one finally hit, it was Matthew Etherington and even then he only caught me in the small of the back, which goes to prove that I may act like a big fat arse but I haven't actually got one.

Sometimes my messing around has been a bit near to the mark. In 2000, the former Villa, Bolton and Palace midfielder Sasa Curcic was getting a bit of stick for an interview he'd given to the press. In it, he'd apparently claimed that English women were ugly, which had understandably caused a bit of a stink, so we decided to make a stand on behalf of the nation's ladies on *Soccer AM*. We were filming at Upton Park and showing off the fantastic hospitality rooms. If you haven't been there, they're unbelievable: each one has a cracking view of the pitch and they double up as hotel bedrooms.

I was showing the cameras around one of the suites, pointing out the fact that it was a bedroom as well as a corporate hotspot where you could watch the game and enjoy a meal beforehand. A straightforward guided tour would have been boring, so without telling the lads and ladettes in the studio, Lovejoy had hired a sexy glamour model called April to spice things up. When the cameras panned around the room, our busty lass emerged from the bathroom wearing nothing but some rather unflattering underwear – pink bra and black knickers (my type of girl, I have to say). April gave me a saucy look.

'Chris, are you coming back in?' she cooed.

'April,' I said. 'I've never seen you before in my life.'

Helen shouted down the line 'How do you know her name if you've never seen her before in your life!'

Suddenly, the phone in the room began to ring. I stared at it in panic. A phone call to the room wasn't part of the gag. Quick as a flash, I picked it up, and I could tell it was someone else having some fun. In fact it was the stadium manager at Upton Park, who had worked out which room we were in and had dialled the number for a laugh.

'It's my boss, Vic Wakeling from Sky,' I said to the camera, and then, into the phone, 'What do you mean I'm sacked?'

Vic told me later he was sat at home, bent up with laughter. He even sent a note to *Soccer AM* saying, 'A bit near the knuckle but absolute quality,' which is much better than a P45. April was a really good sport and that was the closest I ever came to scoring at Upton Park!

It's usually the managers who get the rough end of the stick when I'm causing trouble on *Soccer AM*, as Harry Redknapp found out to his cost. One Saturday morning, when he was manager at Portsmouth, Harry gave me complete access to the ground, even though it was only one hour until his 12.30 kick-off against Leicester City.

'Go anywhere, Kammy,' he said. 'It's not a problem.'

This was a big mistake. When we went live at Fratton Park, I decided the first port of call would be the manager's office – after all, Harry had said it was access all areas, so I figured, why not?

At that time his office was also home to his assistant manager, Jim Smith. Outside there was a sign which quite clearly stated, 'Do not enter unless you knock.' After one bang with the knuckles, I was in, though in hindsight I should have waited for an answer. As I burst through the doors – complete with a cameraman – I caught Harry and Jim both engrossed in reading the *Racing Post*. I couldn't believe my luck. Kick-off was only hours away and outside on the pitch Pompey defender Arjen de Zeeuw was working through a late fitness test. In the meantime Harry and Jim were both checking the form guides. What made the moment even funnier was that

Soccer AM was playing on their telly in the corner, but the sound had been turned down. They had no idea I was about to pay them a visit.

'I thought you were supposed to be discussing today's important issues?' I said.

'We are,' replied Jim, nonchalantly peering out from the top of his paper. This relaxed attitude was typical of them both, as they looked up laughing to see themselves onscreen.

Harry is a proper wind-up merchant. When he was the manager at West Ham, he invited me to play in a training session with the first team. I took the cameras down and Harry just said, 'Come on in, Chris, the training ground is yours. Do whatever you want.' This was brilliant, I had a great day and we even had a small-sided game. What I didn't realise was that Harry and his assistant, Frank Lampard Snr, had told their Israeli midfielder, Eyal Berkovic, that I was going to kick him during the practice match, and clearly it had scared him. I was playing on Frank Lampard Jnr's team. Berkovic lined up for the other side and, sure enough, just before we kicked off, Harry and Frank apparently warned him to keep away from me.

'He's going to kick you, be careful,' said Harry. I still hadn't a clue what was going on. Berkovic then jogged towards me.

'You play with us, that's OK,' he said. 'But no kicking.'

I looked over at Harry on the touchline – he was laughing his head off. As it turned out, though, Eyal had nothing to worry about. I was too old to catch someone as nifty as he was, never mind give him a whack. I just thanked my lucky stars I wasn't lined up against John Hartson. Come to think of it, I bet Eyal wished he never had been been either.

After Harry closed the session, the squad disappeared to get some lunch. Well, everyone except Paolo Di Canio, who changed into his running gear. While the rest of us ate in the club café, Di Canio was outside in his running shoes, sprinting and jogging, performing all sorts of exercises. It was pretty impressive stuff. You could tell why Harry regarded him so highly.

'You don't coach him,' he told me that day. 'You don't need to say to him, "You have to do this", or "You have to do that", like you do with the English lads. He just does it. He's a fantastic example for my young players.'

As if to prove Harry's point, during that same visit to West Ham, Rio Ferdinand's mum rang in to say he was ill. He wouldn't be coming in to train that day.

'See what I have to put up with, Chris?' said Harry, as he put the phone down. 'Who'd be a manager, eh?'

I presume Harry got another call from Rio's mum months later to say her son wouldn't be in for training again because he'd buggered off to Leeds United.

⚽ ⚽ ⚽ ⚽ ⚽ ⚽ ⚽ ⚽

I'm surprised that Micky Adams, the former Leicester City gaffer, talks to me at all these days, especially after I stitched him up at Filbert Street one morning. Leicester were playing Birmingham. It was a midday kick-off and Micky invited me into his office for bacon sarnies in the morning. He even agreed to give us access to the changing-rooms, complete with an interview alongside his striker Marcus Bent, when we went on air after 11 a.m. His only condition was that we didn't reveal the team line-up by revealing the names on the backs of the shirts that were hanging in the dressing-room.

When we went inside, Marcus Bent was sitting there alongside Micky Adams, good as gold. But when the camera lights came on and we linked up with Tim and Helen in the studio, Micky decided to do a runner. He flew out of the dressing-room and refused to be interviewed. He'd obviously decided to stitch me up, so I decided to pay him back.

'As you can see, it's two hours before kick-off,' I said. 'Ricky Scimeca sitting down there, Marcus Bent as well. Tony Adams … I mean Micky Adams has told us not to reveal who's playing today [I then turned a shirt over to reveal SCIMECA 21], but seeing as the lads are here, we can show one or two [I turn another: STEWART 11], can't we? Micky's only in the other room, he's bottled coming out so … [another and another: FERDINAND 9, DAVIDSON 14]. If he wants to tell me off, sorry Micky.'

Micky, who had headed back to his office to watch the programme, could do nothing to stop me.

'Look, Steve Bruce,' I shouted down the camera, 'Scowcroft's playing. So is Isset, and Marcus will be starting up front.'

Moments later I bumped into Micky's goalkeeping coach, Tim Flowers, a Premiership winner with Blackburn Rovers and another former team-mate of mine from Swindon. We had a quick chat for the camera (after he'd almost dropped a ball I'd thrown at his midriff to test his reflexes), and I dropped him in it too.

To camera I said, 'One of the best goalkeepers I ever played with ...'

'You lying git,' he said, not realising what I was about to say.

'... was Mervyn Day,' I added quickly, scarpering to the away dressing-room.

Dennis, the Birmingham City kit man, had also laid shirts out for the players. Unfortunately, he had never seen *Soccer AM*, so he had no idea that he was supposed to say no when I asked him to turn the shirts over. He just shrugged his shoulders and told me to get on with it. By now, Helen and Tim were in hysterics as I read out some more names for the telly. I turned over the first shirt and it belonged to Clinton Morrison. 'Oh dear,' I laughed. 'I must be at the rubber dubs' [subs] end.' As soon as the Birmingham players streamed into the ground, Clinton came looking for me. He cornered me by the pitch. Like many of the current pros, he loves the programme and knows we're only having a laugh. They all realise I'd never be vindictive or nasty, but he was a bit miffed all the same.

'Somebody rang me on the bus and said you took the mickey out of me this morning,' he laughed. 'Well I'm not on the bench. I'm playing today and I'm going to score.' He did as well. Clinton later agreed to an interview after the game for *Soccer Saturday*. He couldn't stop himself from rubbing my nose in it.

'You said I'd be with the rubber dubs this morning,' he said. 'But I've proved Morrison is the man.' Clinton was laughing his head off. Fair play, for once it was me who had been caught on the hop.

CHAPTER SEVEN

KAMMYOKE!

Like a lot of Premiership stars, the *Soccer Saturday* lads like to have a bit on the side. Now, before any of the 'Sky WAGs' start throwing the crockery around, I'd like to point out that I'm talking business interests rather than Page 3 models, G-list pop stars or Jordan. Jeff, for example, presents *Countdown*, where he presses a button and sets off the famous clock several times a day. It doesn't look like a lot of work, but he gets to look at the pins of Rachel Reilly, his glamorous assistant, so you can't knock it. It's also better than looking at the pins of Matt Le Tissier and Thommo on a Saturday afternoon, I reckon.

Meanwhile, Paul Merson has made a name for himself as an entertaining speaker on the after-dinner circuit. There's a lot of money to be made from reliving stories from your glory days and a lot of Arsenal players have some great tales to tell from the eighties and nineties when Merse played. Ray Parlour was telling me recently about a time when the Gunners were away at Liverpool. Ray wasn't in the squad, so he went to the

Kammyoke!

Carlsberg Lounge with Andy Linegan and a few of the spare parts for a beer. The lads were on their fourth pint when assistant manager Stuart Houston dashed into the bar.

'Ray! Ray! One of the lads has got injured in the warm-up,' he shouted. 'Get changed, you're on the bench.'

Quick as a flash, Andy Linegan turned around. 'Stuart, have a heart, at least let him finish his pint first.'

Ray said he sat on the bench with his legs crossed for the entire half, praying that he wouldn't get on. Merse was part of this boozy culture at Highbury – it put him in rehab – so he has loads of these stories to tell with plenty of punters willing to listen.

It may come as a surprise to learn that I've made a name for myself as a club singer. Most readers will have winced at my booming tones over the course of the show on a Saturday afternoon. Some of you might even be thinking, 'How could that shouty bloke from the telly possibly hold a tune?' – but the weird thing is, I can. I've even cracked a few a cappella numbers on *Soccer AM* in a section of the show called 'Kammyoke'.

I first sang in front of an audience after making my debut for Leeds, a friendly against the Irish team Shelbourne, although we nearly didn't make it across the Irish Sea at all. Two days after I'd signed for Leeds we headed off to Leeds airport for the short trip over. With the winds raging at over 70 mph, Leeds managing director Bill Fotherby was told by airport officials that the airport was to be closed. At the time, Leeds United needed the cash that this lucrative and popular friendly would bring in, and Bill could see this slipping away. He begged for the airport to allow us to fly for our evening kick-off and eventually the powers that be duly obliged. The small aircraft, no more than a 30-seater, powered by the gale-force winds, weaved its way down the runway, reminiscent of a drunk staggering home on a Saturday night. The look on the faces of my new team-mates was of pure fear. Once airborne we were subjected to the delights of the plane bungee-ing its way across the Irish Sea. Defender Peter Haddock and striker Lee Chapman were both feeling very ill and were unable to hide the fact when their pre-match lunch made a reappearance. Gordon Strachan's face told the story that he had never endured anything like it before, for all his previous globetrotting with Manchester United. Our team-mates Mel Sterland and Imre Varadi continuously looked over to Vinnie Jones and me for reassurance that all would be well. The nervous laughter they were rewarded with did nothing to hide the fact that the two 'hard men' of the team were also crapping themselves!

Despite the worst flight of our lives we won 3–1 that evening, and afterwards the squad stayed at the fancy Burlington Hotel near the centre of Dublin. After a couple of beers, I spotted a pianist in the hotel bar and soon convinced him to give me the microphone for two Elton John numbers, 'Your Song' and 'Don't Let the Sun Go Down On Me'.

This was my way of introducing myself to the lads. According to team captain Gordon Strachan, a number of players actually exchanged worried glances as I began to perform. The lyrics probably didn't help: 'It's a little bit funny, this feeling inside/I'm not one of those who can easily hide/I don't have much money but boy if I did/I'd buy a big house where we both could live.' According to Gordon, the common consensus among the Leeds squad that night was, 'Who's this shy bloke Howard has signed!'

Word soon got around that I was a bit of a crooner. I was later asked to sing on a charity album called *In a League of Their Own*. The recording sessions had been organised by legendary gaffer Ron Atkinson and also featured Gabby Logan and Ally McCoist on vocals. Former Villa striker Dion Dublin played a mean saxophone, so he was roped in, as was Blackburn striker Matt Jansen on piano and Chelsea and Leicester City's Frank Sinclair on drums. It was like Band Aid, except none of us got to play at Wembley afterwards.

I sang two songs on the album, 'Summertime' by George Gershwin and Van Morrison's 'Brown Eyed Girl'. And while the album barely dented the hit parade, it got some pretty good reviews. 'Chris Kamara sings "Brown Eyed Girl" better than Van Morrison,' wrote one reviewer. 'But then Van Morrison was a better football player than Chris Kamara.'

I later scored a regular gig at the Pigalle club in Piccadilly in London through some mates of a mate, Tim Ellerton and Joe Stillgo. Once a month I'll sing three to four songs at a night called 'Kitsch Lounge Riot' hosted by Johnny Barran at the Café de Paris, which holds 500 people. It's always packed out. Just before Christmas 2009 I had the honour of doing a duet with former *EastEnders* star and comedian Bobby Davro, which was cracking. I've got quite a repertoire of songs, but generally I belt through 'Stuck in the Middle with You' by Stealer's Wheel, Elton John's 'Don't Let the Sun Go Down On Me', 'Summertime' and 'Brown Eyed Girl' (naturally), before I finish on a real belter: 'Born To Be Wild' by Steppenwolf.

Mr Unbelievable

One occasion I was quite pleased not to be called on stage to sing was when Robbie Williams spotted me among the crowd during his concert in front of 90,000 people at Roundhay Park in Leeds. God knows how he caught sight of me, but halfway through his set, he looked over to where I was standing and shouted, 'Chris Kamara, do the Rudebox!' (Robbie fans will recognise this as one of his singles). At first I thought I was mishearing things and then he said it again. 'Chris Kamara, do the Rudebox!' Everyone around me went mental. For the first time I can remember, I was almost star-struck. I just waved like an idiot and Robbie gave me the thumbs up. The adrenaline rush was as good as scoring a goal.

Elsewhere I've done the odd charity gig – I once crooned to a massive audience in the Birmingham Symphony Hall for a sold-out show to raise money for Marie Curie and The Prince's Royal Trust. For the most part, though, I stick to banging out a few numbers in The Hole in the Wall, a boozer I have an interest in at Parque de la Paz in Tenerife. After a few beers I'll get on the mic and run through a few favourites with Irish crooner Fergal Flaherty. The punters seem to love it, but I don't think Simon Cowell will be getting excited any time soon.

CHAPTER EIGHT
JEFF AND THE CRAZY GANG

The camaraderie among the *Soccer Saturday* lads is second to none, and the banter is as fierce as in any football club dressing-room I have been in. The panel has Charlie Nicholas on one side, Paul Merson on the other, and in the middle Phil Thompson, a nose between two thorns.

Our very own Bonnie Prince Charlie loves a wind-up and any mistakes are quickly jumped on, there is no hiding place, apart from behind Thommo's hooter. Charlie has lived a few lives and, when he hit the bright lights of London as the best Scottish footballer of his era, he did things that would make your hair curl! He would be the first to admit that the lure of the West End took a bit out of his game. I'll say no more but if he'd taken up rugby instead of football he would have been a hooker!

David Moyes, the Everton manager, was once talking on *Goals on Sunday* and said that the nearest thing he had seen to Wayne Rooney was when Charlie was starting off at Celtic as a kid, and we're now back talking football. He could also do things with the ball which others could only dream of, and was light years ahead of his time. That may be so, but in the eight years I have known Charlie I have yet to hear him talking about his playing days. He loves his flights down from his native Scotland to London, ready for his weekend stint at the Sky studios, and enjoys the crack with the lads on Friday nights in the hotel bar.

Paul Merson is a one-off. For someone to have had as many ups and downs as he has had is amazing. His helter-skelter life would pass as a ride at Alton Towers, but the guy has amazing bounce-back-ability. He has coped with gambling, drinking and drug use admirably. When I played for Luton against Arsenal on Boxing Day 1992, David Seaman took a goal-kick. My team-mate Trevor Peake was marking Merse and I was just in front of him. When I went up for the ball to head it away, I accidentally elbowed Merse on the nose. When I turned round to apologise Merse sneezed in my face. I am telling you now, that was the best I felt for a fortnight after. I played against him a few times and it was apparent that he was someone who just loved playing the game. He reminds me of another old team-mate of mine, Stan Bowles, who shared similar problems, but once they both stepped over the white line on to the football pitch, their troubles were left behind.

Phil Thompson is the biggest ex-player football fan I have ever met. His passion for Liverpool has no boundaries. People often ask me if it is just an act for the cameras. It is definitely not: the old saying is true in his case – if you cut him open he would bleed Red blood! Tee hee! He is the same as all the *Soccer Saturday* boys – he does not take himself too seriously and is fine about Jeff poking fun at his hooter.

Jeff and the Crazy Gang

Matt Le Tissier, or the god of Southampton, is laid-back but has a wonderful dry sense of humour. The most amazing thing I found out when talking to Tiss is that when I was at Leeds, Luton and Sheffield Utd in the early nineties, I was earning more money than him, even though he was enjoying so much success and banging in the goals for his beloved Saints. His managers knew that he would never want to leave Southampton, so the new contract negotiations were never stressful. Tiss made it easy for the club to take advantage of his loyalty – shame on them! It was lucky for them that Tiss never learnt he could fly home to his native Guernsey from places other than Southampton airport when he felt a bit homesick. The only way Tiss was going to leave SFC was to go to KFC, and his manager at one time, Glenn Hoddle, did actually have to go into KFC in Southampton and tell the staff behind the counter not to serve him the meal for two unless he was with someone and definitely not during half-time at St Mary's! The late great Alan Ball, another manager of Tiss's, used to tell what he said was a true story when doing the after-dinner circuit. He said that during a match he shouted to Tiss, 'Warm up!' And when Tiss asked, 'Why?' Bally replied, 'Because I am bringing you off!' Laid-back on the pitch, maybe, but a genius and a cracking fellow.

Alan McInally is my partner for three days each year, when we take our chance to mingle with some fabulous characters from the horse-racing world at the Cheltenham Festival, and we have a hoot. 'The Muncheon', as he is known to the lads, because of his time playing at Bayern Munich after leaving Aston Villa, is top draw, and because of his larger than life persona gets plenty of stick from the boys. A lot of the younger people who watch *Soccer Saturday* often ask me what Alan was like as a player, so I thought I should ring Graham Taylor, who managed him at Villa. I asked Graham about his strengths and weaknesses.

'He had the strength of a dray horse.'

Not bad, I thought.

'The speed of a racehorse.'

Wow! But hang on, there's more.

'The movement of a polo horse, and the spring in his feet of a showjumping horse.'

'And what about his weaknesses, Graham?' I asked.

'The brains of a rocking horse,' came back his reply. McInally is great company and there is never a dull moment when he is around.

Now for the man who holds it all together, Mr Jeff Stelling. What can I say? He is something else. And a great fan of his home-town team Hartlepool, just in case this fact has managed to slip by any regular viewers to the show. He cannot contain his excitement or passion as a Monkey Hanger. He is the memory man, though I have to say, when that well-publicised incident occurred with that fellow walking into the police station at Seaton Canoe – sorry, Seaton Carew, near Hartlepool – and said he was clueless, had no idea of who he was or where he had been for the last five years, I had to ring Jeff just to make sure he was OK.

Jeff and I have done all sorts together – adverts, after-dinners, voice-overs, you name it. People have really bought into our relationship on *Soccer Saturday* and it has been brilliant for us. He is a friend for life.

Jeff and the Crazy Gang

We had the trip of all trips when we went to the World Cup in Japan in 2002. It is fair to say that Jeff might well not be working for Sky now if he had been the first England fan arrested and deported from Japan, as he very nearly was! He wanted a bit of culture while we were there in Japan, so we left the city life in Tokyo after England had drawn with Sweden in Saitama. Jeff wanted to see some of the real Japan, so we headed off to the temples of Kyoto. After visiting two temples Jeff agreed with me and our other travelling companion and the producer of *Soccer Saturday*, Ian Condron, that once you had seen one temple you had seen them all. That evening after sampling some of the local cuisine, beer and wine in a recommended local restaurant, Jeff and I headed off for the obligatory one more beer, and Condo headed off for bed. We found a bar with quite a few people in it, many of whom were playing a version of 'spin the bottle'. Whoever the bottle points at after being spun has to down their beer in one. This was tailor made for me, as I didn't mind the forfeit to be paid, but Jeff was finding the punishment really tough. He suggested we find somewhere else for our 'one more beer' before he became legless, so after enjoying an hour or so of fun we left our non-English-speaking friends behind. Unfortunately, Kyoto only had one late bar in the whole of town – the one we had just been in. So, after walking round and round, and trying to converse with the locals, we found ourselves back at the bar where our friends were still the spinning bottle.

Outside Jeff um'd and ah'd about going back in, thinking he'd perhaps already had enough. Whilst he was standing (or swaying) there, making his decision, he staggered backwards off the kerb into a parked motorbike. It was a Harley Davidson type bike with big handlebars. Jeff let out a scream, and for a second the world stood still. We both watched aghast as the huge, shiny machine toppled, as if in slow motion, towards the car parked next to it. Jeff lunged forward to grab it but stood no chance as (a) the bike was far too weighty, and (b) Jeff was far too boozy! There was not a thing we could do as the handlebars made contact with the rear windscreen of the car. Bang! What a noise, and what a mess, as the glass shattered everywhere. Disbelief was etched on our faces as we just stood there staring at each other. It is surprising how quickly you can sober up instantly in a panic situation such as the one we were facing. The bike and the car possibly belonged to one of the gang we had been drinking with earlier in the bar, so we did what all good citizens would do – we scarpered!

During the Japan trip, whenever Jeff and I went out jogging to sweat the alcohol from the night before out of our system, Jeff was always lagging behind. Not this time, he found another gear and made it back to the hotel before me. Jeff pointed out that hardly anyone spoke English in that bar we had been in, they would no doubt say we were drunk (perish the thought), and also we were English football supporters, so we would stand no chance if we had to explain that it was an accident. So, deciding to turn in for the night, we were quite confident that we had actually spared English supporters yet another black mark against them by doing a runner!

Next morning, though, Jeff was not so confident. He was certain we would be picked up by the police.

Jeff and the Crazy Gang

'You are the only black man in the place,' he said, 'and I am the only fat Englishman around, so someone is bound to have seen us. There is no doubt we will be picked out and arrested.'

Our flights from Kyoto to England's next game against Argentina in Sapporo were not until the next morning. After keeping a low profile all morning, after lunch Jeff was feeling the worse for wear following the fluid consumption of the night before, so he headed off to his hotel room for a lay down. Condo and I allowed him to sleep for a couple of hours. Then I called him from reception on the hotel phone. Using my best Japanese accent I said, 'Erro, Meester Stelling, reception here. I 'ave poleece in lobby. They want to speak with you and beeg black man ovaar inceedent in town last night. Meester Stelling, do you know whaat eet ees I am talking about?'

Solemnly Jeff came back with, 'Yes, I know.'

'Meester Stelling, poleece want to know was eet you or beeg black man who smashed car window?' I continued. Condo and I were struggling to contain ourselves. Jeff had fallen for it beeg-style!

'It was me,' admitted Jeff. 'Beeg, sorry, big black man was with me but it was my fault, it was an accident.'

'Meester Stelling, you must come down to reception queekly, poleece is waiting for you.'

Jeff, pale faced and visibly agitated, appeared in reception to find Condo and me doubled up with laughter and standing by the telephone. To say that Jeff was relieved it was a prank is an understatement, but I was made up that he hadn't turned me in as the villain to save his own skin. We left the next morning for Sapporo unscathed, and if anyone from Kyoto is reading this I should add that, in the meantime, we have applied for diplomatic immunity from prosecution. As for everyone who watches Jeff's stints on *Countdown*, I offer the following nine-letter words that will make Jeff Stelling cringe for ever: arresting, innocence, drunkards, convicted supporter and lucky bugger. I know the last ones aren't nine letters, but lucky bugger Jeff Stelling certainly was.

CHAPTER NINE

EASY LIKE SUNDAY MORNING

People often ask me how come I have a presenting job on Sky? They can understand the punditry role, co-commentating and reporting from games, because that's what ex-players do, but surely, they think, only trained journalists get given an interviewer's role on TV. My opportunity for presenting came about in August 2000. The bosses, Vic Wakeling and Andy Melvin, decided to try out me and Rob McCaffrey with a new programme called *Summer Soccer AM*. The producer of the show was Barney Francis, who is now the Sky Sports boss. His brief to us was to have fun, use our contacts to bring in guests and try to entertain the viewing public for six weeks of the close season. It seemed to go well – so well that the partnership was born. Vic and Andy took the bold bid to give us a prime-time show for three hours every Sunday starting the next season. Rob and I had an almost telepathic understanding from the word go – it was a shame when he left three years ago to seek his fortune in Dubai.

People think that *Goals on Sunday* must be a doddle to put together. Compared to *Soccer AM* and *Soccer Saturday* I suppose it's a calmer and slower day's shift – I'm not freezing in the piddling rain or evading the long arm of the club steward. Instead, my co-presenter Ian Payne and I will analyse Saturday's goals and action for two hours on a lazy Sunday morning. We'll also have one or two high-profile guests sitting alongside us on our comfy sofa. In the studio there's a big coffee table overflowing with newspapers, pastries and mugs of tea. The apples in the big bowl, however, are plastic and polished every week by a work-experience kid and I have to say they don't taste anywhere near as good as the real thing. They don't work in pies either because they make the pastry bumpy. It couldn't be any more relaxed. The show even has as its theme tune, the Commodores' song 'Easy Like Sunday Morning'.

Weirdly, though, *Goals on Sunday* has dropped me in hot water a couple of times. One week I forgot to switch my mobile off. Normally I put it on silent and leave it in the dressing-room. We replay a lot of controversial incidents during the show and managers and players call me up or text, so I am always popping out in the breaks to check it.

Robbie Savage was our guest that day, and five minutes into the show my phone started vibrating in my pocket. My heart sank as I then heard it ringing loudly. Robbie looked at me with a smirk.

'Here, Kammy,' he said, 'is that your phone?'

I winced, guilty as charged.

'Unfortunately it is.'

For some reason, I froze. All the best performers do it, but usually they're laughing on-stage or fluffing their lines and can usually retake them. This was going out live and Robbie wasn't going to let me off the hook.

'Aren't you going to answer it, then?'

It was unprofessional but, worst of all, my mind went blank. At that moment all I wanted was to do to Robbie Savage was what just about every midfield player in the country would like to do to Robbie Savage. Under normal circumstances I would have come out with a quip. I just froze and allowed it to ring and ring.

The producer, Adam Chenery, was shouting in my ear, 'Get rid of it! Get rid of it!'

I just had to allow it to finish ringing, which it did, but then as we cut to a VT, it started ringing again. I managed to look at the number and saw that it was Everton's Phil Jagielka. He had been watching the programme, had seen the embarrassing incident and decided to give me a ring to add to my shame. Thankfully we'd just gone off air, but there was no getting away from it, I had cocked up big-time. I had to relive the embarrassment following a much-publicised press conference at Ipswich Town the next week. Unsurprisingly, it involved Roy Keane. As he talked to the media, a journalist's phone went off. Keano gave him the look of death.

'Are you going to answer that?' he scowled.

The poor bloke told him he was going to let it ring off.

'How rude can you be?' snapped Keane.

When we made fun of the incident the following week, I laughed and said, 'I can't believe anyone would do something so stupid.'

That was the moment the producers decided to replay my gaffe from the previous weekend. I just had to take it on the chin. Generally, the blunders aren't down to me. Over the eight years the programme has been going we have only had a few mishaps and one major disaster. Let's be fair about it, though, we are dealing with football people, and because the environment is very laid-back they can forget where they are. Even though there are TV cameras in full view and production staff running around, guests have sometimes reverted to dressing-room language, which we all do in football. I've had to scold Peter Reid for using the word 'bollocking'; and Tony Adams once managed to say 'Jesus Christ' three times in the space of 30 seconds. That really didn't go down too well with our religious viewers, though I'd rather that than someone like Luis Boa Morte, the Fulham, Arsenal and now West Ham striker, who could only manage the words 'yes' and 'no'. To be fair to Luis, he had only lived in our country for a short time before he bravely agreed to appear on the show. I'd seen David Blaine doing 'yes' and 'no' in an Eamonn Holmes interview, and Meg Ryan did the same to Michael Parkinson, but when it happened to me I really had to think on my feet and get over it. I think we all learnt that day to only book guests who can speak English. It makes for a much easier and more fluent show.

Our disaster incident has to be the moment Stephen Bywater came into the studio. At the time, he was a Premiership keeper with Derby County. We always do a piece in the show and look back through the guest's past. Stephen was talking about his time at West Ham, when he started as an apprentice and his goalkeeping coach was Les Sealey. Sadly Les died in 2001 of a heart attack, even though he was only 43. Bywater later wore the number 43 shirt as a tribute to his mentor.

Presenting with me that day was the lovely Claire Tomlinson, and she asked him to pay his own personal tribute to Les. He said, 'Claire, not only did he teach me how to be a good goal-keeper, he also taught me how not to be a ... er ... er ...' I could see he was struggling for words. Often I can help guests because, generally, I've got the gist of where they're coming from when they're chatting away. When Bywater opened his mouth, I couldn't tell what he was going to say next. I wish I had. I would have stuffed one of those plastic apples into his gob.

'... er ... er ... not to be a -' He paused, and then proceeded to spell out the 'C' word!

I was gobsmacked - it was unbelievable. It seemed to happen in slow motion and I felt like a rabbit caught in the headlights. I couldn't think of a more offensive word to say on air, but by spelling it out, Bywater thought it was OK. In fact both Claire and I were unsure of how bad it was. If he had actually said the word he would have been off that sofa quicker than you could say Usain Bolt, but because he had spelt it out that was probably a television first.

Michael Brown, the former Spurs and Sheffield United midfielder, was sitting next to Bywater on the sofa. He nudged him during the ad break. 'You can't say that, you know,' he said. I could see Bywater turning red as he realised his shocking error. Claire and I decided to carry on as if nothing had been said. We presumed that nobody had been listening in the production gallery, as we had nobody protesting in our ear pieces, and we didn't know what the proper procedure was. So we continued with the programme as if nothing unto-ward had happened, not a thing. In hindsight it was the worst thing we could have done. Because he'd spelt the word out we were in a broadcasting version of no-man's-land. Claire, because she was interviewing him at the time, got a bigger dressing down than me. The people upstairs came down heavily on her. They felt that as a trained journalist she should have handled the situation more decisively. I felt just as responsible. Instead I got a severe rollocking.

Even so, we only had four official complaints. One disgruntled parent rang up Sky and complained to OfCom – the watchdog committee. He said he wanted free Sky because he had to explain to his five-year-old son what the 'C' word meant. He was so offended that he wanted a lifetime's subscription to the channel! In the meantime, Claire took it very badly. It made her very ill and she needed time off to recover, which was a blow because she was on her way up at the time. Now she feels she won't present anything other than *Sky Sports News*.

I haven't spoken to Stephen Bywater about the incident since. I saw him after a match between Boro and Derby and he said hello. I acknowledged him but I didn't speak to him specifically about the incident. I didn't want to. I can't say to him that everything's OK about it, because it's not. After that I don't think Jeff will ever invite Stephen Bywater on to *Countdown*, and if he did he most definitely wouldn't accept a four-letter word!

⚽ ⚽ ⚽ ⚽ ⚽ ⚽ ⚽

Not all of our guests have been top-of-the-range plonkers. In fact, I'm proud of some of the people we've had on the show.

We've had legends such as Gordon Strachan, Kenny Dalglish, David Ginola and Ossie Ardiles on the sofa, as well as managers including Claudio Ranieri, Steve Bruce, David Moyes, Alan Pardew and Neil Warnock, to name but a few. I remember one time when Paul McGrath, the Republic of Ireland hero, came on the show with the former Liverpool goal machine Ian Rush. Paul needed warming up and a little encouragement, but I thought he was a very good guest.

Afterwards we went for a drink in the nearby rugby club. Paul asked for a water, but Rob McCaffrey, who was ordering the drinks, insisted that Paul had a pint even though he must have known that Paul had a drink problem. Paul started to sink pint after pint of Guinness. Then it did occur to me there might be a problem. He left in the chauffeur-driven car for the airport with Ian Rush, but he went missing inside the terminal and missed his flight back to Manchester with Rushie. God knows where he went, but apparently he did not appear back at home for days. Paul had struggled with alcohol problems and I've always felt I should have done more to look out for the big man that day.

We were very grateful when Chelsea and England skipper John Terry finally appeared on our sofa. He'd been promising me for years that he would do the show, and he kept his word when he was out injured for a lengthy spell. I like his attitude to the game – it's old school. When he dislocated his elbow towards the end of the 2008 campaign, you just knew it wasn't going to keep him out of the following game. That was the kind of daft commitment to the cause players showed all the time when I was JT's age. In fact, I still do it now. When I injured the medial ligament in my knee a few years ago I was warned I would be out for six weeks. Like a fool I was down at Stamford Bridge 10 days later playing 80 minutes in a Samsung charity match with Zola, Vialli, Gus Poyet, Glen Hoddle, Ray Wilkins and Trevor Francis. I struggled to walk for two weeks after, but it was worth it. When I see someone like John Terry do it, it restores my faith in the game and its players.

One of my greatest coups was getting Sven-Goran Eriksson on the show when he was England manager, but it nearly put me into a media hurricane when I first met him. We were both out in Amsterdam for a pre-season tournament – me for Sky, Sven looking at his England players on view with their club teams competing there – and we arranged to meet for dinner. The meeting was brokered by Adrian (Adey) Bevington, the FA press man, who is a good friend of mine. Not that much talking was done at first. I seemed to spend most of the night swatting away several ladies who seemed eager to meet Sven. It didn't help that Sven was facing the flight of stairs, where everybody could see him and he in turn could watch the girls go by.

At the time, Sven was a Fleet Street target. He was in the middle of a huge controversy and his job was on the line. Many people wanted him out because he'd had an affair with FA employee Faria Alam. When the story broke a fortnight earlier, the FA issued a denial, though it turned out that the story was true. The twist in the tail was that Alam was also seeing FA chief executive Mark Palios. Unbeknown to us, the new revelations were to hit the news stands the morning after our dinner date.

I had an idea that something was going on. That night, Adey's mobile never stopped. He kept leaving the table to take calls from England, where the early editions of the Sunday papers were already on the streets. According to the *News of the World*, Palios and Colin Gibson, Adey's boss at the FA, had tried to do a deal over the Alam affair. Apparently, they had delivered the full story of Sven's affair in exchange for Palios staying out of the papers. Adey returned with news and a breakdown of the headlines, but Sven shrugged it off. He didn't want to talk about it and insisted we talked football instead.

It was a fascinating conversation. Sven told me about when he first started out as a coach in Sweden. He travelled to Sheffield Wednesday to see Jack Charlton at work. Big Jack did a session on crossing and finishing for an hour, which Sven thought was a long time, even then. He said he learnt a great deal from just that one session on a training ground.

His next stop was Ipswich Town, where he met a young and enthusiastic Bobby Robson. Typically, Bobby welcomed him with open arms. After Sven had watched his first session on a Friday morning, Bobby asked him if he had a ticket for the game against West Brom the following day. Sven said he hadn't but would love to go to the game.

'Tell you what,' said Bobby. 'You can come and sit on the bench next to me.'

No wonder the pair remained friends until Bobby's death. What a remarkable man he was.

That night, Sven also reminisced about his love for Italian football. He said it started back in 1956 when he watched the national team on television. He could even name that first eleven. Sven decided that if he ever got the opportunity to work and manage in Italy, he would take it. This was the reason he turned down the Blackburn Rovers job in 1998. Sven had met with Rovers chairman, Jack Walker, for a meal and afterwards accepted the job. Sven reckoned that Jack, who saw his dream of Blackburn lifting the Premier League trophy come true at Anfield in 1995, was one of the most charming men he had ever met. What Jack wanted Sven to do was restore his club to the top spot in English football.

But within days of Sven accepting the job, Lazio had contacted him to offer him the role as their coach. They also offered to pay compensation to Blackburn. Sven rang Jack and the pair later met in a London restaurant to discuss the new developments. Sven revealed his predicament to Jack. He explained the full details of his love affair with Italian football and his ambition to manage there. When he finally asked Jack how much compensation he wanted from Lazio, the Blackburn chairman tore up the contract.

'I don't want any money from Lazio or from you,' he said. 'Just pay for the meal.'

If only our dinner in Amsterdam had been as simple. Adey's vibrating mobile phone was a constant interruption. The gory news continued to filter through. I wasn't going to ask Sven what was going on. It really was none of my business and he clearly didn't want to discuss it. It was a shame that the content of the *News of the World* article overtook proceedings because he'd just started to discuss Chelsea when Adey dragged him away. For some reason, the papers then turned their attentions to me. They had got wind that I'd spent some time with him and wanted to know what we'd been talking about. One editor even offered money for an exclusive but I turned him down. I even stopped answering the phone eventually, which was unlike me. I called Adey and said I was being pestered to say something and I couldn't deny I was out with them. He was really relaxed about the whole thing. He just told me to tell them it as it was. So I did. And they stopped.

Six weeks before the Euro 2004 finals kicked off in Portugal, Sven and his assistant Tord Grip were good enough to come in as our quests on *Goals on Sunday*. Tord held the fort for an entertaining hour before Sven joined him on the sofa, later admitting that the first hour of the programme was just too early for him. Before he had a chance to settle, I told him I had picked the team for the opening Euro 2004 game against France. For the key midfield area, I'd selected Steven Gerrard and Frank Lampard as the central pair, with David Beckham and Paul Scholes on the right and left. Michael Owen and Wayne Rooney picked themselves up front, and I would have got the back four right too, but for John Terry's injury which eventually handed Ledley King his chance.

'What do you want me to say?' said the England manager. 'If you took a poll and asked 100 people to pick their England team, that would be it.'

'Yes, but in that shape?' I asked.

'We shall have to see,' he said. It was the reply we'd all expected, but that was typical Sven really. Still, he was good company. He seemed very relaxed alongside Tord, which helped. We even had a laugh at his expense when we looked at some of the pictures of Sven in his playing days. I can't imagine for one minute getting the same laughs should we ever convince Fabio Capello to come in for pastries and coffee one Sunday morning.

CHAPTER TEN
NAME DROPPING

Working for Sky has been brilliant. I couldn't ask for a better job, because it has allowed me to keep in contact with all the characters in the game and meet the new kids on the block as the sport changes, mostly for the good and sometimes for the bad. I even get a chance to criticise the referees from time to time without getting a red or yellow card. It reminds me of the old gag:

'Hey, ref, if I called you a complete tosser would you send me off?'

'Course I would.'

'But if I only *thought* you were a complete tosser, you couldn't do a thing about it, could you?'

'No, nothing.'

'OK, I think you're a complete tosser.'

One of the big thrills I have had was being the reporter on the 2003 Cup Final between Liverpool and Manchester United. Sir Alex Ferguson was brilliant to me during my managerial career, but this was one of the few times I had come in contact with him in my new job at Sky. I was supposed to interview the winning manager after the game, which turned out to be Liverpool's Gérard Houllier, but somehow the other reporter on the day got that interview and I was left with Sir Alex. It was not my greatest television moment, and he certainly wasn't impressed.

He had taken a long while to emerge from the dressing-room to face the press, which made me ask the obvious question:

'Has there been a stewards' enquiry in there?'

At that time he had been enjoying huge success with a particular racehorse, Rock of Gibraltar, but things had now turned sour with his partners in Ireland, and it had been well publicised in the press. I maintain to this day that I was not being flippant with my question, but he obviously felt other-wise. I wasn't trying to be clever at all. As a 'horsey' person myself, I always use the phrase 'stewards' enquiry' to refer to the after-match post-mortem. He certainly thought I was being disrespectful, and put me down instantly. It came close to that infamous 'hairdryer' treatment, but this time on live TV. I wasn't really aware of the extent of his annoyance, as it happened, because I was conscious of trying to keep the inter-view going. The next question angered him even more:

'Was the Worthington Cup a priority?'

He answered it by saying, 'Well, we came here to win it, if that's what you mean.' My interview was over.

Many of my friends rang that night to say they'd noticed he was a tad short with me. When I got home I watched the inter-view on video. I don't claim to be an expert at this game, and I have never had any formal journalism training, but I am determined to do it to the best of my ability, learn by my mistakes and try to improve. When I saw the interview again, the hairs on the back of my neck stood up and I felt extremely uncomfortable.

A few days later, my Sky Sports colleague Bryn Law was at Old Trafford and approached Sir Alex for an interview. He shouted down the tunnel, 'Yes, no problem, Bryn, as long as you don't ask stupid effing questions like that Chris Kamara.' Bryn was good enough to ring me straight away and tell me what Sir Alex had said. I'd clearly upset him and he had a problem with me. Determined not to suffer any long-term damage in my distant relationship with him, I wrote to Sir Alex to explain myself. He was good enough to write back and, while upset that I had asked 'an inane question which smacked of ladder climbing', he gave me some good advice and said he would give me 'another crack'.

And indeed he did. These days I enjoy a good relationship with Fergie, having been in his company on more than one occasion with mutual friends. Even though he shot me down, I have been careful ever since not to ask questions which can be misconstrued, and I often declare that in my lifetime Sir Alex is the best manager there has been. But that's only my opinion. Others may say I was a better manager than Sir Alex, but I haven't visited the planet they live on yet and I know I never will. He stands head and shoulders above every other manager.

But when it comes to name-dropping I can almost trump meeting Sir Alex Ferguson with fighting a world champion boxer!

'Please welcome to the ring the Champion, Ricky – The Hitman – Hatton, and, making his way to the ring, the challenger, Kammy – The Khazi – Kamara ...'

Name Dropping

Michael Gomes, a former boxing champion, is introducing the two prize fighters in Ricky Hatton's Manchester gym. I am in for a pasting and I can't wait. Not many people can say they have fought a World Champion, and not many people can say they have fought Ricky Hatton. OK, so it may not have been a real fight, but I can assure you he packs a punch even when he is restraining his thunderous jab.

For a Sky Sports special I travelled over the Pennines from Leeds to Manchester, to film a mock-up fight with Ricky at his gym in Denton. Meeting Ricky, along with his trainer Billy Graham and his fitness coach Kerry Kayes, showed me just what sort of a slog Ricky goes through between each fight, day in, day out, in order to be at his peak for the big fight night. I enjoyed the day, apart from taking the punches, and it was excellent from start to finish. If you'll pardon the obvious pun it was a knockout. The resulting video clip is one of the best I have done since working with Sky, but I was slaughtered for my acting ability! I later told Ricky he didn't frighten me and next time I'd have him, but I was on the phone at the time.

One person I know who has definitely made the best of his acting ability is my old team-mate Vinnie Jones. During the summer of 2009 my wife Anne and I travelled to Australia to meet up with our son Jack, who was having a 'year out' travelling the world with his mates. (Having been a working man since the age of 16, I sometimes find it hard to get my head around this. Do I wish I could have done the same? It never even came up when I was younger, but I was happy for Jack to do it before (hopefully) settling down into a working life.) En route Down Under, Anne and I stopped off in Los Angeles.

Mr Unbelievable

Anne asked if I would mind doing the Hollywood tour, an organised trip in a 12-seat open-top jeep, where you are driven around the streets of Hollywood, the Hollywood Hills, Bel Air, with the guide pointing out the fabulous homes of great Hollywood stars. Our driver Arturo, a Peruvian chap, was fantastic, just the sort of jovial walking encyclopedia of showbiz knowledge that we wanted. In a similar way it's amazing how many pass my own house in Yorkshire on an open-top bicycle. First stop on our tour was at a vantage point for looking out over the Hollywood Bowl, with the famous huge letters spelling out 'Hollywood' opposite us. Arturo rambled on and on as we trundled on in the jeep, showing us the various homes across the valley. As we drove up Mulholland Drive he began raving about the owner of the home which was to be our next stop.

'You may not know this actor's name. But I like him bery, bery much,' he continued in his Peruvian accent. 'He starred in *X Men* and *Gone in Sixty Seconds*.'

I listened intently – it had become a bit of a game to guess the owner of the next house from the clues he had been giving. Our man of the moment then triumphantly divulged the name of his hero. 'His name is Beenie John-ess' he declared. Anne and I looked at each other blankly – no idea. But Arturo was not finished with enthusing about 'Beenie John-ess' and he carried on repeating his name over and over until he pulled up outside these massive black gates where the Union Jack was proudly on display. Then it clicked with me and I blurted out, 'I know him!' Arturo looked at me as if to say, 'Yeah, right.' And Anne looked at me as if I was bonkers.

'How do you know Beenie John-ess?' she asked, 'What sort of name is that?'

'It's Vinnie!' I laughed, 'Vinnie Jones. It's easy when you get over the Peruvian accent.'

I again told Arturo that I knew him and so he began tooting his horn outside the gates and shouting 'Beenie! Beenie! Come outside! Come out and give us a wave!' He really was making a racket – we wondered how he got away with it when he did a similar thing again later outside another celeb house – but there was no sign of 'Beenie'.

We left Vinnie's gates and continued on our tour, Anne and I very impressed with my old team-mate's gaff. As we trawled the roads and avenues of the rich and famous, Arturo got on with his job admirably, pointing out house after mansion – Mel Gibson, Denzel Washington, Brad and Angelina, Oprah, Elton, Rod Stewart, Samuel L. Jackson, Michael Douglas, Michael Jackson (where two weeks later there was going to be more activity than just our jeep outside those gates), we saw it all. Whilst we were drinking in all this splendour I was wondering if the contact number I had for 'Beenie' still worked. Not having seen him for a number of years, I had genuinely forgotten that he was now living in LA and didn't really think I would get a reply when I sent off a text to him telling him I had been outside his gates.

'U've made it pal. Wd u believe the 1st house we stopped at woz yrs!'

Anne and I finished the tour and set off for Malibu and Venice Beach to soak up a bit of sun. We were totally surprised a couple of hours later to get a call from Vinnie saying he had been playing golf with another old team-mate of us both, David Kemp, who also had a home over that way.

'Now that you know where I am, why don't you come over later for a beer?' he insisted. When I put it to Anne she immediately went into panic mode.

'We can't do that!' she cried. 'Not looking like this. There's sand everywhere and we are looking like a couple of typical backpackers. How can we go to a Hollywood home like this?' But we also knew that we didn't get the chance to go to a Hollywood home every day, and possibly never would again, so after consideration we agreed to go.

When we arrived back outside those gates we called out, 'Beenie! Beenie! Let us in!' and he pressed the button and in we went.

Vinnie was great – it didn't seem like we had not seen each other for so long. It was 18 years since we had played together and 15 since we had last met up. That was at a charity event in Southampton, organised by comedians Richard Digance and Mike Osman. At the bar on that particular night there was me, Vinnie, Jimmy Case and Mark Dennis. That's collectively quite a few thousand hard tackles, quite a few yellow cards and a couple of dozen reds. At one point former Southampton manager Lawrie McMenemy walked over to us and said, 'I've never seen so many skilful players (not!) at one time in the same room!'

Up at his LA home Anne was loving it, getting all the info from Vinnie's wife Tania about their life in La La land, and telling Vinnie the whole 'Beenie' story.

Vinnie asked, 'From here whose house did you go to next on your tour?'

'I think it was Ron Howard's,' I said.

'Oh, didn't you go next door?' he asked, surprised.

'No. Why?' We wanted to know. 'Who lives there?'

'Quentin Tarantino,' he replied nonchalantly.

We had a fabulous couple of hours with Vinnie and co, and a guided tour of his palatial home. It was very nostalgic talking with Vinnie about old times.

'Kammy, we had some good times, you were a good mate. Didn't you once lend me some money in Majorca?'

'Yeah,' I replied. 'I forgot all about that. Where's my cash then, Mr Hollywood?' But no, he didn't pay me.

We headed off back to our base at Newport Beach, giggling to ourselves that Vinnie's place had got a mention on the famous homes tour but Quentin Tarantino's hadn't. It's a bit like checking out the big houses of London and missing out Buckingham Palace.

Speaking of which, mingling in the company of Hollywood stars is all well and good, but mingling with royalty is another matter. And I got to do that on a couple of occasions in my managerial career.

The Queen came to Bradford, along with Prince Phillip, for the official opening of the Midland Road stand, which was renamed the Allied stand on the morning of the ceremony. What impressed me was that although she must have been briefed on the journey from the Town Hall to Valley Parade, which is only about a mile, she still reeled off our history, results and the significance of the stand. I introduced her to all the players and she had a little chat with Ben and Jack, who had been given permission to skip school for the day. She made a real impression on us all, but I couldn't help looking at her and thinking how many times I'd licked the back of her head before posting a letter. A charming lady, unlike her daughter Princess Anne. I met her at the Riding for the Disabled Centre in Wakefield which I'd helped to raise money for. We were introduced and she began the conversation

'Where are you from?'

'Middlesbrough.'

She looked surprised. 'No, where are you originally from?'

'Middlesbrough.' I repeated.

Anyone else might have got an earful but I kept quiet, not wanting to be the instigator of a right royal rumpus!

HALF-TIME

KAMMY ANALYSIS AND STATS

CHRIS KAMARA'S UNBELIEVABLE
FOOTBALL CAREER STATS

Year	Club	Appearances	Goals
1975-7	Portsmouth	63	7
1977-81	Swindon Town	147	21
1981	Portsmouth	11	0
1981-5	Brentford	152	28
1985-8	Swindon Town	87	6
1988-90	Stoke City	60	5
1990-1	Leeds United	20	1
1991-3	Luton Town	49	0
1992-3	Sheffield United (loan)	8	0
1993	Middlesbrough (loan)	5	0
1993-4	Sheffield United	16	0
1994-5	Bradford City	23	3
	TOTAL	**641**	**71**

SECOND HALF

CHAPTER ELEVEN
I'M NO ZINEDINE ZIDANE, BUT ...

I wasn't a bad footballer in my day, though everyone seems to have forgotten this fact over the years. Well, everyone apart from me. I guess the show hasn't helped my cause either. When I'm not giggling on camera, or mispronouncing the name of Everton midfielder Diniyar Bilyaletdinov, the studio boys love to brand me as a one-time clogger who drove up and down the motorways from club to club, when I wasn't suspended, that is. It all makes for a good laugh and a joke, but there was a lot more to my playing days than that.

Those of you over the age of 30 may well remember me as a midfield 'dynamo', although I admit we use the term loosely here. You might have even swapped a Panini sticker of me in the school playground, although you would have had a job keeping up with my kit changes. Over a 20-year career I signed twice for Portsmouth, twice for Swindon and twice for Sheffield United. Yes, those three clubs signed me again – they couldn't believe how bad I was first time! It had nothing to do with the clause I used to put in the contracts that if I was crap then they had to give me another chance. I was like a boxer: every time I got knocked down I went back for more. But I must say no club stooped as low as to sign me for a third time. I also played for Brentford, Stoke, Leeds, Middlesbrough, Luton and Bradford, all which spanned the years from 1975 to 1995. It would almost be easier to list the clubs I didn't bloody play for in those years. At one point I was even close to going to Madrid, but that was only on holiday!

For those of you who never saw me play, perhaps in spite of being at games I featured in, I'll do a *Goals on Sunday*-style analysis of my game. I honestly reckon it wasn't too dissimilar to Wilson Palacios (Wigan, Spurs) or Kevin Nolan (Bolton, Newcastle). Actually, make that former Leicester midfielder Robbie Savage on a good day, but without the blond hair and Armani tattoo. Like Robbie, I did the ugly stuff on the pitch and talked myself into a bit of trouble, using words that not even Stephen Bywater knew. Sure, I got away with kicking a few people more than Robbie would have done, but the game was played differently back then. We had to throw ourselves about a bit in the pre-Premiership days.

Seriously, I was pretty handy on the pitch, even though I didn't win that much in the way of silverware – promotions with Leeds, Swindon and Bradford are all I have to show for 23 years in the game. Some fairly heavyweight managers invested in me, including Ian St John, Lou Macari, Dave Bassett, David Pleat and Howard Wilkinson. Alan Ball, my gaffer at Stoke, spoke highly of me (in fact, Bally used to speak highly at everyone) and reckoned I should have played for England. At one point Ron Atkinson even considered signing me for Manchester United, but he bought Remi Moses from West Brom instead. It was a close thing – at least I looked like him. I also played with a lot of quality footballers, including George Graham and England international Steve Foster, both at Pompey, midfield chancer Stan Bowles at Brentford, and Peter Beagrie at Stoke. During the autumn of my career at Leeds I had the honour of occasionally sharing a midfield with the likes of Gary McAllister, Gordon Strachan, David Batty, Vinnie Jones and Gary Speed.

Alan Ball suggesting I play for England? Well, he was close, I have to say. I could have taken a stab at international stardom, though it would have meant playing for a world minnow: Sierra Leone. I qualified because my dad had been born there. I know what you're thinking but, yes, they did have a team. Eleven patriotic devils sharing nine shirts and seven pairs of shorts. Oh yes, Dad's country had a team and I was picked to play for the national side in the Africa Cup of Nations in 1994 when I was a Sheffield United player. They were in the Premier League and I did not want to leave as I knew my place in the side would be at risk. The manager, Dave (Harry) Bassett, gave me his blessing to go for the cultural experience. I wasn't interested, though, mainly because Dad had told me not to bother. He'd been back to his homeland only twice in the 40-odd years since he left, leaving the house with a bagful of clothes and returning with just the shirt on his back and a nasty dose of malaria. He was also forever inundated with letters from 'back home', pleading for him to send money back to Africa. He used to do it too, even though we were struggling to make ends meet in Middlesbrough back in the seventies. You can understand why I wasn't fussed about flying over to Sierra Leone for the 10 days' prep before leaving for the tournament. Harry said, 'Go, Kammy. A few weeks in Tunisia where the tournament is being held will do you the world of good.'

'Thanks, but no thanks, Harry,' I said.

It had taken me since the start of the season to get a regular spot in the Sheffield United side and I had played the last four games, of which we had won two and drawn two. Because of my concerns, the people from Sierra Leone said I could miss the training camp and just needed to report to the team hotel four days before the tournament started. They were bending over backwards to get me there, but I still refused. What an idiot I was – Sierra Leone lost three games in eight days and got knocked out, and Harry dropped me from the team away to Arsenal on 28 December, four days before the tournament started!

On the Boxing Day we had played at home to Liverpool. It was a 0–0 draw and I had a pretty decent game. Good enough to be awarded the sponsor's man of the match award, in fact. After the game I hurriedly got changed and made my way to the sponsor's room to collect my award. On my return to the dressing-room I glanced at the newly posted squad sheet naming those team members who would be travelling for the away fixture at Highbury two days later. I was absolutely astounded to find that my name was not there! Johnny Greaves, the kit manager, was passing me with the skip full of the kit to travel to Arsenal. My anger got the better of me and I directed a kick straight at the skip, leaving a huge dent in it.

I then began shouting at Harry's assistant Geoff Taylor, blaming him for my absence from the teamsheet. Geoff told me to take it up with Harry, who had hit the M1 down to London for a family party. I sloped off home, full of disappointment and anger, the man of the match award paling into insignificance now.

Later that evening the phone went. It was Harry, who had received the news of my rantings from his assistant. 'Kammy, you are thirty-six,' Harry said, 'not sixteen. I pick the team and if you have a problem, speak to me about it. I am upset at your attitude, but then again that's the reason why you are still playing in the Premier League at your age. Don't worry, you will be back in the side against Wimbledon – I promise you that.' I was feeling slightly better after the call – until I looked for the Wimbledon fixture and saw it was six weeks away! But sure enough, I did play.

I was also called up for England in a cack-handed sort of way when Graham Taylor, then manager of the national side, rang my house in the summer of 1992. I was out at the time, but he left a message with Anne, my wife.

'I need to talk to Chris straightaway,' he said. 'I want him to play for England.'

Anne couldn't believe it. When I got home she was buzzing. 'Graham Taylor's been on the phone, he wants you to play for England – those were his exact words to me. He'll call back at seven this evening.'

'Don't be daft,' I said, 'it's a wind-up and you've fallen for it.'

I was always involved in wind-ups with a good friend of ours, Steve Booth, whose family we holidayed with every year, and whilst he fell for almost every one of the pranks, he always vowed to get me back one day. I could not believe Anne had fallen for this.

'When he calls back just laugh at him,' I said. 'He thinks he's got you now.' Seven p.m. came and went: no call. Throughout the evening we were plotting our revenge and then at eight o'clock the next morning the phone rang.

'Leave this to me, Anne,' I said. 'I will sort it.'

'Is that you, Chris? Graham Taylor here.'

'Yeah, yeah,' I said. 'Boothy, you need to do better than that.'

'Is that Chris Kamara?' said Graham for the second time, and to my disbelief I recognised his voice. My heart sank for being so flippant and calling the England manager 'Boothy', but then skipped a few beats as so many things went through my mind. Was this really it? Had I arrived!? After the shock had finally worn off, I figured that maybe there was an outside chance that even I could get a cap. The England manager had been generous in his caps (that's one way of saying it), so maybe he had a special role in mind for me. But the sad truth was that England were preparing for their ill-fated trip to Sweden for the Euros, Graham had found out I was due to be at Lilleshall National Sports Centre in Shropshire to do my UEFA 'A' coaching badge, and he needed some extra bodies for a behind-closed-doors friendly.

'It will be an honour,' I said. 'Thanks for the call and I will see you on Saturday.'

I thoroughly enjoyed the experience, playing alongside the likes of Ian Wright, Paul Merson, Gary Lineker, Alan Shearer,

I'm No Zinedine Zidane, But ...

Stuart Pearce, John Barnes, to name but a few – and I even managed to score a goal past Chris Woods, although that alone should have been an indicator of things to come for our England squad of 1992!

Despite all that it still wasn't my closest brush with international glory. When I started playing for Pompey as a teenager I went for England youth trials, but the chances of making the final XI were slim: I was competing against a group of players that included Glenn Hoddle, Ray Wilkins, Graham Rix and Bryan Robson, and I didn't get a sniff.

Hindsight is a wonderful thing, but I think much of my skill on the park was overshadowed by the brawn in the game in the seventies and eighties. Yes, I did a little bit of scrapping and kicking in the middle of the pitch, but so did everyone. Instead, I gathered quite a bad reputation because of two incidents. I was involved in an incident which saw West Ham striker Frank McAvennie break his leg, and before that I found myself in serious trouble for thumping a player on the pitch.

I'll be coming back to that, but first I'd like to highlight the fact that there's much more to my career than a few mispronounced names on *Soccer Saturday* and my overuse of the word 'Unbelievable!' As a player I fought like a beaver against managers, fellow pros, bigots, authority, the National Front and, once or twice, the long arm of the law. Somehow I made a life for myself in an era of racism, poor wages and even poorer diets, where drinking wasn't discouraged and gambling was an occupational hazard. Looking back it's a miracle I got through it all in one piece. Maybe this is the one time I have every right to use the word unbelievable.

CHAPTER TWELVE
KICK IT OUT

I love going to football grounds all over the country. At Pompey I've seen 11-goal thrillers and been looked after by the fans. The Geordies seem to love me up at Newcastle United and Sunderland, certainly more than they did when I used to play for Middlesbrough. I even have a lot of banter with the lads down at West Ham. Sadly, it wasn't always that way. When I was a player during the seventies and eighties, I was often booed at grounds, just because I was black.

I'll never forget the moment a football fan first lobbed a banana at me. The Kammy you know today would have probably picked it up, eaten it, slipped arse over elbow on the skin and got myself a regular clip on *Soccer AM*. But this is now and that was then.

It was in London and I was playing for Portsmouth against Millwall, a friendly bunch of supporters if ever there was one. I remember seeing a yellow object – why am I saying that, it was a bloody banana – flying out of the crowd and landing somewhere near my feet. I could hear monkey noises and shouts of 'You black so-and-so!' coming from behind me. When I looked up there were hateful faces staring back at me, and that was just my own back four! Seriously, it was bloody terrifying. I wish I could have called those New Zealand rugby players out and equalled the odds a bit. Sadly, it wasn't a one-off. What made it worse when I played there was that Millwall had two black players, Trevor Lee and Phil Walker. I remember talking to Phil after the game and Phil gave his overview:

'Me and Trevor don't exist with most of the fans and we can't believe the abuse visiting black players get, but they leave us alone so we just get on with it.' It seems unbelievable now, but racism was something I had to deal with throughout much of my playing career. As a tough-tackling midfielder I used to put up with vile chants and abuse from opposing fans. Most people didn't like me because I played hard. Maybe I'm being over-sensitive, because fans abused all hard-tackling midfielders on the away side, whatever colour they were, but sometimes I even took crap from my own supporters.

At times, the abuse got me down. It would eat away at me during games, and sometimes I did well to hold my temper. There was a small National Front presence at Fratton Park when I started playing for Portsmouth as a teenager in 1975. Even though I was proudly wearing their club's shirt, they would subject me to racist insults whenever I touched the ball or won a tackle for them. In an era of casual racism and telly programmes such as *Till Death Us Do Part*, with Alf Garnett, and *Love Thy Neighbour*, sitcoms which would never get on the TV today – Google them if you don't believe me – abuse was an accepted part of the game for a black player. I used to think, 'Hang on, I'm playing for *their* team. Surely they should be cheering me on?' I couldn't get my head around it. There weren't any anti-racism campaigns such as 'Kick It Out' or 'Show Racism the Red Card' or any organisation to help us in those days. I certainly wasn't a strong enough character to be the first one to make a stand on my own. If I had done, I'd have probably been viewed as a trouble-maker by managers and team-mates. I would have brought even more negative attention on myself. I simply kept my head down and carried on playing. When I'd reached boozing age, I would be refused entry to bars and clubs. The barman or bouncers ('security' to those under the age of 35) would always give some other rubbish excuse like I was under-dressed or the place was full, but I always knew when I wasn't welcome for the obvious reason. I was often kicked out into the street while pals argued my case.

Sometimes the abuse bothered my team-mates more than it bothered me. One incident took place in the town of Wetherby, near York, in 1975 when I was playing for Pompey. We had played Sunderland in the final game of the season and they beat us that day to win the league and go back to the top division. I will always remember Sunderland captain Bobby Moncur coming up to me at the end of the game and saying, 'I can't believe you're only 17, son. You're going to be a good player.' Wetherby was, and still is, the traditional stop-off point on the way to and from games in the North-east. Fish'n'chips at the Wetherby Whaler have been keeping generations of managers and their players very content on journeys up and down the A1, and now M1, for decades as all the teams who travel to the North-east stop there. That day the Portsmouth squad descended on the Whaler, and while we waited for our order we popped over the road to the pub for a pint. Despite the fact that I was with about 10 team-mates, the landlord refused to serve me. 'We don't let his type in here,' he said to my mates at the bar and ordered me out. Mind you, if they'd known what me and Jeff Stelling got up to in Japan later we wouldn't have been allowed in anywhere, so it's a fair cop.

Racism was something I'd suffered as a fan, too. When I was a kid I followed Boro and Leeds. My heroes were Norman Hunter, Allan Clarke, Johnny Giles and Peter Lorimer, in fact all the squad. Leeds were one of the top teams around, and my home team Boro were in the third division, so I loved them both equally. But going to Elland Road was a risky business, especially for a gangly black kid from the North-east. On the occasions I went it seemed I was the only black face in the crowd and I used to receive abuse from some Leeds supporters, especially if they did not win. My old football coach from Beechwood Youth Club, Alan Ingledew, always took me to the games, otherwise I would never in a month of Sundays have been able to afford to go or even have had the knowhow to get there. He gave up his Saturday afternoons just so I could see my heroes at Boro and Leeds, in return for me playing for his Sunday team, although he loved going as much as I did, along with his son Jason. It was the agreement we came to when he asked me to sign for his team. It was probably the best deal I ever negotiated for myself. I was useless at dealing with contracts as a pro. Taking me to those games was a tough job for Alan because I was black and he was white. As we got

near to the ground the insults would always start, but he kept
me safe.

'Keep your head up, son,' he'd say, staying close to me like
he was protecting his own boy, while dozens of faces stared
and spat abuse.

'Just ignore them.'

It was a fairly eye-opening welcome to football. The prejudice also hit home on the pitch and in professional dressing-
rooms later in life. After I signed with Portsmouth in 1974, I
was singled out for my colour. It sounds amazing to say it now,
but I played with and against some racists. I first noticed it
after training or matches because we used massive communal
baths in those days. The moment I jumped into it, one or two
players would always get out straightaway. They didn't have
to worry, I didn't fancy any of them. They tried not to make it
obvious, but it happened too many times for it to be a coinci-
dence. I would just let them get on with it. Occasionally it got
to me. I'd tell my dad that I was having a problem. He knew
racism would affect me and I'd find it hard to handle. I had two
choices: either put up with it or become a victim, which neither
of us wanted. I put up with it. Despite the one or two morons,
I also had some good pals at the club. I often went out with
England international-in-waiting Steve Foster, him with the
headband, Graham Roberts and David Puller. They were good
lads, but I'd never let on to them that I was having a few problems. When I think back Steve used to have crowd problems
too, what with his long curly hair and headband. Headband?
Big white headband? I bet a few got bothered when he jumped
in the communal bath as well. If Steve Foster hadn't been a

footballer we would never have seen Berbatov, Tevez or Woodgate daring to strut around like netball internationals.

Sometimes I would lash out verbally and on one particular occasion I let myself down massively, which resulted in me being the first footballer to be convicted of assault on the pitch. It's not something I'm proud of, and I wish to this day that I hadn't done it. I was playing for Swindon in 1988 and Shrewsbury Town striker Jim Melrose and I had a few words after a midfield tussle. Jim had taken a bang to the face when a few players went in for the ball just around the halfway line, but it wasn't me that clumped him. His team-mate, Victor Kasule, was also in the heap and his flailing knee had connected with Jim's mouth, cutting it. Nothing was really said at the time, but it became obvious that Jim was angry as he came after me whilst we were waiting for a corner. He came at me aggressively, but I'd seen him out of the corner of my eye, so I was ready for it. There wasn't a huge amount of contact and he just ran off, so I chased after him. Unfortunately words were spoken which resulted in me thumping him in full view of everybody at the end of the game.

The weird thing was, I actually thought I was being professional by leaving it until the end of the game rather than losing it completely whilst play was going on. I didn't want to satisfy him by getting sent off. I wanted to win the game, and I knew there was a better chance of that with me on the pitch. That theory quickly collapsed when Jim later scored the winning goal. As he celebrated, it felt like my nose was being rubbed in it. Sure enough, when the final whistle blew I headed for him. Jim was applauding the Shrewsbury fans on the halfway line, so he was oblivious to me sprinting the length of the field. I'd been building up to it for a while, so the adrenaline was pumping.

When I got close, I hit him and he fell like a sack of spuds. I didn't even look at him, I just jogged off the pitch and went down the tunnel. Behind me it was all kicking off. My Swindon team-mate Steve Foley, who had seen the incident, was trying to pick him up off the floor. Apparently Steve was going on about how there was nothing wrong with him and telling him to get up. Because he had not seen me coming he wasn't expecting a punch, so he was relaxed. That's what made it worse for him – and me. After jumping in the bath in the dressing-room, it was clear something was wrong. The Swindon manager, Lou Macari – who I wasn't really getting on with at the time – asked me what had happened.' Nothing,' I said. 'I've sorted it and it's finished with. It has nothing to do with you.' I didn't want to tell him the full details, so I just got on the team bus. Jim actually walked past us as he set off for the hospital, where X-rays revealed that he had a depressed fracture of the cheekbone. But it had everything to do with Lou. The Melrose incident was the end of our relationship and I missed the rest of the season.

Worse, I was convicted of GBH. Undoubtedly it was the darkest moment of my career. I couldn't play football till the court case was over. I felt crap. I hated myself for what I had done to myself and my family. My dad could hardly look me in the eye – he felt let down. He told me I should have been big enough to put up with anything. He believed I'd learnt that lesson early on in life, but clearly I hadn't. Instead, I'd taken a massive step backwards. I showed a lack of control and I let a lot of people down that day. GBH? Me? How things change – these days I'm scared stiff of speed cameras.

You would think things would have been a little easier to handle once I got into the dugouts with Bradford and Stoke City. English football had moved on in the 1990s and there were more black players than ever before. Sadly, the worst outburst of racism aimed at me came when I was managing Bradford in a game at Oxford United. I kept getting out of the dugout to remonstrate with the ref Steve Baines (well, we all do it), who was one of a small group of people who have played pro football and progressed to referee. One of Steve's former clubs was Bradford, and at the time I felt that as if not to show bias he was giving everything Oxford's way. One Oxford fan in particular kept standing up behind me and shouting;

'Sit down, Kamara!' As the game wore on, he started to get more vicious. 'Kamara! Kamara!' Then it came out. 'Sit down, you black bastard!' he shouted. More unbelievably, this idiot was sitting next to his wife and kids. I went crazy. I saw red. My assistants Paul Jewell, Chris Hutchings, Steve Redmond and Martin Hunter were all on the bench with me and each one seemed to have a hold of a different part of my body as I scrambled over the dugout to remonstrate with him. A policeman even came to see what was going on. Paul Jewell gave the copper chapter and verse, pointing to the abuser. The police escorted him from his seat with his family following in tow, and I was asked if I wanted to press charges but I declined. He wasn't worth it, I reckoned. The club threatened to withdraw his season ticket, but all I wanted was a letter of apology. Although all the people at Oxford were very professional that day, I never did receive a letter. I just assumed the objectionable pillock couldn't even write.

A later incident at Port Vale was handled entirely differently, however. The dugout at Vale Park is some way from the stands, but as I was making my way back to the dressing-rooms at half-time, a fella appeared from nowhere by the side of the tunnel.' Kamara, you effing black bastard!' he repeated over and over. It was unbelievable. I was ushered down the tunnel to deliver my team talk, but I made sure that the stewards had seen the incident. When I got back to the dugout for the second half I was amazed to see the guy was still standing there. No one, it seemed, fancied kicking him out of the ground. I was later told by a steward that he'd been escorted out at the break, but was allowed back in by the chairman because he was claiming that I'd started it. The dugout was at least 10 yards away from the terraces, so I would have been hard pressed to 'start' something with that idiot!

The Football League and the FA got involved days later and apparently investigated the outburst. They received a letter from Port Vale secretary Bill Lodey, who claimed I'd sparked the incident, but when I rang Vale and gave him a piece of my mind, he retracted the claim. Still, it didn't make me feel any better. How had I instigated it? By formerly playing for Stoke (Port Vale's big rivals)? By being black? Or by just being there? I never did find out.

Racism hasn't disappeared from football grounds entirely. There have been some improvements since the bad old days, though weirdly it took a white man to get the ball rolling. When Eric Cantona jumped into the crowd to kick a Crystal Palace fan called Matthew Simmons in 1995, it sent shock waves throughout the game. Simmons had allegedly chucked a volley of racist abuse at Eric, who reacted with a Karate Kid-style kick to the chops. It rattled the football world because it was such an extreme reaction. It also caught the attention of the public. Racism was no longer just a colour thing: where you were born had now come into it. Racism was still prevalent in football grounds and, after Eric's brainstorm, something had to be done.

Plenty of anti-racism organisations have been set up since the formation of the Premiership. They all do a great job, but bigotry in football hasn't disappeared, as the England team discovered when they played Spain in 2004. The Spanish fans made monkey noises every time a black player touched the ball. A year later, their coach Luis Aragones referred to Thierry Henry as 'a black shit' during a Spanish training session. He was only fined £2,060 by the Spanish FA. Ironically, Henry then went on to play for Barcelona in Spain! Clearly, the job is only half finished. It exists among English fans as well. These days, I'm on my guard when I follow England around because a racist element still exists amongst the supporters, albeit in small numbers. When I hear the crowd singing 'No surrender to the IRA' it makes me feel uncomfortable. I've been there when fans have booed Emile Heskey just because of his colour. Sometimes the same people then have the cheek to turn around to me and say, 'Oh, we're not booing at you, Chris. We're booing him, we don't like him. We don't consider you to be black.' In their mind, that justifies the racism. Sadly, I can't say anything, because generally these people are surrounded by other small-minded idiots, all looking for an excuse to kick off. Arguing back will only get your teeth or head kicked in, so you have to bite your tongue and walk away in disgust. Especially if you like your gnashers as shiny and pristine as mine, even though the front left one is capped.

CHAPTER THIRTEEN
IN THE DRY DOCK

OK, first things first: a confession. These days it's common-place to admit to some deep-seated addiction such as boozing, dogging or dressing up in ladies' clothes in the opening chapters of a football autobiography, just to get the reader's attention. Well, not here. You'll get all of that in an Alan McInally book. And while my news is far less controversial – and unlikely to get the tabloid boys drooling – it's still pretty startling.

The truth is, I might never have made it as a professional footballer, goal analyst and 'Soccer Saturday's intrepid roving reporter and football wally de jour' (cheers, Jeff). If life had panned out differently I could have been the admiral of my own battleship, seeking out foreign lands, hunting Red Octobers and fighting Somalian pirates. I could have been commanding cruise missiles and lifeboats rather than listening to Stelling's terrible gags on a Saturday. Most of all, I could have been a hero. I could have been a major figure in the Royal Navy. Lord Nelson was, and he was only four foot ten, so there was more chance of me becoming an admiral than him becoming a decent centre-half. OK, I was four foot ten once, but I was only nine years old. He also only had one eye as opposed to my two, so he would have been crap at corners from the left. I would have walked through the ranks easily. Well, maybe not, but I did join the forces at the tender age of 16.

This happened because of my dad. He had spent a large chunk of his life in the Royal Navy, and he wanted me to follow his footsteps, even though I was a keen footballer at the time. He never encouraged me to support this team or that team. He didn't take me to games or watch the footy with me on the telly. Dad wanted me to get a bit of discipline instead. Still, I admit it, at first I liked the experience of being in the forces. The main benefit to a life on the open seas – actually it was dry dock – was that I had a routine and got a proper hot meal every day for the first time in my life. In fact, life in service was like a bloody holiday compared to what I sometimes had to put up with at home.

I grew up at 29 Aldridge Road, Park End, Middlesbrough; there was me, Mam, Dad and my sister, Maria, and brother, George, who went on to become quite a handy boxer in the army. You had to be tough in our house though. Being the only black family in Middlesbrough in the early seventies meant that life could be pretty hard. As I mentioned earlier, some of the prejudice we had to put up with was incredible. Looking back on it now, I know it would never have been tolerated today. Back then we would stick it out. If we'd taken crap from another family, or someone in the street, Dad would stand up and fight for us, and then we'd all just pray for an end to it. It never ended, though.

Dad was originally from Sierra Leone. He came to England with the Royal Navy in 1949, after the Second World War. Like most immigrants, he was looking for a better life and ended up in Nanny Green's boarding house in Middlesbrough, a shelter for strays in town. Dad – real name Alimamy Kindo Kamara, translated simply to Albert Kamara – found it hard to fit into his new life and regularly came across racism. This often ended with a blazing punch-up. Dad suffered at the hands of the police, and he felt they victimised him throughout his life. If there was something they couldn't pin on a suspect, they'd often turn up at our house to blame him. We were never allowed to shout or complain on his behalf. Dad told me to ride with it and never to fight back against the establishment, but the funny thing was, he would do exactly the opposite. It is very difficult to envisage nowadays, but I only had to step out of the front door to go to school for someone to say something offensive. Often it came from the people you'd least expect. Well, not my sister, so not the very least expected person, but a kindly-faced granny in the newsagents would yell at me to go back to where I came from. Bloody hell, I only lived three doors away! So I just used to nod and go home. Life was tough.

I remember spending hours and hours – probably days in total – waiting for Dad and Mam in pub doorways and sometimes not knowing whether we'd be receiving a hot meal that night. Those times spent sitting outside a Middlesbrough pub and the ones feeling hungry and fed up aren't really happy memories. In fact, I don't remember much about life as a kid in Middlesbrough. Perhaps I've erased it from my head and blocked most of it out subconsciously, but whenever I try to recall my early life, the memories are very much in black and white, like the grainy pictures on an old TV set. There's very little colour, unless I think of a time when I was playing football. It's all just a grey blur, which is a massive shame for any adult.

It wasn't just me that had it hard, either. Life was tough for my mam, Irene, too. Every Thursday she'd walk 10 miles from Park End to the ICI plant at Billingham or Marske to meet Dad, despite the thrombosis in her legs. Later she took a slightly shorter trek to the British Steel works in Grangetown, near Redcar, but each trip was a slog. She'd walk this distance just to collect Dad's wages. She couldn't trust him not to spend it in the bookies before he got home. All too many times he had reached our front door having blown the lot on duff bets. This was usually done without a shadow of remorse. Mam soon got wise to this and would meet him at the factory gates because she couldn't trust him. He couldn't trust himself half the time. I think he quite liked the arrangement, because it became a good excuse for them to go straight out and have a drink together. George, Maria and me just sat and waited at home, praying that dinner was on its way. When the money did run out (in the pub or bookies), Mam would then beg the neighbours for bread, milk and butter. There wasn't a door in our street that she hadn't knocked on pleading for cash too, at some point or another. She would never tell them whether she really needed it for beer money or Dad's bus fare to work. So a warning to you all here: I learnt a lot from Mam in those days, so when my days on TV are over I will come knocking on your door with the begging bowl. I know where you live!

At 16, I suppose the Navy felt like a bit of an escape from all of this. It certainly changed my outlook on life, and the discipline and training didn't feel like a new beginning, more like an entirely new way of life. At first I was reluctant to join, but I couldn't change Dad's mind and I knew he was determined for me to sign up. But once I came round to the idea and accepted my future, I never looked back. It helped that I was allowed to play football for the Navy team, too. At that time, believe it or not, I was shaping up as quite a handy player. Yes, I know what you're thinking and I don't blame you for not believing.

Playing football was just a natural thing for me as a kid, though I was never really encouraged. I played for the team at St Pius primary school and always kicked a ball about in the road with my mates. One of those lads was Steve Gibson, who went on to become the chairman of Middlesbrough, a team we both loved as kids. Later, when I went to St Thomas's secondary school, I was by far the best player among the pupils, and before you say so, no it wasn't a girls' school, but it wasn't a surprise because it was all I ever thought about. Mam would never show my school reports to my dad because they were always bad and I would have been in big trouble. My problem was that I was always looking out of the window at the school pitches. I dreamt about scoring goals for Leeds or Boro.

My dream almost came true at an early age. Around the age of 15, I was good enough to play for Middlesbrough Boys. Dave Richardson, now of the Premier League, was my coach at Ayresome Park and he had a very good team. Former England cricketer Bill Athey was in that team and he was a very good player. In one season we beat just about everybody in our area. We were so strong that we got into the national youth cup final. I was approaching the age where I could sign apprentice forms with a club, and Dave warned me that I'd have to make some choices. There was a good chance that Boro would want to sign me as an apprentice. Dad wasn't so keen. Football never really came into his world at that time, so playing football for a career was never a serious option. It was a different generation back then. Instead, he was desperate for me to join the Navy, because he reckoned it was the best way for me to get out of Middlesbrough and to better myself. When I mention this to people now, a lot of them ask me how I could have let Dad make that decision for me. I guess I always respected his decision. If I'd really wanted to rebel, then I could have quite easily. The only problem was, I hadn't told Dave Richardson of my plans to join the Navy. The youth cup final was looming. He was expecting me to play, and on the eve of the game I left to travel to Devon and my new life. Without Dave knowing, I'd left school at Easter, dropped out of my exams and joined the Navy. Boro went on to win the cup that day. I was about to start a new life away from football. Well, that was the idea anyway.

⚽ ⚽ ⚽ ⚽ ⚽ ⚽ ⚽

I loved life in the services, mainly because I seemed to play a lot of football. In fact I was involved in nearly all the sports on offer. Athletics, tennis, football: you name it, I played it. When it came to vocational training, I was being taught everything I'd need to survive life on the open waves, not that I ever made it on to a proper boat. All my work was taking place in a dry dock called HMS *Raleigh* in Torpoint, Devon. So yes, it was like being a vicar but not working Sundays, I suppose. It wasn't all fun and games. A letter to dad from 'The Captain, HMS *Raleigh*, Torpoint' warned me of the training to come.

Dear Mr Kamara,

Now that your son has arrived at HMS RALEIGH to begin his training in the Royal Navy, I expect that you will be wondering what his life here will be like during the next few weeks. He will spend some four months here with a class of about twenty young men in the charge of a Petty Officer who has been specially selected for training duties. On average, three or four classes are grouped into a Division under the supervision of a Divisional Officer who is my representative for the welfare of the men in his Division. Unless you hear from me to the contrary you can assume that he is getting on well, and that there is no need to worry about his well-being. Slight home-sickness is naturally not uncommon at first, but we find that the vast majority overcome it with sympathy and, best of all, encouragement from home.

Sincerely,
The Captain

The homesickness never came. I was only in the Navy for six months before the chance to jump ship came, thanks to Portsmouth Football Club. I knew I had to take it. The club had seen me playing for the Navy representative team in Portsmouth after I had been transferred there from HMS *Raleigh* to HMS *Vernon*. I was scoring for the Navy (as opposed to in the Navy) and new Pompey manager and former Liverpool legend Ian St John wanted me to join his blossoming trainee squad. A guy called Henry Stenhouse ran the Navy side and had already recommended me to St John, who had only been at the club for a few weeks. St John, youth-team manager Ray Crawford and chief scout Tony Barton liked what they saw and took me on. I remember Tony (who later went on to win the European Cup as Aston Villa manager in 1982) taking me round to my digs in Portsmouth.

Dad still wasn't keen. He insisted that I had a letter from the Navy promising to take me back if things didn't work out with Pompey. He'd already stopped me from joining Boro. This time I was just really grateful he was allowing me to try out with Pompey, though I couldn't have cared less about the letter and his lack of faith in me. I joined Portsmouth full-time as an apprentice on £8 a week and with a £200 buy-out fee to the Navy agreed. It still goes down as the worst deal in Portsmouth's history. I became St John's first signing on 8 November 1974. Pompey were in the old Second Division at the time (now the Championship). I was 16 years old and suddenly it all felt like a very long way from home and my old life in Middlesbrough. It didn't help when the youth-team boss told the *Portsmouth News* that my 'knowledge of the game [was] scanty. He is weak in the air, his marking is wayward and he hasn't got much positional sense.' But I didn't care, I was playing professional football and living the dream. Besides, it was probably one of the nicest things ever written about my playing style. In fact, thinking back, it was the nicest thing ever written about my playing style.

It's always amazing how you make do when money is tight. For years in Middlesbrough, we didn't even have such basic requirements of modern living as a wardrobe or a fridge. Many houses had outside toilets, but when I think back I reckon we had an outside lounge. When I was a kid, my brother and I used to hang our clothes on a length of string which dangled across the length of our bedroom. We called it 'the rope'. I remember when Anne first visited our Middlesbrough house I had joked with her that she would be getting all the hanging space for her clothes that she could ever dream of. I was in my twenties and playing for Swindon by that point, but Mam and Dad seemed to be stuck in a time warp. 'The rope' was still hanging across my old room. They didn't have a fridge or basic storage units for the kitchen either. There was no heating, just a coal fire burning all day in the front room, and it was on all year round. Dad worked in the blast furnace and he came from Africa, so he was always cold in the house. Even on the warmest summer day he'd have the fire blazing in the front room. To help out, I decided to give them an unwanted fridge, just a small one with a little flap-down icebox in it. We had brought it from our house in Swindon, and when we took it into their house, Mam and Dad walked round it like it was a spaceship which had just landed unannounced. They stood back when I opened the door and cooed at the light inside. Anne explained how it worked before filling it with food.

Mr Unbelievable

I guess they had never entertained the idea of needing a fridge because there was no central heating in the house, and they reckoned the pantry was cold enough to store any dairy stuff, along with Dad's meat for the curries. It had always been that way. They wouldn't buy something when they didn't need it. Mam always purchased food at the corner shop to eat that day. Her theory was, 'Why buy today what you won't need until tomorrow?'

Anne explained that all food could be kept fresh in the fridge, although whenever we went back for a visit, the meat for Dad's legendary curries would still be left on the cooker, rather than in the fridge. We then told Dad how the icebox worked in the freezer and how you had to defrost it if it got clogged with thick ice.

It went in one ear and out the other. The next morning we walked into the kitchen only to find Dad peering into the unplugged new fridge with a bowl of hot water in the upper section. Overnight, a thin film of frost had formed inside the freezer compartment. He must have thought, 'Christ, what have they brought this contraption for? If I have to go through this palaver every morning I wish they hadn't bothered. I'll stick to the pantry.'

Anne put him right about when the fridge would need defrosting, but it was too late for Mam. She was scared off for life. As far as she was concerned, the pantry was good enough for her.

A few years later Anne and I went to visit Mam in Middlesbrough and instead of the usual trip out for lunch that I always liked to treat her to we thought we would stay in, so we went armed with pizzas to have later. Mam said she had tried pizza before and wasn't keen but would give it another go. As the time ticked by and we began to feel peckish, I asked Mam if it was OK to put the oven on. 'What for?' she asked. 'To cook the pizzas, of course' I replied. She looked confused and then said, 'Oh, is that what you have to do with them? Cook them in the oven? No wonder I wasn't keen.' It turned out she had eaten uncooked pizza – yuk! I can assure you, the survival instinct in Mam was such that there was no way she would ever leave anything but an empty plate, so I know for sure that she had devoured the raw pizza to the last crumb!

CHAPTER FOURTEEN
(NOT) THE LAST OF THE INTERNATIONAL PLAYBOYS

I loved Portsmouth and a part of me still does. I would not be where I am today if I had not gone there. From the moment I'd signed forms with Pompey, I was as happy as a pig in the brown stuff. Sometimes in the Navy, when I was not doing sport, I had to get up at six in the morning and wouldn't finish work until eight in the evening. In those long hours I was learning the ropes in dry dock, taking on physical challenges and assault courses, and working on the basic training programme, with football and other sporting activities thrown in on top. Half the time I was bloody knackered.

At Pompey, I could have a lie-in. I lived in digs in St Ronan's Avenue, Southsea, with the Penneys, Keith and Hazel, and their two sons David and Jeremy. I lived like a king – Hazel treated me as one of the family. We had to be at the club for nine a.m., where I'd clean the boots, sweep the terraces and wash out the dressing-rooms. This was probably quite arduous for some of the apprentices, but to me it was a doddle. We'd play football from 10.30 to 12.30 and for another hour after lunch. I thought

I was on holiday. I had a cracking laugh, too. I quickly made friends with trainee defender Steve 'Fossie' Foster, who later went on to play for Brighton in the 1983 FA Cup final and for England. You'd remember him from the photos, where he often sported a big broccoli haircut and that headband.

Fossie was great fun and we were forever messing around. I remember when the first team were playing against Aston Villa. All the lads were doing the work after the game – cleaning the baths, collecting the kit for washing – but Fossie and me had sat in the away dressing-room. We were talking about the game as Villa winger Ray Graydon was getting dressed after the game. He was their big name at the time. He took one look at us sitting there and laughed.

'You two must be the star players at this club,' he said.

Fossie looked up at him and said, 'Why's that?'

'Because you're sitting there doing naff all, that's why. Everyone else is working their bollocks off.'

Fossie couldn't help himself. 'You got that in one, Ray.'

At that moment our youth-team manager, Ray Crawford, popped his head round the door. We both jumped up, quick as you like, and started sweeping the floor furiously. Graydon couldn't keep the smirk off his face.

It was all a good laugh. As an apprentice you're the butt of the jokes, and most of it was good-natured banter from the pros. I was hammered, big style. I got extra stick because I was a gangly kid, straight out of the Navy, with hair like the wild man of Borneo. They must have taken one look at me and thought, 'What the bloody hell have we got here?' These days, I look back at the old team pictures and can see their point. I was never going to challenge George Best for the 'Best Looking Footballer of the Year Award', if an award like that had even existed.

It didn't help that George Graham and Peter Marinello were at the club at the time. George was known by everyone in the game as 'Gorgeous George' because of his suave good looks and stylish clothes. Marinello, meanwhile, was nicknamed 'The Cat' by the lads at the club. I'm not entirely sure why. Maybe he could sleep anywhere. I reckon it was probably because he was out all night and nobody ever knew where he'd been. The fans called him 'the Scottish George Best' because of his style of play at Hibernian before joining Arsenal. Despite being offloaded by Arsenal, Peter was still a class act on the pitch, but he was lazy and would often do his own thing. He always wanted the ball and was lightning quick, but if you laid a pass in front of him rather than to his feet, he wouldn't bother chasing after it. It got frustrating for the more senior players in the team. I wasn't bothered and I certainly wouldn't have dreamt of saying anything to him. I was just happy to be there.

George Graham, meanwhile, was coming to the end of his career. He had made a name for himself at Arsenal and Manchester United and was 32 at the time. He arrived at Fratton Park having been swapped with Ron Davies, who went the other way to Old Trafford. His legs had gone but he was a terrific bloke and a massive influence on all the young lads at the club. We all looked up to him. In those days, he was nothing like the strict disciplinarian he would later become as a manager with Arsenal, Leeds and Spurs. He was fun-loving George. When United had offloaded him, I think he must have felt like playing out his final professional days in comfort.

Boozing wasn't considered a red-card offence in football back then and George liked a beer.

George was always centre of attention with the ladies. The WAGs weren't really around in those days. Today, the modern player has the pick of the girls, but in 1975 that wasn't the case. Fossie and I weren't earning that much cash, so the hot, single lasses of Portsmouth probably didn't think a lad like myself, on £10 a week, was much of a catch. I was hardly the doorway to a life of leisure. And anyway, no girl wanted to snog a gangly bloke with a broken tooth. They made an exception for George. He was rich(ish), famous and good-looking.

It was the same for Peter. He had long straight hair with a side parting, just like George Best, and was a bit of a budding fashion icon too, often seen in a trendy white mac. There were always a lot of girls around him. He had a missus when he was at Pompey, and I mean his own missus and not someone else's, but if there was a lads' night out, the opposite sex always gathered around him. Because of that, Fossie and I thought these were great blokes to be around, though Fossie probably did a lot better than me with the girls at the time. Thanks to my appearance, I didn't get a look in.

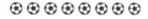

Walk into the car park of any Premiership training ground and you'll see some pretty flash motors. Beemers, 'baby Bentleys', those fancy little sports cars that hairdressers love so much – the car is the first thing most footballers worry about when they sign a professional contract with any club. It won't surprise you to learn that I wasn't any different. Once I'd started to make a name for myself at Pompey in the 1975-76 season, I went out and got myself the best car my wages could buy: a Ford Cortina. Of course, it was a pile of crap but it had a handbrake. Having passed my driving test I splashed out a few hundred quid for my dream runaround – one previous owner, Pompey team-mate Bobby McGuinness. I paid in cash and Bobby disappeared in a puff of smoke. Amazing really, because the car performed a similar trick less than 24 hours later when I proudly drove home to Middlesbrough to show it off to Mam and Dad.

Even now I can recall the horror of feeling the car die on me. After the final training session of the week, I set off from the digs in Portsmouth in my new pride and joy. By junction 28 of the M1 near Mansfield, the engine was spluttering and the seats were shaking. I called a mechanic, who said he could only fix it the following morning, so I had to spend the night in a nearby B&B. The next day, the mechanic did just enough to get me home. The car coughed and choked its way into Aldridge Road, but when I arrived (very noisily) Mam and Dad didn't mind. After attention from another mechanic the car was sorted for £150, and I drove them around Middlesbrough like royalty for the entire close season.

It was funny, but after I started to play regularly in the Portsmouth first team, Mam and Dad really took an interest in my career. I guess they didn't think it was a serious voca-tional choice until I'd signed professional forms and got myself a classy bottom-of-the-range Ford Cortina to drive them around town in. Once I began a new life for myself in football, they looked at my passion differently and came to as many matches as possible. Their place in the stands was mainly down to my old Beechwood Youth Club coach, Alan Ingledew, who drove them to the Pompey fixtures, home and away, whenever he could, including my debut.

I loved them being there. When I was a kid playing for different teams across Middlesbrough, Dad only ever saw me play once. Whenever I played a schoolboys game, I'd look along the touchline where most of the other lads' mams and dads were standing, praying that he would be there with them. He never was, except once. The image of him watching me on the sidelines that one time is crystal clear to this day: I was playing for St Thomas's school. It was the final of the Schools' Championships at Clairville Stadium in Middlesbrough. He turned up on his bike halfway through the first half. I can still picture him, silhouetted against the sunlight at the top of the stand. There was a cycle track all the way around the pitch and he was standing up at the top, astride his bike. He was finally watching me. I was running around the pitch with elastic bands held across the toe-caps of both boots to stop the tongues from flapping around. I probably didn't look very different when I played my first game for Pompey a few years later in 1975.

Thinking back, I hadn't grown up too much by then, either. Away from the pitch I was always fairly quiet and unassuming. When I signed at Fratton Park, I realised that I was really a very different person when I played football. I believed in myself. I was almost fiery. And the more I played, the more confident I became off the field. When I started at the club, I scored goals regularly for the youth team and played for the reserves in the South East Counties League against up-and-coming star players like Glenn Hoddle.

The coach of the youth team was Ray Crawford, who in his day had been a striker with Ipswich Town and won the First Division Championship in 1962. He also played for England. Ray was a joy to work with – but then he began picking on me, or so I thought. It was his way of trying to improve me, but I could not handle it at times. After a blistering start as a goalscoring midfielder the goals dried up, which affected me mentally.

Like every lad at every club at that crucial stage in his career, I worried about blowing it. I'd have nightmares in which I was being kicked out of Portsmouth and heading back to the Navy. I suddenly realised that after all, despite my earlier presumptions, I hadn't enjoyed the forces so much that I wanted to go back. It really would be a case of being all at sea if Pompey dispensed with me.

Before our next youth match Ray, sensing my anxieties, took me aside and assured me that if I continued to listen and learn, I could become a regular in the reserves and even make the first team in my first year in football. Now that would be some achievement. From there I could go far in the game. It felt like a fresh start, and his message stayed with me for years. Despite what he'd said about me in the local paper when I joined from the Navy, and despite what he said about me during the training sessions, I suddenly respected the words of the championship-winning England international who I should perhaps have listened to in the first place

Later that day we went two down to Fulham's youth team, and after scoring one goal, I set up the winner in a 3-2 victory. I was back on track.

In that first season together we eventually won the Youth Cup. After settling down in the youth side, I made more reserve-team appearances and, at 17, was in the first team for a pre-season friendly against Brighton. If you think that happened quickly, I then made my debut at the end of August 1975 against Luton Town. It was all happening so fast, but winger Mick Mellows was out with a knee injury and manager Ian St John didn't want to upset the rest of the team by moving his more experienced players into unfamiliar roles. It was time for him to delve into the apprentices for a striker – and he came up with me.

His hand was forced really. In those days, Portsmouth FC was run by husband and wife team John and Dolly Deacon. They had no money to give to the manager for new players, so the club survived on scraps in the transfer market. When St John couldn't do that, he relied on the club's youth team. Players like Fossie and me were quickly chucked into senior action. It wasn't ideal, but the board really gave him no option. That's probably why I've always had such a soft spot for Portsmouth, as they survived in football living off scraps, just as my brother and sister and I had done in those early days in Middlesbrough. We had that as a common link, and perhaps that's why it hurts me so much to see them suffering the plight they are in today. Poor Pompey: good days, bad days, just like when Dad won or lost at the bookies. No wonder I love the place.

Mr Unbelievable

I knew the Luton game was a real chance to impress and earn a regular first-team place. When St John first named me in the squad, I thought it was for a bit of a kickabout. Then I thought I was just going to get a quick run-out at the end. But no, the manager reckoned I could do a job for the side and wanted to play me for the entire 90 minutes. I went back to the digs and called the Newmarket Pub in Middlesbrough. In those days it was the only way to get in touch with the family, because Mam and Dad were usually in there. I told them I was playing. Somehow I managed to get them together with Alan Ingledew, who took them to the game. I tried hard to take it in my stride, but the day flew by me. I was in cloud-cuckoo-land for 24 hours beforehand. I didn't sleep a minute the night before. Thankfully I had returned to earth by the time of the game. My strike partner that day was George Graham, and Peter Marinello was also in the side. To be playing alongside those two was incredible. I didn't want to let them down and I certainly didn't want to let Ian St John down. That afternoon, George gave me plenty of advice on the pitch – where to stand, who to mark and so on. We lost 2-0 to Luton that day, but I was chuffed to have played my first game as a pro. I went out that night, determined to celebrate making my debut. On my wages, it wouldn't have been much of a party, but George looked after me and Fossie in the pub. He was richer than us, so he was buying. I'd also been chosen as man of the match, but I'd picked up a booking in the last minute. It was a sign of things to come. Still, Ian St John and the papers had been impressed with my debut and I was kept me in the side for a few more games. The results didn't improve, but I managed to make my mark against players like the late, great Bobby Moore, then at Fulham, and Bobby Moncur at Sunderland. This added to my reputation. I soon became a first-team regular. The Saint liked my hard-working attitude, and some of the fans loved it even more.

⚽ ⚽ ⚽ ⚽ ⚽ ⚽ ⚽ ⚽

Mam and Dad were there when I scored my first goal. It took place in my second game for the club, but I got extra satisfaction from the fact that it came against a Bolton team that featured several handy players, including Sam Allardyce and Peter Reid, the future England international. My first strike came when Bobby McGuiness (who was probably still feeling bad about selling me a duff Ford Cortina) fired the ball across the penalty area. I made space past Big Sam and hit the ball into the back of the net. Afterwards I just ran and ran. It was hardly the most sophisticated or rehearsed of celebrations – no shirt off, no finger up to my lip to silence the crowd, no triple somersault, I just ran and ran. I didn't jump into the crowd either, I didn't need to discover more ways of getting booked, thank you very much. I smile when I watch them do it now, yellow card guaranteed. As I say, I just ran, but happy as you like.

Big Sam also gave me lesson that night in how to give someone a bruising. It was early in the game and a long ball came through the air towards us. I knew he was nearby, but I also I knew I would be first to the ball. As my forehead made contact with it, he followed through the back of my head with his head. There were stars in my eyes and tweety birds flying around my bonce. I remember thinking, 'What's this all about?' as I rubbed the back of my head, convinced it would be bleeding. It wasn't, but it left one hell of a bump. Sam, meanwhile, walked away looking as if butter wouldn't melt in his mouth. Despite my goal, we lost 4-1 and it felt like a massive blow. With our mixture of old legs and inexperienced heads we had fallen to second bottom of the division. The team was in free fall, and Ian St John was suddenly under pressure from the board and the fans.

Mam and Dad were sadly also on hand to catch my first sending off – one of eight in my 20-year career. It came at home against Plymouth and I only had myself to blame because I'd lost control. Plymouth midfielder Mickey Horswill cut me off at the knee. I retaliated by turning round to kick him. I could hardly say he goaded me, because he just chopped me in half, but he'd got the reaction he wanted. I was going for an early bath and Ian St John, who was quite rightly furious, could barely speak to me after the game. It was a hard lesson, but despite the red cards to come later in my career – not to mention the disciplinary hearing at FA headquarters in Lancaster Gate, London – this was my only dismissal for retaliation. I learnt very quickly that if you played hard and gave it out (like I did), then you'd better be ready to take it back as well.

That didn't make me feel any better about the trip to the FA. During my playing days, discipline was still dished out through the bookings-points system and I made a second visit to the Football Association months later when I topped the 40 points mark. I always dreaded that journey on the train to the capital with the manager. It was usually done in silence. I always felt like a naughty schoolkid. And yet the only indiscretion that really landed players in trouble during those days was dissent. You could poleaxe someone and snap them in two, but woe betide anyone who answered back to the referee. Still, the first red card was a terrible experience for such a young player. I missed the Youth Cup semi-final against Aston Villa because of it.

Ian St John was far from chuffed, but he decided that suspension was punishment enough. He called me into his office, told me it was a lesson and advised me to get on with my game. I had a lot of admiration for him, particularly after he had the faith to give me my debut and keep me in the side when I played well. That was typical of the way he tried to handle me. He came from Motherwell with an excellent reputation after being recommended by his old Liverpool boss, the legendary Bill Shankly. Still, he found it tough at Portsmouth, mainly because of the limited finances. The Pompey supporters rallied around and raised cash for new players with a trust fund, but St John still fielded the youngest ever side in a 1-1 draw against Port Vale that season. Despite the donations, he couldn't buy older, more experienced players. Perhaps it was no surprise to outsiders that we were relegated in 1976, or to the fans, but St John believed he could save the club from another relegation in 1977 until the very end. He was sacked with three games of the season to go. We'd failed to win in 12 games and it looked like we could drop into the Fourth Division for the first time in the club's history.

The Saint's successor was Jimmy Dickinson, a lovely old man who was very much in the mould of Sir Bobby Robson. He wasn't much younger than Sir Bobby was when he took over at

Newcastle United. Once the initial shock of the sacking was over, I did what all players do when a manager is fired – I got on with my own life. Jimmy took over and it was soon a case of, the Saint is dead, long live the King. Jimmy stuck with the blossoming young talent at the club and managed to keep us up even though we lost our final game of the season away at my new club-to-be Swindon. We were awful in the first half, going three goals down. Jimmy told us in no uncertain terms that we had to play the second half for our lives. He shouted and hollered at us like he never had before. It frightened the life out of me. We were inspired enough in the second half and I scored two penalties in five minutes in a 4–3 defeat. Thankfully, the other results went our way and we stayed up. I celebrated hard that night. It seemed natural that some of our players should leave, given that Pompey had narrowly missed relegation to the Fourth Division. New blood was needed. There were also money problems and the club were banking on selling their most promising talent. I was one of the names heading for the door because I could fetch a profitable market price. I was soon in transfer talks with Swindon Town in the summer of 1977, just months after I'd given that man of the match performance against them on the last day of the season. I had played 63 league games for Pompey by the end of my second year there. It had been a season-long struggle under Ian St John and not a lot changed under Jimmy Dickinson. I was frustrated at the inconsistency of myself and the team, so I wasn't unhappy at the thought of moving.

Swindon boss Danny Williams offered Pompey a massive £14,000 (my head was spinning – £14,000!) and a tidy little deal for me. The basics were a £500 signing-on fee and wages of £30 a week, which was a big improvement on my contract at Pompey. At the time I was wondering what I'd do with all the dough. I must say I have every sympathy with the big hitters of today trying to spend their millions. The club also offered me a massive £2,000 in travelling expenses until I relocated, which was usual with most jobs then, but I was still surprised at the generous amount being offered. The club had even found digs for me with a lovely lady called Phyllis Smart and her ex-policeman husband Jack. They had housed players for many years and were old hands at looking after young footballers.

It doesn't take an Einstein to realise that this was hardly living the life of Cristiano Ronaldo, but I was tempted by the move all the same. During talks, I actually asked for a few days to think about the move. I met up with Ian St John and George Graham at a Hampshire county cricket match to discuss the transfer over a few beers. They were always on hand to give me advice. George and The Saint both told me to quit Pompey for what they felt was a better club for me at this stage of my career. Sod it, I thought – I'm off. I agreed a deal with Swindon quickly and picked up my boots from the dressing-room. It wouldn't be the last time I'd leave a club in such circumstances. In the same way that I left the Navy, I pulled away from Portsmouth, not knowing then if I'd ever return. My life's parallels were mapping out. I had to leave the club that struggled for money as my parents had. Swindon offered me the move and the freedom I'd first experienced when I joined the Navy.

CHAPTER FIFTEEN

CSI: SWINDON - DEATH THREATS AND POLICE ESCORTS

You're always going to take plenty of verbal when you leave a club, but death threats from your old fans can come as a shock. When I left Fratton Park for Swindon in 1977, I knew I was moving from a team in decline to a better side. I thought this would annoy some of Pompey's supporters. I also knew that my transfer would give the more bigoted fringe of the Portsmouth crowd an excuse to have a pop at me. What I didn't expect was a series of sinister letters from fans promising me some serious harm. The worst of these even gave the police cause for concern before my first game against Pompey. To be honest, after my shocking performances in some of the games I played for various clubs, I'm surprised I didn't get more death threats ... from my own fans.

I can remember the day of the game vividly. It was Saturday, 27 August 1977, and began as a normal morning in club digs. It was a home match, so I woke late, around 11, on the low, single-mattress bed. It wasn't the most glamorous of surroundings, but Phyllis the landlady had the *Western Daily*

CSI: Swindon - Death Threats and Police Escorts

Press ready for me downstairs, as always, and breakfast was on the go: a good old fry-up to steel me for the game. Arsène Wenger would have had a fit as the second fried egg collided with the sausage halfway down my stomach. Modern coaches would have had me sucking on a slice of kiwi fruit and a bowl of nuts, given the chance, but this was Swindon, many years ago, and I was no Henry or Walcott.

The only difference that day was the three extra mugs of tea on the table. My police escort to the game had arrived. Look, don't get me wrong, nobody likes to be the target of a hate campaign, but I figured the notes sent to Swindon were the work of a couple of nutters rather than any serious effort to have me knocked off. Swindon's club secretary Bob Jeffries was having none of it, though. These were pretty heavy threats, not just some idiots carrying out a prank. As soon as he learnt of the threats, he called the police. They were alarmed enough to get in some plainclothes coppers to look after me. When they arrived I tried hard to persuade them to leave and not to escort me, insisting the extra protection was unnecessary. I also thought the fuss might give the impression that the threat had unsettled me, which was the last thing I wanted. In the politest possible way I was told to shut up and sit in the unmarked car that would take me to the doors of the home dressing-room at the County Ground. Swindon Town FC and the local police were taking no chances. I had to lump it.

The police released the story to the papers on the day of the game (it was on the whole of the back page of the *Daily Mirror*) to unnerve the culprits. They wanted to show them that they'd been rumbled. I suppose it just emphasised the seriousness of the threat at the time, but I reckoned it had given whoever was behind it some extra notoriety. I really didn't believe anything would happen to me, and I certainly didn't want anyone thinking I was scared.

I was used to walking to games on a match day. Being driven in a cop car was as good as a chauffeur-driven limo. Danny Williams did his bit to help me by naming me as team captain for the day. Psychologically it was a massive boost. I emerged from the tunnel bursting with pride, and the hostile reception from Pompey's fans bounced off me. It also helped that the club had doubled its police presence at the game to around 130 officers. This came at considerable cost – about £600 – but it proved a wise move because around a hundred home fans invaded the pitch before the kick-off, and from the first kick to the final whistle the visiting support booed my every touch.

We won 3-1, and the atmosphere was hardly serene when I scored the game's opening goal after six minutes right in front of the Pompey fans. I ran the full length of the pitch to celebrate in front of the Town End where the hard-core Swindon fans always stood. As I was still going back to Portsmouth on a regular basis I did not want to annoy them any more than I seemingly already had. Pompey fans began scrapping among themselves in the Stratton Bank end. Was it over me, I wondered, as the police waded in to put a stop to it. Had some of the Pompey fans applauded my goal and been set upon? I will never know. Like any goalscorer I was very, very happy, so this time the hate fell on deaf ears, and I was oblivious to the pandemonium and arrests until I scanned the papers in

Phyllis's kitchen the following day. Even then, it never crossed my mind that I was in any way responsible for the chaos.

If any positives came out of the grief, it was that Swindon's fans became more appreciative of me. I think they were shocked by the level of abuse being chucked by fans who, three months previously, had regarded me as one of their own. It was a small consolation; the result hadn't made me any safer. When I left the dressing-room after the game, my three new mates in blue were waiting for me. I put my foot down and insisted they could leave. I was desperate to enjoy a drink with my old team-mates in the players' bar, and the coppers agreed to go. One did stick around, but he kept a healthy distance and I was free to enjoy myself. Looking back, I was young and naive and the whole thing was a pain to me. I didn't really even thank the plainclothes officers or the club for their concern afterwards, which was pretty short-sighted. Who knows what might have happened if they hadn't put those precautions in place to ensure my safety?

Anyway, a month later the threats started again when Swindon and Portsmouth met in a League Cup tie at Fratton Park. This time I was determined there would be no overreaction, but that didn't stop three tabloids completely distorting the story on the day of the game. Apparently I was again under police protection, and the latest death threats were being treated seriously. Thankfully, it was all news to Hampshire Police, who took no such precautions. In fact, the police presence was kept to a minimum. There was a short cordon of officers from the bus to the players' entrance at Fratton Park, which was just as well. The noise was incredible when I emerged from the bus, a cacophony of boos. It was an intimidating atmosphere. I tried hard to rise above it, but it's not easy to ignore thousands of supporters jeering your every move. Still, I grew used to the noise during the game and, in the end, I buzzed off it. I made sure the Portsmouth fans knew I was enjoying it, too. We got a replay thanks to a David Moss goal.

In the replay at Swindon we eventually went through. I scored the first goal on the way to a 4–3 win, while the Pompey fans kept to their script and booed me again. It was a terrific match, but I'm sure some of those fans were too busy concentrating on me to appreciate the drama. I thoroughly loved it, although it came to an abrupt end when I earned the second sending off of my career. Perhaps the abuse had got to me – during the last few minutes of the match I'd gone in late on Portsmouth left-back Keith Viney, one of the lads I had grown up with in the youth team and reserves at Pompey, and World Cup referee Clive Thomas sent me down the tunnel. Thomas wasn't the ref to misbehave in front of. He wouldn't have hesitated to send off a pigeon for flying over the ground, let alone get rid of someone who'd gone in with a late tackle. With the possible exception of Jack Taylor, Clive Thomas was the first of the celebrity refs who loved controversy.

Still, I hadn't finished getting my own back on the boo boys, and in the fourth game against Portsmouth during that campaign – a return League match at Fratton Park – I ran myself into the ground, despite another two death threats through the post. I scored the winner too, an unstoppable shot that flew past goalie Phil Figgins. The downside for me was

Top left Butter wouldn't melt in my mouth
Top right Riding my bike outside our house – I think the bike was a bit small
Bottom left Looking very pleased with myself at my confirmation. I was born on Christmas Day – hence my first name, Christopher. Then my parents gave me the confirmation name Columbus – so I was Christopher Columbus
Bottom right My brother George and me with our sister Maria at her confirmation

In the Navy

My mam and dad

Top Relaxing at home with my horses
Below left With Anne, Ben and baby Jack
Below right With the boys at Anne's brother's wedding

Opposite

Top The boys and me with a shark in Mexico
Centre Jack graduated from Birmingham in 2008
Bottom Ben graduated from Durham in 2005

My playing career took in spells at Portsmouth (**centre left**, © *Portsmouth & Sunderland Newspapers Ltd*), Swindon Town, Brentford, Stoke City (**top right**), Leeds United (**top left**), Luton Town, Sheffield United, Middlesbrough and Bradford City

Centre right The closest I got to playing for England – keeping a close eye on John Barnes in an England training session

Bottom Enjoying a night out with my good mate Steve Foster (far right) in our Portsmouth days

Play-off jubilation with Bradford City

Top Enjoying the moment with the players (© *Empics*)
Centre Sharing a word or two with chairman Geoffrey Richmond (© *The Telegraph & Argus*)
Bottom left Introducing my players and staff to Her Majesty The Queen – a very proud moment
Bottom right Revelling in the open-deck bus parade in the city (© *The Telegraph & Argus*)

Top With my great pal Steve Gibson, chairman of Middlesbrough FC

Above Making a meal of it for the 2009 *Soccer Saturday* Christmas special. Back row, from left to right: Matt Le Tissier, Alan McInally, Charlie Nicholas, Phil Thompson and me. Front row: Aldo Zilli, Jeff Stelling, Gino D'Acampo

Right Presenting *Goals on Sunday* with my good friend Rob McCaffrey (© *Andi Southam/ Sky Sports*)

that the result pushed Portsmouth nearer the relegation zone. Despite the small minority who made themselves heard I still loved the club. 'He did rub salt into the wound, didn't he?' moaned my old boss Jimmy Dickinson in the papers, but I wasn't one to gloat. I'd always reckoned on keeping my head while everyone else seemed to be losing theirs, police escort or no police escort.

⊛ ⊛ ⊛ ⊛ ⊛ ⊛ ⊛ ⊛

My very first league game for Swindon had endeared me to the fans immediately. I scored on my debut away at Sheffield Wednesday, managed at the time by Jack Charlton, one of my heroes. I hit a 20-yard right-foot shot in the 14th minute – and I felt like I'd justified my move.

Manager Danny Williams was a lovely bloke, but his man-management left a lot to be desired at times. Every Friday morning he'd allow coach Frank Burrows to take the final training sessions and, as his number two put us through the set-pieces, Danny would pin the team-sheet on the notice-board in the dressing-room. Then he'd quietly sneak out of the back door and head home before training ended, leaving Frank to face the wrath of any player whose name wasn't on the list. I was only familiar with Danny's routine on Fridays because it happened to me so often. Despite my impressive debut, he was always leaving me out.

On away trips, his match-day preparation was just as annoying. It was team policy that we would only stop over in a hotel if it was a trip of three hours or more. Even then the club wouldn't stretch to pay for a meal in the hotel restaurant, so Danny would give every player a quid to buy fish and chips from the nearest takeaway, and on reflection I don't think Arsène Wenger would have been too impressed with that either. The stars of tomorrow would be gobbling down their greasy pre-match meal in a freezing car park. It didn't help that we'd usually then spot Danny and the directors eating from the à la carte menu through the hotel window.

On one trip to Carlisle, we found Frank Burrows berating Danny, club chairman Cecil Green and his directors, as they ate in the hotel dining-room. He was voicing his disgust that they were feeding their faces with the finest food while the players, who had to perform the next day, were outside eating junk food. Frank refused to take a place that was set for him alongside them at the table. Instead he came outside, full of apologies for the disgusting manner in which we were being treated, and tucked into cod and chips. It was no surprise when Frank eventually left the club. Even though he was standing up for the players, no one likes a trouble-maker, least of all football chairmen. That was something I'd discover to my cost later in my career.

The 1978–79 season at Swindon hardly got off to the perfect start for me either. New manager Bobby Smith was quickly on my back after a defeat at Sheffield United in our second game. He had decided to give me a few home truths. He accused me of dereliction of duty, saying I'd taken my eye off the ball because I thought I'd already made it in my profession and I didn't need to listen any more. Some of that was true. I was spending more time at the bookies and drinking to alleviate the boredom and drudgery of living in digs. The bookies and the booze were entering my life and I was ignoring the consequences. I wasn't the only one, though ... a lot of the other players did the same. Back then, most players would play a game on a Saturday afternoon and have six or seven pints immediately after the match. They would stay in the pub until closing time and head to a nightclub for a couple of spirits and then finally grab something to eat from a takeaway on the way home. After a good lie-in, Sunday lunchtime meant a few more pints and a full roast dinner with all the trimmings. I was the same, except that on Sunday night I'd go for a sauna to sweat it all out - barely drinking any water to counteract the loss of fluids - before training in a black plastic bag on Monday morning to complete the weight-loss process. What I didn't realise, and none of us did, was the drastic effect it was having on my energy levels. I was forever dehydrated and exhausted after games and training.

Nowadays players' diets and fluid consumption have changed dramatically. The regime we used to follow is simply no longer possible. In the seventies, it was almost unacceptable to live a healthy lifestyle as a footballer, just as it was later for Graeme Le Saux to be reading the *Guardian* or Frank Lampard to be reading *The Times*. I remember hearing about former Middlesbrough player Craig Johnston, who introduced his own diet of vegetables and pasta after signing for Liverpool at Anfield, the home of the champions. He was ridiculed, not only by his team-mates, but by the coaching staff as well. It was bad enough Craig having a long girly hairstyle and a pair of his self-designed boots, but bloody pasta?

He was having a laugh. There were lots of good fish and chip shops in Liverpool and they didn't do Ian Rush any harm. Lou Macari, a manager of mine at Swindon, was totally opposed to alcohol consumption; he realised it deprived the body of the minerals needed to aid performance in matches and training. But even he drew the line at telling us what to eat, as he owned a chippy named after him outside Old Trafford.

I only became fully aware of correct dietary habits later, when I arrived at Leeds in 1990 and was managed by Howard Wilkinson – one of the pioneers of the health regime in football. He encouraged us to eat the correct food such as carbohydrates in the build-up to a match. He wanted us to drink vast quantities of water to replenish the body. He was ahead of everyone else. I wish to this day that I'd been introduced to these better habits earlier in my career. I reckon it would have made an enormous difference to my game, particularly with consistency and stamina in the early years, and I would have saved a fortune on beer and fast food.

Those words from Swindon manager Bobby Smith did the trick, and I never looked back after that. The side was flying and we were looking certain to maintain a push for the promotion places. However, it was as cup experts that we really made our mark in Swindon's history that year. After fine wins over Chester, Stoke and Wimbledon in the League Cup, it was on to Highbury for Arsenal in the quarter-finals.

CSI: Swindon - Death Threats and Police Escorts

I grabbed two goals for Swindon in the 1979-80 League Cup quarter-final replay against Arsenal and thought I was Roy of the Rovers - a comical thought on reflection. Sadly, when the match reports came out the next day (and I was fully expecting to see my name in lights), both strikes were credited as own goals by Arsenal's John Hollins. I'd hit two long-rangers, only for them to fly in from deflections. We had won 3-2 and in my head I'd grabbed the glory, but the press had other ideas. Strange that, I could have sworn they were both heading for the back of the net before Hollins got his backside in the way.

When we first drew Arsenal in the cup at Highbury we knew we were in for a tough game. The Gunners were full of world-class stars, Pat Jennings, Frank Stapleton and Liam Brady among them. They were also playing at a world-class stadium. Highbury was a ground full of history, which was enough to set the butterflies going. But I was only 21 at the time and, when I got out there, I loved it. I thought it was going to be like that every week from then on, as you do. All the more so when we managed to get a draw from the game and took them back to our place a week later.

The return fixture was a big deal. The County Ground was sold out and the world and his wife wanted tickets. I managed to look after Mam and Dad, as well as one uncle and some cousins, which was better than most players did. The problem was finding them somewhere to stay. I only lived in a one-bedroom flat at the time with Anne, so we gave over our modest home to the family and bunked down with friends in the flat downstairs. It was hardly the best preparation for the biggest game of my career. It also didn't help that Anne hadn't met my folks before. The nerves were jangling for all of us.

When we awoke at about 8 a.m. on the morning of the game, Anne and I headed straight from our temporary digs to join my folks for breakfast before I was due to set off for training at 10.30. As we began to climb the flight of stairs we were hit by a wall of sound which I quickly recognised as Earth, Wind and Fire's 'September'. I began to sing along, much to Anne's annoyance. Then we suddenly realised that the racket was coming from our place. Anne was shocked. 'What about the neighbours?' she said. I couldn't get the front door open quickly enough. I was thinking 'What the bleeding hell is going on here?' In my mind, the flat had been overrun with disco-mad squatters. The communal hall sounded like a nightclub from the 1970s (well, it was still the 1970s) but inside, nothing was trashed. When I scanned the bedroom, I could see my bleary-eyed folks, and they were looking none too happy. Mam waved a noisy alarm-clock radio in our faces. It was still pumping 'September' at full blast. The alarm-radio was a new gadget at the time and it woke us up to the sound of our favourite radio station every morning. They're common now, but were a rarity back then when disc jockeys had jump-leads on their turntables. Certainly the Middlesbrough contingent hadn't seen one before.

We presumed it had only just gone off, at our usual wake-up time. But after I'd rushed over to stop the party, and the noise had stopped, Dad started to shout at Mam. 'I told you that's what we could have done last night,' he said. It turned out that for some reason the alarm had gone off just before midnight - and Mam wouldn't let Dad, Uncle Derek or anyone touch it. She didn't want anyone to break my new toy. This meant it had been blaring for eight hours at least, when just yanking the plug out of the wall would have silenced the racket. God knows what the neighbours must have thought of me after that.

That win over Arsenal took us into a two-leg semi-final with Wolves. Wembley was only two games away. We drew with Woves 1-1 at the County Ground, but a goal from Andy Gray at Molineux knocked us out. The dream was over.

⚽ ⚽ ⚽ ⚽ ⚽ ⚽ ⚽ ⚽

Despite the result against Wolves, I had now grown up as a player, and even though, at 21, I was one of the youngest players in the team, I took over as Swindon Town captain for the beginning of the 1979-80 campaign. Sadly, the club embarked on one of its worst starts to a new season at the same time. After five straight defeats from the opening game of the season, Bobby Smith was handed his P45. It wasn't exactly the start I wanted as skipper.

As captain I felt partly responsible for Bobby's departure - it was hard in those days not to take your role in a team personally, even if our poor form was down to the entire team, not just me. Even so, I was determined to play my part in recovering the season. Bobby was replaced by Swindon legend John Trolloppe.

John had never been very outgoing as a player, and his longevity on the pitch came from a single-minded approach to the game. It meant that he always looked after number one. Naturally, he couldn't change his persona and he carried that attitude into management. By appointing a legend, the board had kept the fans at bay after our horror-show start, but there were problems in the dressing-room. Even as a senior pro, John rarely had his say in team talks. Often you'd look for experienced men to see you through the difficult times as a player. You would need to hear their voices at half-time when you were losing. John would never speak up or rock the boat in team meetings. Then, all of a sudden, coming to the end of his career, he decided to go into management. It was a situation where we needed him to be strong and opinionated, but he struggled to do it.

I guess the problem was that John was too nice to be a manager. Still, we worked well together and I loved the responsibility of being club captain, even though we had a difficult season. John did well to guide us to safety after a horrible start. At the end of what was a hard season I was on the move again.

⚽ ⚽ ⚽ ⚽ ⚽ ⚽ ⚽ ⚽

Given that some of their fans had threatened to have me knocked off, it will probably be a surprise to some readers to hear that I moved back to Pompey. Yes, the boy from the Royal Navy had indeed returned safely and docked a second time, as suggested earlier.

Frank Burrows, my former coach at Swindon, had got his first managerial job with Portsmouth and came back to

CSI: Swindon - Death Threats and Police Escorts

Swindon and sat with me for hours, persuading me to go back. I was a bit apprehensive at first, but after chatting with him there was nowhere else I wanted to go. I felt like a million dollars even though the fee was only 50 grand. By this time the mood had changed: the fans were delighted to see me back and I was happy to be going. So as not to spend any of my relocation money the club placed me in apprentice digs while I looked for a more permanent home for me and Anne. The level of care in the digs left a lot to be desired. I had progressed to eating steak and vegetables on the night before a game, and on match days I considered it sensible to have scrambled egg on toast for breakfast. But the day I moved into the new digs, a couple of young apprentices came up to me and complained about the food at the house. They pleaded with me to sort it out because they were too frightened to say anything to the landlady.

They had a point. Everything we ate came with chips. The meal on my first evening there was fish fingers and chips. It wasn't good enough. I only stayed for two weeks, but the day after I left to move into a flat with Anne I felt it was time to help the boys out. I decided to do what any good senior pro would do for the young lads at the club to ensure they looked up to him: I rang Anne and asked her to sort it out! (A taste of things to come, she would say ...) She listened to the depressing scenario and eventually agreed to give the digs a call.

Our landlady was not impressed. 'I've done this job for 20 years, the past three for footballers,' she moaned after Anne's call. 'No one has ever complained before.'

Mr Unbelievable

The following morning Frank Burrows called me into his office. He told me my landlady had been on the phone to him in tears. Although he understood where I (or Anne!) was coming from as regards the inappropriate meals, he still made me go back with a bunch of flowers to apologise. I felt terrible, but the young apprentices told me it had done the trick – last night they had had boiled potatoes and tonight it was going to be spaghetti bolognaise. 'No problem, boys,' I said, 'just glad to be of assistance.' I couldn't tell them it was Anne who had sorted it, could I?

I was quite shocked to be on the move again. It was October 1981 and I'd only been back on the south coast for a few months. I'd started to settle at Pompey and was playing well. The call from club chairman John Deacon came from nowhere. His advice was clear: sign with Brentford and move to London, whether you like it or not. It turned out that Brentford's manager, Fred Callaghan, and his chairman, Martin Lange, were desperate to sign me, while Pompey were keen to sign David Crown from the Bees. I was part of a swap deal and had to pack my bags once more. But at least I'd never have to eat a fish finger again.

⚽ ⚽ ⚽ ⚽ ⚽ ⚽ ⚽

During the 2006 World Cup in Germany, England were playing Trinidad and Tobago in Nuremberg. At the time I was Coca-Cola Football League ambassador and I was a guest of Coke's sponsorship manager Tim Ellerton. I kept getting asked for photos by England fans around the ground. After a while I could see Ellers was getting fed up with being an unpaid cameraman, so we hid behind a beer cabin and started to sink a few pints and talk about the England game. Would Crouch be playing, was Stevie G going to be fit, and so on. Wherever I went in Germany, as had happened in Japan in 2002, England fans had been shouting, 'Unbelievable, Jeff!' This time we thought we had found a hideaway behind the beer cabin, but after the first cry of 'Unbelievable, Jeff' I was rumbled.

Amongst all the people who approached me were two Pompey fans in their early fifties. At first I thought they were after autographs. Then they dropped the bombshell.

'Er, Chris,' said one. 'Do you remember those death threats you were sent when you signed for Swindon after leaving Pompey in the seventies?'

'Yeah?' I replied quizzically, wondering where this was going to lead and what had made them mention this after so long. I honestly hadn't thought about the threats for a long, long time. As far as I was concerned it was a closed chapter in my life.

'Well, we sent them,' he said.

I couldn't believe it. I knew there was no way in the world that they were making it up, because it had happened nearly 30 years previously and I had not spoken about it to anyone for as long as I could remember. I was in shock, Ellers and the rest of the gang from Coca-Cola were aghast, but the Pompey fans were happily telling me how they'd written the notes and sent them to the club, obviously aware of the publicity at the time but probably completely unaware of the trouble they'd caused. They explained they were young, stupid and naive and seemed apologetic about the incident.

Mr Unbelievable

As they stood there in front of me I literally could not believe what I was hearing. Here were two perfectly respectable-looking, middle-aged guys, probably with grown-up lads the same age now as they were when they penned those threats. It was definitely another 'unbelievable' moment, but I assured them that it was all water under the bridge. The people I was with couldn't believe I was being so forgiving, but that was then, this is now. I said that no harm was done and they seemed really nice blokes. In a way it was nice to put an end to that episode in my life. Then I smacked them both in the gob! ... only joking.

CHAPTER SIXTEEN
BUZZING WITH BOWLESY

At Brentford, I played alongside Terry Hurlock in the middle of the park. Manager Fred Callaghan had bought him from non-league Wealdstone. Terry was Fred's first signing, and even though he was an amateur, Fred was determined to mould him into a pro. The trouble was, as far as Terry was concerned, there were no rules on the football pitch. Imagine Vinnie Jones and Mike Tyson rolled together, then think of someone who'd pick on that mixture in a fight and pound them into submission and there you have Terry Hurlock. This man was never going to be Billy Elliot. Like me, he probably wouldn't have lasted five minutes in today's football. His style was so robust, which is a diplomatic way of putting it, that in a non-contact game like modern football, he'd probably get booked just for putting his boots on.

Yet, despite Terry's inexperience, the other players looked up to him, and not just because he'd deck them if they didn't. His commitment had an impact on everyone around him, particularly me because I was often very close to the epicentre of his crunching tackles. We could play together, too, and at Brentford we were regarded for our technical ability as well as a fearless streak. Terry eventually ended up at Glasgow Rangers in 1990 after a big-money move, and you didn't get signed by a club like that without a whiff of talent. Before that, between 1987 and 1990, he played for Millwall, a team he loved. Unsurprisingly, he became one of the Lions' greatest legends.

I'll never forget the sunny afternoon, years later, when during my second spell playing for Swindon I came up against him at The Den – the old, snarling pit that was previously Millwall's intimidating home. As I've said before, playing in front of Millwall fans was a bowel-quaking experience for any player, but if you were black it was a hundred times worse. During the game, Terry and I went for a loose ball in midfield. Typically, we were both determined to win it, no matter who was in the way. As we hurtled together, it must have looked like one of those King Kong versus Godzilla movies, as two titans stepped up to battle. Even the most hardened Millwall fans (what a stupid thing to say – everyone knows that all Millwall fans were hardened. This was the time when you couldn't even get a season ticket if you had two ears and 10 fingers. Anyway, to continue ...) even the most hardened Millwall fans cowered in their seats as the pair of us collided at a hundred miles an hour. We both missed the ball, a minor point really, and ended up in a concertina of mangled legs and arms. Terry jumped to his feet and I was tearing at his shirt as we squared up to one another. Before we knew it, the ref had whipped out his red card, no hesitation. We were both off. What struck me as funny was the reception given by the fans. As Terry stalked back to the dressing-room The Den was on its paws dishing out one of the most enthusiastic standing ovations I'd ever heard. There was none of that for me, though. I went down the tunnel accompanied by a volley of abuse and spittle. We shook hands straight after the game and I bought my good mate Terry a pint in the players' bar. As I handed his lager over, Terry's dad, a terrifying sight at the best of times, came from nowhere and threatened to knock my block off. I was right the first time: Terry would never, ever, ever have become Billy Elliot. Thankfully, Terry stepped in and calmed down his old man and my teeth remained intact. That was the Hurlocks for you.

Getting treatment for injuries at Brentford's Griffin Park was a risky business, and the players had a running joke that the medical staff were more dangerous than the tackles. I once took a nasty gash in my knee that needed treatment. It had happened just before half-time, so our club doctor, Radley Smith, took a look at me in the dressing-room. He was a brain surgeon – a complete waste of time in my case unless he traded old ones in for new – and a very clever man, though he was getting on a bit. The lads used to pick him up on the team bus at his home in Teddington when we went to away games, but all we really knew about him was that we'd never want him messing around in our heads, thank you very much. I needed eight stitches in the wound, but once he'd put them in I was in complete agony. I looked down and noticed a long, thin bulge protruding from my knee. Dr Smith had sewn me up expertly, but he'd left a needle in my leg. After more open-knee surgery, my limb was back in working order and I promised to keep his little mistake quiet, which I have done until now.

Mr Unbelievable

In hindsight, I'd been pretty lucky. During the same game, my team-mate Francis Joseph took a knock below the shin. Dr Smith gave him the once over and told him to play on. He even promised him he'd be fine for the next game. An X-ray taken later in the week revealed a broken leg. Unbelievable. But in all fairness to Dr Smith, his other leg was fine and Francis Joseph wasn't a two-footed player anyway.

Thinking back to that medical man, who ranks alongside Dr Crippen, I'd probably have done just as good a job if I'd treated myself. I certainly knew a trick or two when it came to first aid after my time in the Navy. I even had to give the kiss of life one night in the Brentford social club, when some away fans from Bristol Rovers started a fight. They hadn't been allowed in, and when Brentford's winger Gary Roberts left the bar, he was attacked by the mob. A few of us ran outside to see what was going on but it had all kicked off. After the fight had broken up, I noticed that this one fan, Stan Willis, had fallen to the ground. I ran over to pick him up, but he wasn't breathing and I couldn't feel a pulse. Thankfully, I had taken life-saving courses and was able to resuscitate Stan and bring him round. Anyway, that's my story and I'm sticking to it, and I can assure you that the kiss of life that night didn't involve tongues, even though I started on the neck and then the ear before I reached his mouth. Never learn first aid in the Royal Navy.

Despite my medical expertise, I hated being injured. I'd rather play in pain than sit in the stands. When I went back to Swindon with Brentford for an FA Cup tie in 1983, I smashed into someone during the game. I was in agony afterwards. I didn't say a word, and it later turned out that I'd broken a rib, though

Buzzing with Bowlesy

I only realised after attempting to play through the replay like an idiot. We were convincingly beaten and I had a crap night. It was one of those games where every touch seemed to go astray. The harder I tried, the worse it got. Every challenge was agony and I could hardly wait for the final whistle, but I still didn't want to come off. But I was like that as a player. I always played when I was injured, and if a cortisone injection could sort the problem out temporarily, I'd take one. I had countless jabs in my career and I was a fool to do so, because there have been reports of negative side effects, such as thinning of the bones and increased blood pressure. So far I've been fortunate, as there doesn't appear to be any long-term damage (although the *Soccer Saturday* panel might have a different take on that). What I do know is that, throughout my time as a player, all I cared about was playing. I couldn't get enough of it.

At Brentford I also played alongside Stan Bowles, the one-time England maverick and long-term gambler. Stan had been, and still was, a great player, but if he could have passed the bookies the way he passed the ball he'd be a multi-millionaire today. Sadly, the man who had all that talent is potless today. With my extra cash I allowed myself the luxury of winning and losing with one of the game's worst gamblers. Stan and I hit it off immediately. Nowadays I am the face and voice of Ladbrokes and frequently front their advertising campaigns.

They once asked me to do a voice-over, which was played through their tannoys all over the UK, and which came back to bite me on the backside. I was minding my own business in Ladbrokes at King's Cross and my own voice rattled through the speakers.

Mr Unbelievable

'Hello there, it's Chris Kamara,' I bellowed in a weird, out-of-body experience. I crept to the back of the shop, praying nobody would recognise me. My virtual tones weren't finished, though.

'Unbelievable! Here's your chance to win a million pounds ... All you need to do is pick ten correct football scores ...'

Suddenly, a bloke sat in front of me watching the 2.30 at Doncaster looked up at the tannoy.

'Sod off, Kamara, you tosser,' he shouted. 'I can't pick one effing winner, never mind ten, you scum bag.'

Dear old Stan. When it came to betting, Bowlesy taught me a lot of what not to do today. We once went to the Cheltenham Festival with Brentford manager Fred Callaghan, who took the whole squad along. I noticed that Stan's ex-manager at Carlisle United, Stan Anderson, who was an idol of mine when he was Middlesbrough manager, had a share in a horse that was running that day called Badsworth Boy. It was running in the Queen Mother Champion Chase and I urged Bowlesy to have a word with the other Stan to see if it would win.

'Yes,' came the reply, 'fill your boots. And when it wins you and your mate can come and join us in the winners' enclosure.'

Off we trotted to the bookies' pitches situated near the main stand to place our bets. The race began, and soon I was jumping up and down as this beautiful horse waltzed to victory. I was overjoyed – it was my first winner at Cheltenham – but looking over to Bowlesy it was obvious that something was amiss, and it turned out he hadn't backed it! He told me he had fancied something else and lumped his money on that, even though we had been told Badsworth Boy was a certainty. 'Please don't let on to Stan Anderson that I have not backed it,' said Bowlesy as we joined the happy co-owner for a celebration drink.

Stan's main problem was that he loved it all. Horses, dogs, the pools, cards – you name it, he would bet on it. And if he won a lot of cash, he'd spend it all straightaway. If Stan ever had a night at the White City greyhound racetrack, he'd very rarely leave with a penny for his cab home. If he finished quids in, the champagne was on him for the night.

We had a great time betting together. When we weren't in his local (which was actually the exterior used for the Nag's Head in the BBC comedy *Only Fools and Horses*), we'd frequent a gentlemen's club in Shepherd's Bush. When he was there, Stan regularly played a card game called Kaluki, which he was pretty good at. He would blow all his money on the horses, because he couldn't pick a winner to save his life, but he was a wizard at that game. I always used to sit at the back, watching in amazement as he tore into real card sharps.

Stan clearly had skill, judgement and intelligence to burn. Sadly, winning on the horses involved guesswork and luck, and he didn't have a lot of that. Because of his bad fortune, I became the Royal Bank of Kamara, dishing out no-interest loans to help the recession-struck gambler. To pay me back, Stan would take me along to the Kaluki card school and give me his winnings. We had a good business relationship. Stan was never afraid to ask me for a loan, and I never turned him down because I knew he'd repay me when he could. Sometimes he'd end up borrowing the money he'd just repaid, just to complicate matters, but that was fine by me. It became an endless cycle for us both. After one particularly successful afternoon in the gentlemen's club, Stan insisted on repaying me with his winnings. Then he told me to spend it straight-away, just in case he was tempted to ask for another loan. I took him literally and went into an antique shop next door. For some reason I'd always fancied owning a rocking chair, and there was a nice one in the window. Five minutes later, I was sitting next to Stan, rocking away, while he scooped up more cash.

Stan was a hell of a trainer. He could stay up at a card club until the break of dawn and be the last off the training ground in the afternoon, having turned in a masterclass of dribbling and Hollywood passes for the benefit of the club's bewildered youngsters. He was wonderful to watch sometimes. Stan loved to take the mickey if he could. He was always keen to keep up his performances, because victories brought more dough. The club offered bonuses for wins, but Stan soon devised a scam with Brentford's secretary, Christine Matthews, to siphon off the bonus cash from his wages because he didn't want his girl-friend to know about the extra payments. It didn't help. Stan was still skint most of the time and would go into Christine's office on a regular basis to get an advance on his pay cheque. Christine ensured that the advance never went beyond what was due to him, for obvious reasons: the man was an accoun-tant's nightmare and would spend it as soon as he was paid. The sad thing was, he never learnt from his mistakes. It wasn't unusual to find him rooting around an empty envelope or staring forlornly at a payslip.

On the pitch there were highs and lows at Griffin Park. Amongst the characters I played with during my spell with the

Bees were Ron 'Chopper' Harris, Mickey Droy and Bill Garner, all former Chelsea legends. The first man to be famous for his long throw at Chelsea, Ian Hutchinson, was also involved at Brentford, with the social club. Arsenal legend Charlie George came down for a few weeks too, but he didn't stay.

During my third season at Griffin Park in 1983–84, we were struggling. Brentford slipped into a relegation battle and Fred Callaghan left the club. His replacement was Frank McLintock, a former Arsenal legend and later a colleague of mine at Sky. At first, we all felt sorry for Fred, because he was such a nice bloke. This made it a little harder for Frank, of course, but it soon became apparent that he was exactly the sort of gaffer we needed. In many ways, Frank was ahead of his time as a manager. At the end of every league campaign he would write to his players and give them a series of gentle exercises and running programmes to maintain fitness during the summer break. Of course we all knew his reputation as a player and a man, and he didn't disappoint. He imposed his likeable character on the club, and on the whole we responded.

His preparation paid dividends: during his first season at the club he took us to Wembley for the Freight Rover Trophy Final in 1985. However, his preparations for our big day were a little unconventional. He took us on holiday to Corfu for a week. Four days before the final, Francis Joseph, he with the broken leg on one side and the unbroken leg on the other, who hadn't expected to be fit, told Frank that he thought he might make it. Frank said that he would have to do a fitness test. The problem was that we were on the promenade next to the beach bar at the time but, sure enough, Jo put down his

Bacardi and Coke and started to run up and down the promenade between the tourists! He was wearing just his shorts, loafers (no socks) and sunglasses. Frank sat back and let him get on with it, and the rest of us laughed at the bar. A bit of an unconventional fitness test, to say the least. Unsurprisingly, Jo never made it to Wembley.

Corfu was hardly an ideal way to prepare for a cup final, though. We occasionally trained between the boozing. Often we partied as if our season was over and we'd already won the cup. It was a big mistake. The Freight Rover Trophy Final was the first time a Brentford side had reached the twin towers in 43 years. It came thanks to a 6–0 thrashing of Newport County in the Southern Area Final, so mentally we were on a high. Sadly, we thought we only had to turn up to win.

Maybe this was the manager's fault as well as our own. Frank was not hard enough, which is perhaps why he went on to become such a fantastic number two with John Doherty at Millwall (John was his assistant at Brentford, but the pair swapped roles when they moved on to The Den).

Our opponents for my only Wembley appearance as a player were a young Wigan side, managed by my former Swindon coach, Bryan Hamilton. They included up-and-coming players like Steve Walsh, Mike Newell, Warren Aspinall and Paul Jewell, who would go on to become my team-mate and later assistant coach at Bradford 15 years later. It was a red-hot day and we wilted in the heat. Terry Hurlock and I were dying on our feet as the young Wigan team skipped around us on that enormous pitch. We just didn't perform for the Brentford fans. More than 20,000 travelled the short distance to see history being made, and we let them down badly. Wigan won 3-1.

That night as we drowned our sorrows in London, I was thoroughly miserable, and out of contract too. With the club only prepared to offer me one additional year and a £10 a week rise, I made my mind up there and then to get out. It was time to leave.

CHAPTER SEVENTEEN

MY RETURN TO SWINDON ...
(OR, HOW NOT TO BE A PROFESSIONAL FOOTBALLER)

When I made my escape from Brentford and returned to Swindon – yeah, forget that *Escape to Victory* movie, this was the real thing – I really thought my career was on the up (even though I was to play in the old Fourth Division for the first time in my career). Their team had been revamped from the touch-line by former Manchester United hero Lou Macari, and he seemed to be instilling new ideas into their training and tactics. Results were good and Lou's work pushed the club from the bottom tier into the old Second Division. After I'd signed for him in the summer of 1985, we had some good times and a few bad times. Two promotions back to back were the high points. But a shocking start to my Swindon career (part two) and one flashpoint in particular ended my days at the County Ground. Still there were plenty of lessons to be learnt, and to help any budding pros (or interested readers), I've put together a little manual, simply entitled 'How Not To Be a Professional Footballer'. Take note, it could save your career. Or leave you shaking your head in despair.

RULE NUMBER ONE: TRY NOT TO SIGN FOR A CLUB WHILE SERIOUSLY INJURED

Following Brentford's Wembley defeat in the 1985 Freight Rover Trophy Final, the exit door was on my mind. My contract was up, but Frank McLintock dug his heels in because he wanted a fee for me. It was the pre-Bosman era, after all. He knew I was determined to go, whatever contract he put on the table. In the meantime I'd heard that Lou Macari was interested in me for his new-look Swindon team, and I was up for signing – I still had a home there.

All the same, I had to go through pre-season with Brentford. Frank wanted to mount a proper campaign for promotion that season, and at the end of May he sent out letters to all the players. Each of us was told to go through a daily routine of exercises, stretches and runs in order to be ready for the first day of training. It's a sign of my ignorance at the time that I binned the letter immediately. I spent the summer unwinding and enjoying myself with my new family – Anne and I had got married in 1982 and our first son, Ben, had just been born. I should have taken Frank's notes more seriously really. Here was a manager, like Howard Wilkinson, who was ahead of his time. He was introducing an innovative training programme picked up from his days at Arsenal. I figured I knew better and was too blinkered to see it.

In my defence, fitness came naturally to me in those days. I didn't see what extra stretches and runs would have done to ease me into the swing of things come July, but I was mistaken. The first day back kicked off with a six-mile cross-country run around Richmond Park. I shot off as I did every summer, but after four miles of leading from the front, my left knee suddenly seized up and I couldn't walk for days. I went to see Brentford's physio, Eddie Lyons (thankfully not our brain surgeon friend, Dr Radley Smith), who worked on the knee constantly for three weeks. When his treatment failed to bring results, he told Frank he thought I was pulling a fast one. He claimed I was forcing a move from the club. The truth was, I'd ruptured a hamstring tendon, but nobody at Brentford could diagnose it. Eventually, the club agreed a £12,500 fee with Lou Macari, even though Swindon knew I was crocked at the time.

Lou didn't believe in medicals. He reckoned he would have me fully fit in a fortnight. But two days after signing for Swindon I was sent on a run around the track at the ground, with Lou watching. I barely got further than a few yards. The club doctor, who had just returned from a holiday, arranged for me to have an X-ray, plus an MRI scan, which revealed one nasty torn hamstring. He told me I wouldn't play for at least four to five months. Lou wasn't chuffed, and I guess this could have been considered a bad start in our working relationship, even though I eventually played 23 games and was never on the losing side in the 1985–86 title-winning season that pushed us into the Third Division.

RULE NUMBER TWO: AVOID ACCEPTING ANY CASH DELIVERED IN A BROWN PAPER BAG

When I signed for Swindon, I was invited to a meeting at the County Ground with Lou. He got straight to business: the club couldn't afford my wages. At £400 a week with Brentford I was one of the best-paid players in the Third Division, but a drop to Division Four with Swindon would mean a drop in salary. The club devised a way to pay me my worth using some kind of supporters' co-operative fund which basically meant I was paid a certain amount by Swindon Town and a further amount by the fund, in cash. The first I knew that we faced problems over the payments was a couple of years later, in 1988, when I had moved on yet again to Stoke. I got a call from Bill Bradshaw, a journalist with the *Sunday People*. He said he was investigating irregular payments at Swindon Town and I was implicated. Bill, who is now the *Daily Express* sports editor, said there was evidence that some players had received back-handers. I told him I had no idea what he was talking about. A couple of weeks later I saw my contract reproduced in the *Sunday People*. I don't know to this day where Bill got it from.

As far as I was concerned, my contract was the club's responsibility. I didn't have an agent in those days, but I was happy to sign for the club because I trusted them. The funny thing was, I didn't have one conversation with the Swindon chairman, Brian Hillier, about how my wages would be paid, and yet he was the poor-sod who eventually went to prison for dodgy payments. I was implicated in the scandal, and the police even dragged me to court to give evidence, though I was later cleared thanks to Gordon Taylor from the PFA, who got all the players involved immunity from prosecution as long as we fully cooperated with the tax man. Lou Macari was acquitted.

Thankfully, I was cleared of any dodgy dealings, though on my way to the trial I secured yet another trip to court by being pulled over for speeding. I was travelling from my home in Stoke to Winchester Crown Court for the Swindon trial. It was quite an early start and I didn't want to arrive late and be in contempt of court. When it came to facing the transport cops, I was represented by Peter McCormack, who later went on to defend Jonathan Woodgate and Lee Bowyer during their trial for assaulting Sarfraz Najeib in Leeds.

The omens were bad. I met Peter at Heathrow Airport to drive him to Basingstoke Crown Court and unbelievably managed to prang my car en route. An old lady in a Morris Minor had stalled at a roundabout, and the Volvo in front of me and my Beemer Three Series went straight into the back of her. The front of my car was crumpled on the Volvo's tow bar. What a saga. But Peter did his job brilliantly and got me off.

RULE NUMBER THREE: NEVER TALK BACK TO THE GAFFER, TEAM-MATES, REFS, TEA LADIES ...

With Lou working like a sergeant-major behind the scenes to get the best out of his side, we carried our impressive league form into the Third Division. Becoming a regular in the fittest Swindon team of all time was some achievement. I managed to miss just four league games, despite a few run-ins with authority during the 1986–87 campaign.

Dissent was always the offence which caused the most offence with referees. I did not have the honour of the captain's armband under Lou. Colin Calderwood was Lou's captain at Swindon, which was a bigger problem for me than I'd initially realised. I'd always relished the skipper's role when I was at

Brentford and during my first spell at Swindon. In those days, when the captain approached a ref to discuss a decision – in other words disagree with one – they were more than happy to talk to you. If you weren't a captain, you were booked for opening your gob. I couldn't get it into my head that I wasn't a captain any more, and so the cards came down like confetti.

There were some high points in that season, though. I made my 400th League appearance at Ayresome Park, Middlesbrough, of all places, which felt like a landmark. Weirdly, for the first time in my career, I'd failed to rise to the occasion. Surrounded by my smiling mates and Mam and Dad in the Ayresome Park players' bar that night, I wasn't my usual outgoing self.

Lou was happy though, as he'd managed to get us into the Second Division via a nervy play-off final. We had to face Gillingham over two legs, and after losing the first at Priestfield 1–0 we clawed back the second with a 2–1 win. The final then went to a third game at Selhurst Park, home of Crystal Palace. I actually missed that game because 15 minutes before the end of the second one I was on my way to hospital. Gills striker Tony Cascarino had kneed me in the backside and a blood clot had swollen my right buttock to four times its normal size. It isn't the most glorious of war wounds, I have to admit.

RULE NUMBER FOUR: DON'T OPEN AN OFF-LICENCE

During my first stint at Swindon, Mrs Kammy and I took quite an unusual business decision: we opened an offie. Annoyingly, it also proved to be a bit of a distraction, even though it was a much easier way of getting a six-pack.

With hindsight, putting an old-school footballer in charge of a grog shop might seem a bit like handing Paul Merson a casino loyalty card, but it was quite a tidy earner in those days. Footballers weren't making millions in the early eighties after all. We opened the store near the County Ground. Anne worked in there day-to-day and I helped out when I wasn't training or playing, which must have been a shock for any Swindon fans picking up a four-pack of Skol for the evening.

To be honest, the off-licence was a bit of a dump, and although we put a new kitchen in and spruced the place up, it was a struggle, and we had no time to ourselves. We'd also heard that there had been a problem with rats in the past. Well, I blame the previous owners. If they'd refused to serve them in the first place they would have pushed off to the fish and chip shop down the road.

One evening a young girl came in, loading up on her fags and scotch I wouldn't wonder, and said she'd actually seen a rat in the side street. This put the willies up Anne, so when our dog Sasha started barking at something in the garden late one night, she lost it completely. She'd convinced herself that whatever was lurking out there was fat and cheese-loving with a very long tail. I managed to calm her down, but through the hysterical tears I heard those chilling words:

'Chris, sort it out.'

My heart sank. I puffed out my chest and told Anne I'd sort it. Then I rang her dad, Roy. He came round like a man on a mission with his best mate and after some serious rummaging and thrashing about in the hedges, he found a hedgehog minding its own business in the middle of our garden whilst I (and Sasha, the daft dog) cowered in the doorway. Strange stuff, I didn't even know hedgehogs drank lager.

RULE NUMBER FIVE: AVOID GAZZA

We drew Newcastle away in the 1987-88 FA Cup fourth round after a good win over Norwich in the third

After we'd travelled up to the Gosforth Park Hotel on the outskirts of the city, Lou took us to an Italian restaurant in central Newcastle. He kicked us out of the restaurant at half nine and told everyone they had to be back on the coach at ten. So there we were, 16 grown men in football club tracksuits, standing like lemons on a busy Friday night in Newcastle's city centre.

This was a few years before the Quayside became a 'Booze Britain' hotspot, but Geordies know how to enjoy themselves anywhere, any time, any place. If it's in the middle of Newcastle, all the better. We stood outside the restaurant watching life go by, while the coach weaved through traffic towards us. Wild groups of women cheered us. Groups of lads, most of them gobsmacked, took the mickey. We all stayed together like a pack of scared zebras as the lions circle, because no one had the balls to go into a pub for a drink of lemonade! (Well, it was a Friday night, the eve of a game.)

The following day another Geordie took the mickey: Gazza. He scored two great goals in a 5-1 win and went down in my book as the best footballer I'd ever played against.

Mr Unbelievable

I always had a lot of time for Gazza. When I was the manager at Bradford City in 1996 he came down as Chris Waddle's guest, who was playing for us at the time. It says something for his standing as a true legend of the game that he was absolutely worshipped by Bradford fans that afternoon. The reaction was so mad that Chris asked if Gazza and a friend could watch the game in my office, which overlooked the pitch. I was only too happy, knowing that Anne and and my son Jack would keep an eye on them, although Gazza and his mate Jimmy Five Bellies made a decent attempt at emptying the contents of my fridge. At one point Gazza disappeared to go to the loo and he returned wearing my tracksuit which I'd left hanging behind the toilet door. He discarded his own tracksuit and appeared on the pitch at half-time to draw the weekly raffle wearing my gear with the CK initials on the breast.

That was the last Anne saw of him. Apparently, he disappeared in a car with Jimmy and Chris after the game. I believe it was the start of his infamous bender with Danny Baker and Chris Evans in London – and he was wearing my bloody tracksuit! It was the nearest I ever came to getting on the front page of a tabloid, because afterwards the papers ran photos of Gazza, blotto, eating a kebab, along with headlines like 'Pittafull!'

My other son Ben had to miss out that afternoon. He was away on a school trip. Gazza was one of his heroes, and Ben was gutted at not meeting him, so I promised to bring home as a souvenir Gazza's own tracksuit which he had left behind in my office. It was one of those things that just kept slipping my mind. By the time I rescued it, the top stank. When he had been in my office I had ordered sandwiches in for everyone. It turned out that Gazza had filled the pockets with sandwiches, which had since gone mouldy. Anne washed it and Ben kept it. These days I use it to muck out the horses, and it still smells a lot better than it did after Gazza slung it on.

RULE NUMBER SIX: DON'T THUMP A FELLOW PRO, GET BANNED AND CONVICTED

As I've already mentioned I was the first footballer to be convicted of assault on the pitch when I thumped Shrewsbury striker Jim Melrose. Sometimes I actually forget that I've got a criminal record because it happened 20 years ago. Occasionally I get reminded. I was once pulled over by a traffic cop flying down the M1. I thought I'd been fortunate, because he was a football fan and a Sky Sports fan, too. I was about to get off with a warning – until he checked my details.

'The computer says you've got a criminal record,' he said. Hearing it from a man in uniform really hit me.

Back in 1988, the build-up to the trial had been relatively quiet in the press. Most of the fuss had died down over the months, and although I was naturally apprehensive, I was relieved that the media interest appeared to have cooled. Well, that's what I thought. When I got out of the car at Shrewsbury Crown Court, the cameras and journalists descended from every direction. I had never seen anything like it and nothing could have prepared me for the fuss.

It was a grim day all round. I took the guilty charge and became the first player to be found guilty of an offence on a football pitch in a court of law. It's a label I will have to live with for the rest of my life. There have been similar incidents since. Arsenal's Paul Davis was banned for nine matches for hitting Glenn Cockerill, but he received full backing from his club. I was on my own.

The only consolation was that the judge was very complimentary about my behaviour in the courtroom and the way I'd handled myself in the build-up to the trial. I was ordered to pay £250 compensation to Jim, as well as £50 court costs and an additional £1,500 in solicitors' fees. Lou, to his credit, did appear in the witness box for me and tried to explain how the club had taken their own action against me immediately at great cost to the team. Swindon were going for promotion to Division One (then the top flight) at the time, and it was a blow to have one of their most experienced players unavailable, even though I was fit. Later, the FA hit me with a £250 fine and I was on my way out of Swindon.

Immediately after the incident, I didn't think I would ever speak to Jim Melrose again. He was never going to be on top of my Christmas card list. But time is a great healer and he was at Lancaster Gate for the FA hearing. To his credit, Gordon Taylor, mediator for the PFA, made us shake hands.

'Chris has suffered, Jim has suffered, you both need to get back on with your football careers,' Gordon said.

I reluctantly put my hand out and Jim took it, agreeing to forgive and forget so we could both get on with our lives. Gordon was right, we both had careers to think of. I later ran into Jim again when I was manager of Bradford City. I was trying to sign John McGinlay from Bolton Wanderers and when

I looked into it, Jim was his agent. I had no hesitation in ringing, and the pair of us dealt with the matter like professionals. We spoke a few times on the phone and he seemed a decent bloke after all the crap we'd been through. He came into my office at Valley Parade while John was having his medical. We shook hands again, but nothing more needed to be said as far as I was concerned.

RULE NUMBER SEVEN: TRY NOT TO SIGN FOR A CLUB WHILE SERIOUSLY INJURED (AGAIN)

At the end of the 1987–88 season I made my mind up to leave Swindon. The players and the supporters at Swindon had stood by me throughout Melrosegate, but deep down I knew it was time to make a clean break and rebuild my career elsewhere. Lou then offered me a new, one-year contract, which was a blow. I was hoping to leave the club on a free transfer. I wasn't short of offers.

I refused Lou's offer and went on the transfer list. Crystal Palace, Sheffield United and Wimbledon all got in touch to see what the situation was. Whilst on our family holiday I was contacted by ex-England skipper Mick Mills, who was then Stoke City manager. I was naturally chuffed and relieved that Mick Mills was a big fan and wanted me to lead his club's charge to the top division. What impressed me even more was that when we met for the first time, neither Mick nor his assistant, Sammy Chung, made any reference to Melrosegate. I was used to that punch being mentioned whenever I was in the supermarket, bookies or pub, so it made a refreshing change not to have to relive the horror of it all. They both knew the whole episode had been out of character, and was unlikely to be repeated. I knew I didn't want to let anyone down again.

Still, my move wasn't straightforward. When I first arrived at the old Victoria Ground in Stoke, news had spread that Mick was making a signing. The gossip was unbelievable really, given that this move took place nearly 20 years before Sky Sports News's Super Duper Transfer Day Deadline 24-Hour Final Countdown to Midnight with Jim White and Georgie Thompson. But with the rumour mill working hard, a few supporters were waiting in the car park to see Stoke's new arrival. They must have thought, 'What the hell is going on here?' – because when I pulled up in the car I had to struggle to the club entrance on crutches. My former Swindon Town team-mate Peter Coyne had driven me up to Stoke for the meeting with Mick. I should have taken the opportunity during my ban to get a cartilage problem sorted out, but I'd waited till the end of the season to have an op – and it went wrong. It was an operation I'd needed for some time, so a few days after the season finished I had it carried out. I'd also heard that Rangers hotshot Ally McCoist had undergone a similar operation and was spotted playing 10 days later.

'That'll do for me,' I thought, and went under the knife. The following day I walked to the travel agents to book a holiday to Menorca with my family, Anne, Ben and one-year-old Jack. After all the headlines and press attention, I knew I had to get out of the country for a little while. Menorca seemed like the ideal place to escape and recuperate. That evening I drove to Middlesbrough to see Mam and Dad, less than 24 hours after surgery. With the benefit of hindsight, this wasn't the best move. My leg started to bleed internally, and by the time we got to Teeside, I couldn't straighten it.

I was in bloody agony. We barely had time to say hello to my folks before Anne turned the car around and drove back to the surgeon in Swindon. Ben and Jack and I were all in the back of the car, but I was moaning and crying more than the kids. The doc was not impressed when he saw the grotesquely deformed limb, which had ballooned to the size of a grapefruit. My knee was drained, I was put in plaster, and the dream of returning to the training ground in 10 days, fit as a fiddle, was kicked into touch. I was facing two months of rehabilitation at Lilleshall, the sports-science academy and former FA School of Excellence. I still went ahead with the family holiday, but it was a nightmare for Anne. Our room was positioned 100 stairs away from the bar, and she had to help me up every single step to bed!

I arrived at Stoke and loved the sound of Mick Mills's plans and tactics from the off. Despite selling the influential defensive duo of Lee Dixon and Steve Bould to Arsenal, he was planning on rebuilding his team. He wasn't bothered with my disciplinary record and he didn't care about the knee injury. Mick just wanted me to play a pivotal role in the centre of midfield alongside tricksy winger and current *Soccer Saturday* reporter Peter Beagrie. 'Beags' was a player renowned for his flair and incisive running. I was going to be the muscle alongside him.

My Stoke career got off to a flyer, too. After 44 minutes of my debut against Ipswich at the Victoria Ground, I scored with a header and started to repay Mick's faith in me. Days later, though, Lady Luck was kicking me in the knackers once again when my face collided with the bonce of Bradford defender Dave Evans. The clash fractured my cheekbone, and the swelling inspired one smart-Alec journalist to nickname me 'the Phantom of the Opera'. Mick Mills couldn't believe it when I told him I would play the next match against Wolves, even though the doctors had told me I should rest for a month until my cheekbone healed. And, sure enough, I played.

Still, the 1988-89 season had gone well for me, despite the bruises. Stoke fell away towards the end of the campaign, finishing just above halfway, and there was some unfair stick for Mick Mills, mainly from the fans and the media, but we were right behind him. The players knew we had better results in us. We were also a promising side. Peter Beagrie, for example, had a great season, and was the best winger in our division at the time. But to Peter's dismay I won the Stoke Supporters' and Southern Supporters' Association Awards for player of the season! I still have the letter from the Stoke Supporters' Club informing me I'd picked up more than half the votes.

It had been a good season. I could count the bad games on one hand. My mood couldn't have been any more different from how I'd felt 12 months earlier. There had even been a great moment on my return to Swindon on 6 May at the end of the campaign. Ben - who was just four - had been made mascot for the game against Swindon at the County Ground. It felt like a happy end to a horror movie.

CHAPTER EIGHTEEN
FRANK McAVENNIE: THE TRUTH

Football fans of a certain age will remember Frank McAvennie: marauding West Ham striker from the mid-eighties, who built a profitable partnership with fellow Sky Sports pundit Tony Cottee. They were part of West Ham's most successful team ever, who were known as the Boys of '86, a side that also included another Sky colleague, Tony Gale. A few more reminders: he turned out for Scotland, went back there to play for Celtic, was a bit of a playboy and had a *Charlie's Angels* haircut, as did most of the girls he went out with. He loved London life for much the same reason as another Scottish striker, Charlie Nicholas. By all accounts he would have fitted in well with our Friday night drinks gathering before we go to air on Sky.

I always rated Frank as a player, because he could give you a hell of a game on the park. He was smallish for a striker, and so was Tony Cottee. Actually Tony still is – he's the only one who actually stands behind the desk on *Soccer Saturday*. But it's unlikely I'll ever make it on to Frank's Christmas card list.

Mr Unbelievable

For over 20 years he's held a grudge over a 50/50 tackle at Stoke's Victoria Ground in 1989 that left him with a nasty broken leg, some nuts and bolts in his bones and nine months out of the game. He's been reported in the papers claiming that this freak incident was deliberate. Sadly, some people have taken those words as the truth.

The challenge that hurt Frank really was an accident: a ball came in from midfield, we both went for it, and Frank ended up on the deck. The ref was a yard away. A few minutes later, when the ball went out of play, Frank was still down. Nobody could have envisaged his horrific injuries, certainly not me, even though I was the one involved in the tackle. Nobody, but nobody, in the ground at the time pointed any fingers at me. The incident has become something of a myth as the years have gone by. And if you don't believe me, there's a clip of the incident on the YouTube website (www.youtube.com) for you to make up your own mind. Just type in Kamara_McAvennie.avi and you'll see what I'm talking about.

Immediately after the game, I spoke to the press boys waiting outside the dressing-room and gave them my side of the story. I pleaded my innocence when it became apparent from their questioning that things were a lot more serious for Frank than any of us had thought. Frank refused to go to the hospital in Stoke, instead insisting that he travel back to London on the team coach. That evening a friend of mine in London, Christine Mathews, phoned round every London hospital to find out if he was there, so that I could enquire how Frank was and send him my best wishes. This is something I would have done even if I hadn't been involved in the challenge. It is the last thing you want to see, a fellow professional with a serious injury. When I heard back from Christine, she had located him, but the news was not good – he was undergoing surgery.

The next day, the tabloids were full of it. The Hammers captain, Alvin Martin, added to the drama, reportedly claiming in one paper that the tackle was late and then reckoning in another that he never saw it.

Before I knew it, the Royal Mail were delivering sackloads of hate mail. Nearly all of them carried an east London postmark. A battle was brewing. The thing was, Frank wouldn't let it go because he was hoping for compensation in the courts, but nobody would take him seriously, mainly because there wasn't any evidence to back his claims. I was having to get my head round what looked like some pretty serious accusations from Frank, printed in the *Daily Express*: 'I'm not going to let Kamara get away with this. I've had a three-and-a-half-hour operation on my left ankle and I was told my career was in doubt. Eight pins and a plate have been inserted in the damaged area and hopefully everything will work out. I'm out of football until at least January and it's a shattering blow. I'd never felt better at the start of a new season. I will be approaching Stoke for their video of the match and will be speaking to my lawyer with a view to considering legal action.'

Frank's solicitors wrote to me and to Stoke, but their threats came to nothing. It seemed like Frank was on his own. West Ham refused to stand by him, Mick Mills defended me at Stoke, and even West Ham manager Lou Macari defended me in print. I'm delighted that now, thanks to the development of computer technology since those days, as I said earlier, you can see it for yourselves.

But the damage had been done by the *Express* article. Because of the reported outburst, vitriolic letters from Hammers supporters continued for months. I think our postie nearly collapsed under one particularly large sackful the week before the return league match at Upton Park. As you can imagine, that fixture against West Ham had hazard signs flashing all over it. By the day of the game Frank had dropped the charges against me, and Mick Mills had left Stoke after only four months in charge. The side had struggled, we were in the relegation zone, and former England legend Alan Ball had taken over. Bally told me he'd keep me in as captain for the West Ham game because he had no intention of dropping me, despite the fuss that was beginning to kick off.

Frank had, in my view, stirred up the fans in the press on the day of the match and claimed he had dropped the legal charge 'for the good of the game' rather than because he didn't actually have much of a case. Despite my innocence, a lynch mob was out in force at Upton Park that day. Everybody hated me, because they believed I'd deliberately injured a hero of theirs. In fact, even though a police officer had to sit next to me on to the bus for the final leg of the journey into Upton Park, I was oblivious of the abuse from the moment we arrived at the ground to the moment we left, with a point in our back pockets. I do remember the West Ham fans screaming at me each time I went near the ball, but I just ignored it. I played as if I wasn't their target and shut them out. I was a professional, I had a job to do and I was just determined to get on with my normal game. I got through the 0-0 draw unscathed. My police officer mate made sure I got back on the coach and out of east London in one piece.

I figured Frank was finally over it when I saw him some nine years later. We were both part of a squad that had been invited over to Trinidad and Tobago, along with our families, to play in a Masters-style tournament. As we headed off on our flight from Heathrow, I must admit to feeling a little uncomfortable, but the moment I saw him Frank smiled and offered me a drink. It seemed like the incident was water under the bridge, and we even had a laugh on the long flight over the Atlantic. For the duration of the tournament/holiday we partied like old mates.

Our paths crossed again in April 2004 at the International Masters in Cardiff. It was a good night with the old fogeys. Chris Waddle, Ian Rush, Neville Southall and John Collins all played, and Frank was there too, this time in Scotland colours. I couldn't join in because I was on commentating duty for Sky, but I was asked to interview him for the show. It wasn't a problem for either of us – this was work and a chance to prove we were grown men. Frank was in great form, cracking jokes, even though his team had been knocked out.

'It's not been a good night for Scotland, Frank.'

Frank smiled. 'The night is young. Ask me in the morning if I've had a bad night.'

That was him all over, a joker and a rogue. I liked him. In fact I wish he'd been around in the old days, I have a feeling him and me would got along, and I'm delighted I've been able to draw a line and wish him my best.

CHAPTER NINETEEN
SERVING SERGEANT WILKO

My dream as a kid was to play for my home town Middlesbrough or Leeds United. My favourite player for Boro was Eric McMordie and my hero for Leeds was Johnny Giles, who down south had become a modern cockney rhyming slang item, and quite aptly so because the London clubs considered him a complete pain in the backside. The way he passed the ball was incredible as he linked up with Peter Lorimer and Eddie Gray on the wings. Giles bossed that midfield and he was a god to me, so when I was a small boy playing footie with my mates I was always Johnny Giles – also at that young age I was the same height as the little fella.

When I heard in 1990 that the Leeds manager, Howard Wilkinson, fancied signing me, I was interested to say the least! There was a nice problem, though: Boro had also tabled a £150,000 bid for me. Their timing couldn't have been worse. If Steve Gibson, my old school-mate and the Boro chairman, had come in for me at any other time, I'd have jumped at the chance of signing at Ayresome Park, their home ground back then. They were my home-town club and I watched them more than Leeds when I was a kid getting 'a squeeze' in the boys' end with my saved-up paper-round money – a squeeze being two people going through the turnstile together at the ground, with the kind turnstile operater only charging for one.

I had really enjoyed my time at Stoke. I was the captain and the fans loved me, but I had been approached by Leeds. I was told, 'If you get permission to speak to another club, would you ring this journalist, David Walker, who is a big friend of Howard Wilkinson.'

As far as Alan Ball was concerned, I was signing for Boro. I was even called into Bally's office for a long phone conversation with Boro manager Bruce Rioch, who made a pretty good case for why I should sign for him. Judging by our conversation, Rioch was a manager with big ambitions. With the help of Steve Gibson he'd performed a minor miracle on Teesside. The club had been transformed into a halfway decent Second Division outfit (for the benefit of younger readers, this was what the Championship is today). I would also be joining some players with exciting potential – Gary Pallister and Colin Cooper among them – and Rioch reckoned my experience would push his side to the next level.

Alan Ball figured I'd been charmed by Rioch's PR campaign. He even gave me copies of all the documents relating to the transfer, which included details of how Boro would pay it. He told me to travel north and take in a game at Ayresome Park against Newcastle which promised to be a tasty local derby. I was to have a ringside seat with Rioch and Steve Gibson. Somewhere in the script it said I would sign for Boro that evening. But I had other ideas.

Mr Unbelievable

As soon as I got home I rang David Walker, the journalist.

'Sit by the phone for a while,' he said. 'I will speak to Howard.'

After what seemed like an eternity but was only 10 minutes he phoned back, saying that on my way to Middlesbrough I should stop off at Elland Road, the home of Leeds United, for a meeting with Howard Wilkinson. The car journey was a real tug-of-war as far as my conscience was concerned. Thankfully I was familiar with the road up to Middlesbrough. The M6, M62, A1, then the A19 – a stretch of road that leads from one side of north Yorkshire to the other and takes you closer to two contrasting images of Teesside. The greenery of the Cleveland Hills looks great on the right, and the industrial towers of north Middlesbrough and beyond sit imposingly on the left. That night I didn't get close to any of that. My car stopped at Leeds and didn't go any further north.

The good news when I arrived at Elland Road was that Bill Fotherby, the Managing Director of Leeds, had cleared the proposed meeting with Stoke chairman, Peter Coates. I was free to talk to Howard Wilkinson and thrash out a deal. The bad news? Nobody had told Alan Ball. The next day, when the details of my meeting with Leeds came through to him, he reckoned the board had acted in an underhand way. In truth, they hadn't. It was not only the deal I got that convinced me to sign for Leeds, it was their position in the league that did it. At the time, Leeds were top of the old Second Division and looked odds-on for promotion. Boro were doing well but were down the table and just above the relegation places. Signing for Leeds was a no-brainer.

Serving Sergeant Wilko

Despite having these points on his side, Howard still did plenty of talking when I arrived at Elland Road. He desperately wanted me for his team, he said. They were going to win the First Division in the next couple of years. That aside, the real bonus was the prospect of playing in the top division after years of graft in the lower leagues. The money he was offering me was fabulous, tripling my basic wage at Stoke. There was also a substantial signing-on fee and a promotion bonus. I was up for it and told Howard and Bill I would sign the following day, but I wanted to do the decent thing and meet with Rioch and Steve Gibson, just so I could tell them face to face. Howard didn't want me to leave his office without a finalised contract. He was worried that I might change my mind.

'I have to talk to Middlesbrough,' I said, trying to reassure him. 'I have to do the right thing and see them.'

What I had not told them was that Steve Gibson was a mate of mine and that signing before seeing him would in my mind be a betrayal of trust.

Howard and Bill looked at each other and went out of the office. When they came back they offered more money – another £10,000 per year on top of an already great deal which, I reminded them, had already been accepted! I couldn't understand what they were doing. I suppose they must have thought I was using Boro's offer to up my money. In those days I didn't have an agent, and negotiating money never has been one of my strong points.

At most of the clubs I'd been to, I happily accepted the first offer. I was the manager's best friend and never knew it. The massive irony here was that I was sitting in Howard Wilkinson's office playing my best ever poker hand and I didn't even know.

'I'd still like to sign it on my way home from the Boro tomorrow,' I said.

They refused to listen. Bill decided he wasn't going to let me out of Elland Road without me putting pen to paper. God knows what must have been going through Howard's head. Up until that point I'd resembled a man happy to crawl across broken beer bottles to play for him. The now disgruntled duo disappeared again, asking me to sit tight for a minute while they had another discussion. The door closed, voices were raised. I sat there looking at the pretty pictures on Howard's wall.

When they returned, I greeted them with a smile but their demeanour had changed dramatically. The laughs and the small talk had gone. Bill marched over.

'This is our final offer,' he shouted, slamming his fist, contract and all, down on the table, Alan Sugar style. 'Take it or leave it, because it won't be there tomorrow.'

I looked at the numbers. The money had been upped again. I could ensure my family was financially secure for a few years at the very least. This was an offer I couldn't refuse. The fact that I was signing for my boyhood team was an added bonus. I grabbed a pen and signed the contract before Howard and Bill changed their minds.

I knew I had made the right decision signing for Leeds almost immediately, mainly because playing under Howard Wilkinson was a dream come true. Well, most of the time. That night, he introduced me to the club by outlining his plans for the future: first to build a Leeds team with plenty of experience at its core, but with a number of highly talented youngsters on the fringes. My role was to provide some of that experience. Howard's ultimate vision was to build a young Leeds team for the future. From the second I had scribbled my name on the contract, I wanted to drive to Stoke to get my boots and start training.

There was one problem. I had to tell Bruce Rioch and Steve Gibson that I wouldn't be signing for Boro. Making the phone call to Ayresome Park that night wouldn't be easy. I rang the club, asked to be put through to the boardroom and caught Bruce Rioch in a foul mood.

'No one does this to me or Middlesbrough Football Club,' he shouted, smarting at my decision. 'You will be a very sorry young man. You will regret this for the rest of your life.'

My gut instinct was that I'd betrayed Steve even though I knew Leeds was the best possible move for me, my career and my family. I knew that face to face Steve would have been hard to turn down, because he was genuinely excited about the prospect of us being reunited, as was I. When I got back to Stoke that evening, Anne and I should have been celebrating. In a way we had won the lottery, but I thought I might have lost my friendship with Steve, so we were both flat. Then, around 11.30 p.m., the phone rang. It was Steve. I felt awkward as he spoke:

'How much have they offered you?'

I told him and he was honest enough to comment: 'We couldn't have matched that ... Remember when we were kids? We were either Boro or Leeds players? You go to Leeds and have a great time.'

Steve showed his class and his deep friendship. I put the phone down and I couldn't have been happier. My pal Steve had come up trumps for me, so the time had finally come for me and Anne to break open the champagne.

My league debut for Leeds against Hull City was a classic game that ended 4–3 to Leeds, with Gordon Strachan scoring the winner in injury time. I played out of position at right-back, a definite first, but I didn't care because I was just so chuffed to be playing for Leeds in the league. Wherever the manager asked me to operate was fine by me. I would have played in goal if Howard had asked me to. I'll go even further: I would have sold the bloody programmes so long as my name had been on the team-sheet. I played the next two games, both 2–2 draws against Ipswich and West Bromwich Albion, at right-back until Howard's first choice, Mel Sterland, came back from injury. Mel was an occasional England international. He made the position his own again with no grumbles from me. The 2–2 draw with West Brom (as right-back) brought me the greatest goal I ever scored for Leeds – indeed it was the only goal I ever scored for Leeds, but who's counting? And in fairness I missed some absolute crackers, so my goalscoring form at Leeds was swings and roundabouts, but without the roundabouts and with only one swing. I still remember that header ... it went in. It was one of those moments I'd dreamt of when pretending to be Johnny Giles as a kid. Doing it for real was something special: a Strachan corner, my forehead connecting, thumping the ball into the back of the net. I reeled away to the Leeds fans with a big grin on my face, and Vinnie Jones grabbed me round the neck – it could have been worse when you think of what he did to Paul Gascoigne. It wasn't one of my best goals, but it was certainly the most memorable.

Vinnie was one of the first players to welcome me to Leeds. When I arrived at the club, he came over to me and hugged me on the training ground. I was in digs in Headingley, and Vinnie was in the same place. We would often go out together. He was a real good lad from the start. He was also a much better player than people gave him credit for. He was influential in the middle of the park and would never take any nonsense. Vinnie knew what he had in his locker in terms of being hard, and he would never back away from anyone. It's amazing what he made of himself after football.

Howard had told me when I signed that he thought David Batty could blow up for him at any time, as it was his first full season, but Batts had other ideas. He was playing out of his skin, so I wasn't a guaranteed pick for the starting line-up as I had been at Stoke, Pompey and Swindon. Also in the midfield was Vinnie. Howard had pieced together a squad that also included former Man United legend Gordon Strachan and Welsh international Gary Speed. Five into four wouldn't go, and I looked like number five in the pecking order. He later also signed Gary McAllister. For the first time in my career – well, since those early days as a naive teenager at Portsmouth and Swindon, anyway – I wasn't an automatic first-team choice for the gaffer. But I grafted away and I knew my time would come. First Howard dropped Gary Speed away at Oldham and played me wide right, whilst Strach switched to the left. Oldham had a plastic pitch in those days and were very adept at passing the ball in and around you. At half-time in that game the gaffer had a pop at Gordon Strachan for pulling out of a 50/50 ball. Strach just looked over at me, Vinnie and Batts, and screamed at Wilko, 'That's not my game, that's what you have those three for!'

He was right, us three fierce midfielders were Lock, Stock and Two Smoking Barrels long before Vinnie went into movies as a modern-day Shirley Temple. So how did he get into films and not me, I hear you asking. He was better than me: Vinnie had been acting all of his life.

The next game was against Sheffield United, managed by Dave (Harry) Bassett, who were lying second in the table. There was only a point in it with six games to go. Batts was dropped and I was put into my favourite position in the centre of midfield. We won the game 4–0 and I received the man of the match award. At last things were going well for me. We drew 2–2 the following Saturday at Brighton. When we were 2–1 up, Howard took me off with 20 minutes to go. I thought I was having a decent game, but I was replaced by Batts, while Vinnie Jones, who hadn't kicked a ball all game, stayed on. My frustrations boiled over as I walked past the gaffer on the touchline:

'What have you brought me off for?'

'Because I'm the manager, that's why,' he said.

'I know you're the manager, but I'm doing all right,' I shouted. 'Vinnie's not doing anything out there.'

He turned round to me, pointed his finger and told me to shut it.

Spotting the tension brewing, Mick Hinnegan, the first-team coach, stepped in. He could see the writing on the wall for me.

'Come on, sit down, Chris,' he warned, pulling me to one side. 'You'd better keep your mouth shut.'

'No, I won't. There's one rule for one and one rule for the other here. I've worked my socks off to get in this team and I'm playing well and now you've dragged me off,'

Howard looked angry. 'You better shut it now, or you won't be at this football club tomorrow,' he hissed. Then he turned his back on me and went back to the game.

Mick and a couple of the lads ushered me away. I sat at the end of the bench with the subs. Thankfully I was back in the side the following week. Barnsley looked a formality but we lost 2–1, which left us needing victories over Leicester and Bournemouth in the last two games to be sure of promotion. Two wins would also mean we'd won the Second Division title and I would be picking up my first League winners' medal. It was squeaky bum time for all of us, thankfully without the Johnny Giles's.

Howard Wilkinson was a visionary. A manager so influential and imaginative that he reshaped the way a lot of the Leeds players looked after themselves on and off the pitch. He was also a master of man management. A lot of plaudits have been heaped on Arsène Wenger in recent years – and rightly so, for his revolutionary attitude towards diet and nutrition – but Howard was quietly implementing the same sort of practices at Leeds, only several years earlier. The methods he used at Leeds in the late eighties and early nineties were ahead of their time, certainly in this country. He even introduced psychologists to the Leeds coaching staff at a time when most people thought that Leeds players needed psychiatrists rather than psychologists, and animal trainers rather than personal trainers.

When it came to preparing us for big games, Howard was just as ingenious. We'd got a great result against Leicester City, beating them 2-1, but not before we had had a scare. Gary McAllister scored to put the visitors 1-0 up in a game in which I should have had a hat-trick, but the ever-dependable Strach scored the winner in the last five minutes. One game left to play and we needed to beat Bournemouth to win the Second Division title. In the run-up to this showdown game, it became clear that our striker, Bobby Davidson, wasn't fit. Bobby was a massive player for us. His 11 goals that season had been invaluable, and he had been sorely missed when he sat on the sidelines for three months with an ankle injury. The prospect of losing him again was a blow to Howard, and his only fit alternative was Carl Shutt.

Carl was a smashing lad and he had bags of ability, but he'd only scored two goals as Bobby's stand-in. He could also get a bit nervous on those big-game days. Howard knew that if Carl was told about his place in the starting line-up against Bournemouth, the biggest game of his career at that time, he would get so nervous we'd need to make sure he was wearing two sets of pants under the team's white shorts.

On the day before the game, Howard organised a meeting with me, Bobby and Strach. I was only privy to this information because the gaffer wanted me to room with Bobby that night. He had a plan: despite his injury, Bobby was going to start the match and come off after about five minutes. Carl was going to replace him. But Howard made it clear that not a word was to be uttered to Carl; we were sworn to secrecy. Footballers love a good gossip, and sometimes there's nothing better than being in the know when everyone else is in the dark, no matter who they are. But Howard was adamant. we had to keep our gobs shut. The title possibly depended on it.

Howard's plan worked, too. Bobby Davidson succumbed to the inevitable after five minutes. Shutty barely had time to warm up when he was called on, although I think Howard made sure he wasn't too comfortable as he sat on the bench – he was probably warming up from the minute we'd kicked off. Leeds ran out 1-0 winners, following a Lee Chapman winner, which I had helped to set up.

At half-time it was 0-0. Harry Redknapp's side needed to win to stay up, so the game was nervy, but I was loving it and was bombing forward in the second half trying to make things happen. With 20 minutes to go Howard shouted at me: 'Sit in midfield and hold your ground.'

I ignored him.

'Sit in midfield and hold your ground. If you don't I am bringing you off,' he shouted.

I still ignored him. I saw him telling David Batty to warm up.

'If you make one more run I am bringing you off!' he shouted. At that point I made a burst down the right wing from a pass from Chris Fairclough. I looked up and saw Lee Chapman on the far post and pinged a pass right on to his head. Chappy powered his header past Gerry Peyton in the Bournemouth goal. Now I would sit! The job was done, Leeds was back in the big time and I was a part of it.

When I signed for Leeds, I hadn't considered the wider impli-
cations for my family. Mam and Dad had taken a lot of flak after
I'd turned down my home-town club, and there had been a lot
of tension in our street, where they still lived. One night their
house was attacked, and stones rained down on the windows as
they sat watching television in the front room. Offensive graf-
fiti were painted on to the house walls. Mam was almost too
scared to go out during the day, but Dad was different. Anyone
coming anywhere near the house was interrogated. If Dad
didn't like their reason for being at his door, they soon knew
about it. It stopped the trouble, and the tension eventually died
away after they had suffered for four miserable months. I know
that deep down he was happy the move to Middlesbrough
hadn't worked out and that he felt my success at Leeds justified my decision, but he still took a lot of stick because of it.

Now, by beating Bournemouth, we'd helped Boro to remain
in the division. They'd been involved in a relegation scrap with
Bournemouth, and our three points against their enemy at
Dean Court saved them from Division Three. With Boro saved,
I figured that the timing was right to make peace with the
Middlesbrough supporters through their local press.

'I was pleased to set up the goal for Lee Chapman because
I had been praying for Boro to win,' I told the *Evening Gazette*.
'I couldn't understand why they were down there in the first
place, but I knew we could do them a favour at Bournemouth
and I went into the game with my fingers crossed. It was great
to beat Bournemouth and then see that Boro had won, and I
think they'll prove next season that they were in a false position. Perhaps the most important thing is that I'll be able to go

out with my pals in Middlesbrough without having to worry about the backlash. It has always been my ambition to play for Middlesbrough. I went to school with Steve Gibson, and the first thing I did was to phone him and congratulate him, but it has also been my ambition to play in the First Division and that is why I joined Leeds. Hopefully I will achieve that ambition now that we are promoted. Howard Wilkinson is likely to buy big again this summer and there's going to be a right battle for places.'

The promotion to the First Division meant everything to me. I more than played my part in delivering that dream to the supporters at Elland Road, and none of us will forget the scenes in Leeds city centre for the victory parade.

The summer months naturally brought some serious transfer activity to Elland Road. Howard was keen to add to the squad after our promotion, because he believed we could really make a name for ourselves in the First Division. He was also happy to show a few established faces the door. Vinnie Jones was sold to Sheffield United where he hooked up with his old mate and mentor Dave 'Harry' Bassett, the manager who famously took Wimbledon's 'Crazy Gang' from the Fourth Division to the First. Vinnie felt like he was going home.

Before Vinnie's exit from Leeds we had the obligatory end-of-term 'rest after a long hard season' on a sunny beach in Majorca. It was a great trip. It was good to see the likes of Gordon Strachan, Lee Chapman and Mel Sterland letting their hair down. One evening the whole team – apart from Vinnie – was sitting in the pub opposite the hotel waiting to go out for something to eat. Suddenly a police car pulled up outside. One of the lads said, 'I bet Vinnie's in there.' And we all laughed. But, sure enough, he was. Two police officers pulled him out of the car. He was handcuffed and looked rather the worst for wear and a bit miffed to say the least. They all sat down in the hotel foyer. As his room-mate, I went over to find out what was going on.

'You all right, mate?' I asked.

He nodded. Apparently, he'd been drinking on the beach all day. A couple of punters had started on him and he had sorted them out. 'I'm fine,' he said, 'but I need some money. These coppers want paying off and I haven't got any Spanish money on me. They need 2,000 pesetas.' I loaned it to him, and he promised to pay me when we got back to Leeds, but I never did see it again. Within an hour he had showered, changed and was back with the rest of us lads in the bar opposite!

⊛ ⊛ ⊛ ⊛ ⊛ ⊛ ⊛

On paper, Vinnie's departure was good news for me. The deal went through with only two weeks of the 1991-92 season played, and I figured that Howard would use me in Vinnie's place. What I hadn't contemplated was that Howard would splash a cool £1 million on Gary McAllister from Leicester City. Macca was a creative playmaker who later went on to become an ever present for the club. He was also one part of Howard's new midfield blueprint which featured David Batty, Gordon Strachan and Gary Speed.

Howard put me on the bench again, though I soon got a spot at left-back when injuries left him short before the game against Aston Villa. This was a scary prospect for me, because Villa had a right-winger called Tony Daly. Some of you may remember him as one of the first players to wear cycling shorts under his regular kit. He was so bloody quick that the Lycra kit was needed to support his hamstrings. Days earlier, he had torn Inter Milan's defence apart in a UEFA Cup fixture. My job that afternoon was to make sure that Tony didn't get a sniff. He didn't either, and my performance convinced Howard that I was worthy of a place in the side at left-back. I was looking at a nice run in the team if I played my cards right.

You can almost see the bad news coming, can't you? In an away game against Coventry City I twisted my ankle after jumping for a header, and at half-time Howard gave me the option to come off.

'No, a strapping will do,' I said.

Physio Alan Sutton patched me up, then in the second half Micky Gynn (short guy, quick, 'tache) flew past me on the wing. He went one way, I went the other, and my ankle tried to do both. The studs in my boot stuck in the turf and my weakened ankle went for a holiday. Little did I know then that I would be out for 11 months. My world was about to fall apart.

For a professional footballer, let me tell you, there's nothing worse than a long-term injury. It was a thoroughly depressing experience. I couldn't play, and I got up every morning with nothing to look forward to other than a couple of hours in rehab at the training ground. Meanwhile, my mates worked on set-pieces outside, played small-sided games and planned for the next match. You also have plenty of time to think. Often I worried: Would I be the same player when I got back? Would I have a place in the side? Was my career over? Mentally you have to be pretty tough to get through it.

I missed the banter in the dressing-room. I wasn't involved in the match-day tension as much as I'd been used to. The in-jokes and new nicknames went over my head. Sometimes I felt like a peripheral figure; when the team was winning games, I wasn't part of their success. And watching Leeds play from the stands was unbearable. Unsurprisingly, I fell out with the manager and just about anyone who came into contact with me. I even considered retirement.

Help came eventually, but only after further frustration. Whenever Gordon Strachan suffered an injury at Leeds, he turned to a fellow called Harold Oyen. Harold recommended that players should use diets, training routines, stretching exercises and post-match relaxation techniques to prepare for games. He introduced Gordon to bananas, yogurts, seaweed and energy drinks when the rest of us were downing lagers and eating pies before and after matches. Gordon had been introduced to him at Old Trafford and really believed in him.

I was extremely sceptical. Given the impact such practices have made on the game in this country in recent years (and the fact that they're now part and parcel of every team's preparation), I'm not proud to admit that I would not have normally gone to see someone like Harold for help. In my defence, this was a totally new world to me, even though I'd just entered my thirties. I believed there was very little wrong with the pie and pints approach I had followed for over a decade.

But now I was desperate. I'd been out for eight months by this point and couldn't see a light at the end of the tunnel.

Serving Sergeant Wilko

Howard Wilkinson suspected I was pulling a fast one, after nearly a season on the sidelines. The medical staff had convinced him that I wasn't injured and they reckoned I didn't want to play any more. Howard thought I'd slipped into a comfort zone. He kept pressurising me to try the injury in practice games and seemed unusually keen to get me fit. He even made me play in a reserve match against Liverpool when I could hardly train. At that time, getting out of bed took me five minutes and walking was a real struggle. I wanted to prove Howard wrong. So when he suggested I should see Gordon's guru, I jumped at the chance.

My trip to see Harold was a real eye-opener. One of his tricks was to spend a few minutes slagging you off as he loomed over you, holding your arm at a right angle. He'd call you every name under the sun, then he'd ask you to push his arm away. You'd be fuming inside, but no matter how hard you tried, it was impossible to push him away. He'd then turn the abuse on its head and praise you to the hilt. When his tone changed, shoving his arm was much easier. The problem was, I knew the script. I'd been warned what to expect by some of the lads who had already visited Harold, but his psychological techniques still angered me.

'You don't want to play for Leeds, do you, Chris?' he said.

That was as far as he got. I lost it.

'You don't know me,' I yelled. 'How dare you launch that at me? Has Howard put you up to this?'

Harold just sat there impassively. It was probably one of his less successful consultations. I don't know if it was the reaction he was expecting, but I stormed out of the room and went straight to Howard's office. I was fuming. His secretary, Maureen, stopped me from breaking down his door and politely but firmly told me to sit down. She promised to tell Howard that I was waiting for him and, when he was ready to speak to me, I could go in. I sat there for 45 very long minutes, but the wait just added to my rising anger. I stared at the door, willing him to open it. I wanted to give him what for. Finally Howard called me in. At first he wouldn't even look at me. As I closed the door his telephone started ringing and he answered it, chatting away for 10 minutes. He then buzzed Maureen back into the office. The pair of them nattered away for ages, both apparently oblivious to my steaming ears.

Once I'd been granted my audience, I spoke (well, shouted really) for five minutes straight, hardly drawing breath. I told Howard how important it was to me to play for Leeds and that I was genuinely injured. I didn't appreciate what Harold Oyen had said to me. Eight months was too long for me to be out of action, and if Howard really felt like that then I didn't want to play for him, I was prepared to quit there and then. I even offered to retire, because I was tired of the hassle. I didn't want to be paid by Leeds any more.

Until this time I am not sure Howard appreciated just how much I wanted to play football.

'It's my life!' I shouted at him. I told him the injury was genuine. 'I'm doing everything I can to fix it,' I told him. 'But all the gym work, all the cycling and even the alternative treatments aren't making a difference.'

Howard listened to me and took in everything I had to say. I think he could tell I was angry, frustrated and as low as I had felt for a long time. I wasn't in any comfort zone and I genuinely wanted to get fit. He waited a few seconds and took a pen from his desk and started scribbling. He handed me a piece of paper with a name and address on it: Paddy Armour, a supposed miracle worker based in Wakefield. Apparently he specialised in treating unusual sports injuries. I couldn't help wondering, though, if he was a miracle worker, how come he still had a mortgage and lived in Wakefield as opposed to the South of France.

'Go and see him,' said Howard. He then looked at the paperwork on his desk and began working away. Clearly he had nothing more to say on the matter.

I was prepared to give it a go. Howard had known Paddy since his days at Sheffield Wednesday and used him occasionally to help seriously injured players. By all accounts, he'd been pretty impressed by the results. I have to say that, as I pulled up and saw Geoffrey Boycott's Rolls-Royce parked outside, I was pretty impressed too. I later learned that Paddy had helped prolong the career of the Yorkshire and England cricket legend from his tiny room in Wakefield.

Paddy turned out to be elderly, stocky and wily. He was also more astute than any of the other doctors who had poked and pulled my ankle. It took him five minutes to identify my problem.

'You've got an Achilles tendon problem,' he said. 'You've got arthritis in your ankle and you've got plantar fasciitis.'

The last bit was a new one on me but, on reflection, it seemed so obvious. The condition, which is also known as Triple Jumper's Heel, means it's difficult to even stand because pain sears up from the bottom of the foot, through the Achilles and into the lower back. It explained why I was finding it difficult to put my foot down and why I'd spent an entire 'comeback game' in the reserves running on tiptoe. It was common among road-runners. When I was fit I used to go jogging around the streets of Wakefield. I'd probably made it far worse.

I was relieved to hear a diagnosis at last, and to know it could be treated. All I'd experienced for months was shrugged shoulders and bemused looks. I was even more relieved to hear the relatively short time-scale Paddy predicted for my recovery. He said it would take me three months to get fit. In the end I was back in six weeks and sold within seven.

I thought Howard Wilkinson was a great manager. If there was one flaw in his managerial style, though, it was that he could drone on for bloody hours. If he wrote his autobiography it would have more pages than the history of the Second World War. He also had a painfully pragmatic attitude to the way the game should be played. Today, when I get up at fancy dinners and give speeches (or a song, depending on how good the complimentary champagne is), I tell a tale from when I was doing my 'A' licence coaching badge at Elland Road in 1992. As part of my assessment, I had to take a training session on attacking midfielders. I asked Howard to help, and he organised some drills, using me, Gordon Strachan and Gary McAllister in midfield, defenders Chris Whyte and Chris Fairclough and keeper John Lukic, with Eric Cantona, who had joined the club from Sheffield Wednesday, up front.

During one session, the ball was played neatly in to Eric's feet. He checked his run, lost his man and chipped the ball with his left foot. His shot dropped just under the crossbar, leaving John stranded. The rest of us stood back and applauded. It was a little flash of the genius which Eric would show regularly at Manchester United some years later. Everyone was amazed. Well, everyone apart from Howard, who raced over from the touchline wagging his finger.

'Whoa, whoa, whoa,' he shouted. 'Eric, you had better options there.' He then proceeded to lecture Eric on where he should have passed the ball and how he could have brought Gordon and Macca into play. In Howard's mind, Eric's quick thinking would have been useless in a match-day situation. It was my first big lesson in the art of coaching: sometimes, there's just no pleasing a football manager.

CHAPTER TWENTY

WISH YOU WERE HERE?
(MY LIFE ON THE MOTORWAYS)

If you believe everything you hear on *Soccer Saturday*, you're probably under the impression that I was a journeyman pro for much of my career. Well, can I say right now, not everything Jeff says on the telly is gospel. Sure, I might have one or two more clubs on my CV than most players, but the tag of journeyman probably comes from my last few seasons in the game. In the space of four and a half years, I turned out for Leeds, Luton, Sheffield United (on loan and then a permanent deal), Boro (on loan) and Bradford, where I began my coaching career.

But rather than giving you a detailed, blow-by-blow account of my move from this club to that, I thought it would be more apt to give you a *Goals on Sunday*-style highlights package of my last few seasons in football. So grab a bacon sandwich, cue up the Commodores' 'Easy Like Sunday Morning' on the stereo and read on ...

Wish You Were Here?

LEAVING LEEDS

When Howard Wilkinson signed Eric Cantona for Leeds United in 1991-92, I'd like to think he was a direct replacement for my mercurial talents, but there's a limit to how far the imagination will stretch. Eric was a fantastic player, a class apart - even from me! During the very brief time I played with him in training, he showed many flashes of the talent that would make him such a legend at Old Trafford. And he always had his collars turned up, even then. I remember Charlie Nicholas sometimes played at Arsenal with his collar up, but that was probably to hide the war wounds sustained overnight at some nightclub if I know Charlie. Only joking, of course. I think Cantona was the first to wear his collar up since Allan Clarke at Leeds United.

We never did get to play together. Whilst I was out injured for that long, long stretch I was told that I had to play in a reserve team game against Liverpool. The plan that night was to get through 90 minutes of action, but I lasted no longer than five, I couldn't put my foot to the ground. When I trudged off, I was surprised to see David Pleat - then the Luton manager - waiting for me in the tunnel, although nothing really clicked at the time. Well, apart from my ankle. I was so disappointed with my whole situation that I didn't really think it odd that another First Division manager should be enquiring about my fitness.

'How is it?' he asked, peering down at the suspect leg.

I was in a right mood. 'It's a nightmare,' I said. 'The pain is exactly the same and I think it's shot completely.'

I headed off to change, without realising that my comment had shot me in the other foot. What I didn't know was that David had been willing to take a gamble on me at that time.

I was very, very down following this and Howard was probably not very thrilled either. He felt the time was right to sell me, as I was one of his older players, and now prone to picking up these long-term injuries, probably due to my age. Naturally, when I finally returned to full fitness in the title-winning 1991–92 season, I was delighted to find that after only two games in the reserves I was back in first-team contention.

I found myself on the bench for an away game at Notts County. I came on for the last 20 minutes when Gary McAllister got injured, and we went on to win the match 4–2. I was back and buzzing – I thought my Leeds career was on the up again.

The following Tuesday we played Tranmere Rovers in the Worthington Cup and I started my first full 90 minutes for nearly a year. I must have got by on adrenaline because it definitely wasn't due to my fitness. All the same we progressed through to the next round and I had a decent enough game. The next morning Howard called me to break the news that he had agreed a fee with David Pleat for me, but that before letting me go he needed me for the Saturday home match against Oldham. The reason he was telling me this was that he felt I was the type of character who would be able to carry out this unusual request.

I was absolutely gutted! I had worked so hard to get back, even threatening along the way to quit, but at last I had done it. Leeds were second to Manchester United in the final year of the old First Division, now the Premiership, and Man U weren't playing until the Sunday. Leeds had the chance to go to the top of the table for the first time in 20 years and I had envisaged being back to keep them there. I went home to give the news to Anne. We never even thought about or discussed Luton as a club. I was just so, so disappointed to be leaving Leeds. I told Anne I would be playing my last game on Saturday against Oldham, but secretly I was hoping to play a blinder and force Howard into rethinking his future plans to include me.

By Thursday the proposed move had hit the papers: 'Kamara poised to leave Leeds for Luton.'

The bad news for me came on Friday morning, Gary McAllister passed his fitness test and I was only required on the bench, in case he didn't make it through the full 90 minutes. I came on for David Batty, thank you Howard, when the score was 0-0. Brian Kilcline scored the decisive own goal that day, but the winner actually came from my cross. I turned to celebrate with the Leeds fans and they started chanting, 'You'll win eff all at Luton!' It was a bittersweet moment and one I've never forgotten. I didn't want to leave Elland Road and the fans knew it.

Within two days I was a Luton player. I was gutted to leave Leeds, but determined to stay in the First Division with David Pleat, whose team were in a relegation scrap at the time. On the morning of my debut I received two telegrams from Leeds. The first was from Howard.

'Good luck from everybody at Elland Road,' it read. 'And remember, "Stay on your feet!" The Gaffer.'

The second was from my former team-mates: 'Good luck today and for the rest of your career. See you soon. Gordon and the boys.'

Those telegrams went some way to softening the blow of being sold. Rejection is tough for anyone to take, especially a footballer in his mid-thirties. Sometimes it can feel like the beginning of the end.

LUTON TOWN (1991–3; 49 appearances, 0 goals)

If I'm being honest, I only did OK at Kenilworth Road. David Pleat wanted me because Luton were struggling to avoid the drop. His team had slipped into the relegation places and they needed all the muscle they could get. At £150,000 I was viewed as a much-needed reinforcement, but my short time there was a mixture of small highs and big lows. Let's go over to Kenilworth Road ...

✪ ✪ ✪ ✪ ✪ ✪ ✪

HIGH! David Pleat had assembled a good, strong team at Luton which included midfielder David Preece and centre-half Trevor Peake, an FA Cup winner with Coventry City in 1987. Despite Luton's lowly position in the division, I loved playing with them. Striker Mick Harford also added plenty of brawn in attack, so on paper we should have been good enough to stay up. Our main problem was that at Pleaty's insistence we always relied on entertaining, skilful football. At times it was too good, and I think we over-played, which cost us vital points.

Wish You Were Here?

One occasion when it worked with style was against a very strong Arsenal team, which featured Tony Adams and Merse, Ian Wright and co. The Gunners were champions at the time, but we bought them down with a bump at Kenilworth Road when Mick Harford scored a cracking header to win the game. George Graham, my old Pompey team-mate who was the Arsenal manager, could hardly speak to me afterwards. He was so angry with his players' performance. He didn't hold back in front of the press either. 'Graham: We Were Rubbish' was one headline the following day. Nobody mentioned how well we'd played. Typical.

✪ ✪ ✪ ✪ ✪ ✪ ✪

LOW! I was chasing fitness from the minute I arrived at Kenilworth Road, but by the time it came to playing Leeds at Elland Road, I was getting fitter. Leeds were flying. They beat us 2-0 after a goal from my 'replacement' – ha! – Eric Cantona, and a penalty from Lee Chapman. I was gutted.

The one thing I'll take from that game was the reception from the home fans. They had sent thousands of letters of support before I left, asking me to stay, which made a nice change from the death threats I had received at one of my former clubs. At five to three when my name was called out over the tannoy, they even started singing my name. Those fans meant the world to me, which was one of the reasons why I refused to lead the Luton team out as captain. I left that honour to my two boys, Ben and Jack, to run out with Luton captain Trevor Peake as mascots. They had been Leeds fans when I was there, but they now had to keep the family loyalty and support whoever Dad played for. At the time they were on to their fourth club – after Swindon, Stoke and Leeds it was now Luton.

'At 34 he is a credit to himself and was probably the best player on the pitch,' said Howard Wilkinson afterwards.

I wasn't so happy. 'I would rather have had a stinker and won,' I said. I really meant it, too.

I played football to win. As Mark Hughes found out to his cost. I clashed with the Manchester United striker in April as we picked up a great draw at Kenilworth Road. 'Sparky', as he was nicknamed, was booked for stamping on me when a confrontation between the pair of us got out of hand. The yellow card meant he was suspended for the crunch game of the season against Liverpool, a game United had to win to finish top. My former club Leeds were playing on the same day and won to nick the title, while Liverpool beat United.

I felt genuinely sorry for Mark afterwards. Our ruck was a bit of old-fashioned argy-bargy, similar to what you see in the IKEA sale on Boxing Day. I was booked too, but the stakes were higher for Mark. Maybe his absence the following weekend helped my old club to win the 1991–92 title, who knows? I was just sorry it cost Mark so much.

⚽ ⚽ ⚽ ⚽ ⚽ ⚽ ⚽

HEARTBREAK! I had the pleasure of playing with David Preece at Luton. David went on to play for England 'B', and he was a cracking player and an even better mate. Sadly, he died in July 2007 from throat cancer. He was a top bloke.

During my time at Kenilworth Road, I was in rented accommodation at Luton while the family stayed in Yorkshire. Because I was away from the family, I had a lot of spare time in the afternoon, so I'd go to the local betting shop. David made for a cracking partner at the bookies. We were very often joined for our afternoon entertainment by another team-mate, Steve Claridge. He managed to make my old mate Stan Bowles look like a bingo-loving nun compared to him, but I got on great with him and still do.

After he retired, Preecey developed a good eye for football talent as a non-league manager and coach. 'Mini', as he was known, even rang me when I was the manager at Bradford to recommend a young kid called Mark Stallard. I only needed to take one look at him in a reserve-team game to know that Mini was spot-on. Stallard went on to score one of the goals at Wembley that took Bradford into the First Division. David was a good lad, a good father and husband, and a true professional. His death was a real blow.

❀ ❀ ❀ ❀ ❀ ❀ ❀

LOW! We needed to win on the final day of the season at Notts County to stay in the First Division. We went one goal up, but lost the game 2–1 and went down. The tension and pressure at half-time was incredible. I don't think I'd experienced anything like that in my career before. David Pleat reckoned there was so much at stake for us that day that we froze in the second half and blew it. The fear of losing was stronger than the incentive to win. Funny how the brain works when you're playing for something so important.

On top of the relegation nightmare that day came the news that Leeds had won and clinched the title in only their second season back in the top flight. That made me think, but I was delighted for everyone involved at Leeds United.

Relegation was a massive disappointment to all of us, but I seemed to take it particularly hard. It didn't help that my family wouldn't move south with me. They wanted to stay in Yorkshire, and I had to respect that, but the time away from them was very hard. Nothing can replace being at home with your wife and kids.

Luton's relegation meant that they had to get rid of some of their best players. Mick Harford, Brian Stein, Alec Chamberlain and Mark Pembridge had been sold. I battled on for the start of a new season in the lower division but wasn't happy. Driving up and down the motorway from Bedfordshire to Yorkshire didn't help. I knew the M1 like the back of my hand – I was beginning to leave my legs in the car. I knew it was really time to go.

For a couple of months the Sheffield United boss had been sniffing around me (like a Bassett hound) and I wanted to sign for him. Harry Bassett had taken United into the Premiership and it seemed like an ideal opportunity to move closer to my family. By the middle of October, I got my wish. I was back on the M1, driving north, on the road to a loan deal with United. Sounds like a bad Chris Rea song, doesn't it?

Wish You Were Here?

SHEFFIELD UNITED (on loan 1992-3; 8 appearances, 0 goals. 1993-4; 16 appearances, 0 goals)

Harry Bassett gave me the chance to play Premier League football, but with his rotation system I was hardly a regular at Bramall Lane, even though after a loan spell at the club I was signed permanently.

It was a great club to play for and had a spirit all of its own, which Harry used to encourage. The club had some good characters. Skipper Brian Gayle, whilst not being in my former captain Gordon Strachan's league as a player, had a similar presence and led us well. Goalscorer Alan Cork was a footballing one-off. His idea of a pre-match warm-up was a fag and a cup of tea, so while the rest of us were searching for silverware Corky spent most of his time searching for an ashtray. That's how much the game has changed. Nowadays some players save their not-so-clean habits and hobbies for their private time, at least as private as the tabloids will allow, but I don't suppose many managers these days would allow a player to smoke during the pre-match chat. Corky may have smoked like a chimney but he was the business on the park. In the whole time I was there I never saw Corky do a single stretch to help him into his training session or match situation – it's difficult with a packet of fags and a lighter tucked down your shorts – but then I never saw him miss a game through injury, which is amazing. In contrast, strike partner Brian Deane would be the perfect pro, stretching every sinew in his muscular body, and he wasn't bad either, holding the distinction of being the first player to score in the newly formed Premier League.

You would have thought that our fighting spirit would have been enough to keep Sheffield United in the division, but sadly we were relegated on the last day of the season. We were playing at Stamford Bridge and at four-twenty that afternoon we were 16th in the table, an incredible eighth from bottom. A single last-minute goal from Chelsea's Mark Stein meant we were relegated. One of Dave Bassett's finds, Dennis Wise, crossed the ball into the box, Glenn Hoddle flicked a header on and Steiny hammered a shot past the hapless goalkeeper, Simon Tracey. Even so, being in the position we were at the start of the match, we still thought we were safe. News then filtered through that Everton had beaten Harry's old club Wimbledon 3–2, despite being 2–0 down at one stage. We were down, a devastating blow for all. Harry couldn't believe it.

When I got home that evening, full of disappointment, my wife asked me, 'What did Harry say after the game? When you tell me, be mindful that the boys are here, as well as my mum and dad, so without the swear-words will do nicely.'

I thought for a few seconds and then said, 'Well, in that case he didn't say anything!'

The bad news for me and my old Leeds team-mate Bobby Davison, with whom I had been reunited, was that our contracts were not to be renewed. But the following day we set off for Heathrow. The club had organised a three-week trip to Australia, playing matches all over to help with funds. According to the rules, every player in the squad had to go. Obviously the mood that morning was sombre. None of us had got over the shock of relegation, and for several of us it was a pretty uncertain time. We must have looked like the most miserable bunch of holiday-makers ever. When we congregated at the airport Harry told us he had heard a rumour that the Everton–Wimbledon game had been fixed. Nobody could take him seriously; surely it was just his immense disappointment playing tricks. Years later, when John Fashanu, Bruce Grobbelaar and Hans Segers were implicated in a match-fixing scandal, the Everton–Wimbledon game was one which was mentioned. All three players were acquitted.

When we arrived Down Under, our luxury hotel was turned into a jail scene from the Aussie soap opera *Prisoner Cell Block H*. Harry kept applying curfews. Because we were leaving the club, Bobby and I kept ignoring them. We went out on the first night in Perth, but when we got back, Bassett was parading up and down the hotel reception, waiting to give us an almighty rollocking, and he imposed fines on us. We went out again for the second night, this time with Brian Gayle. When we returned at three in the morning to find Harry keeping vigil in reception again, he gave us another rollocking. Harry was spending so much time in the hotel reception that I was beginning to think he had forgotten to book himself a room.

But Harry's attitude was, if you can't beat 'em, join 'em. On the third night he did join us and we headed straight to the casino. That set the tone for the rest of the trip, but it still took him a long time to get over relegation. We went to Perth, Sydney, Newcastle, Brisbane, Melbourne and Adelaide, and in those busy three weeks the games, the alcohol and the sun helped to soak up the disappointment. It was followed by a week's holiday for the squad in Bali. I flew back to England ahead of this. I needed to find a new club.

MIDDLESBROUGH (on loan, February–March 1993; 5 games, 0 goals)

During my time at Luton I also went on loan to Boro. It was only five games, but playing for them fulfilled another boyhood dream. It also felt like a nice way to repay the club after the transfer fiasco which took me to Elland Road rather than Ayresome Park. Lennie Lawrence was the manager now, but Steve Gibson was still on the board, so I was delighted to be linking up with him at last. Middlesbrough were close to the bottom of the table, but had some good players – Craig Hignett, Bernie Slaven, Colin Cooper and another former Leeds team-mate of mine, John Hendrie.

My debut was at Ayresome Park, and Nottingham Forest were the visitors we lost to. That day I was proud to spot a few of my friends in the Aldgate End, where I used to stand as a kid when I was lucky enough to be taken along by Alan Ingledew. We also lost away the following week at Manchester United, a very difficult game for Boro. We went down 3–0 but it could have been much more. I had a month to prove myself and put in some good performances, as I was hoping to get a deal which would see me end my career at Boro. I played OK but it didn't work out. Boro were strapped for cash at the time and I found myself back at Luton by the end of the first month.

BRADFORD (1994-5; 23 appearances, 3 goals)

I signed for Bradford while coaching at a nine-week 'soccer' camp in the States in the middle of the 1994 World Cup. It was a cracking opportunity – I taught football to some great kids and I caught some brilliant games of football, though I was denied an opportunity to watch Diego Maradona in Argentinian colours. He was busted for a failed dope test the day before his next game against Bulgaria. I was gutted, but probably not as much as Maradona. He suffered a double whammy, failing a dope test and not meeting Chris Kamara – some say he never fully recovered.

Midway through our adventure, I was contacted by Bradford boss Lennie Lawrence. Having signed me on loan at Boro, he was now offering me the chance to join him at Bradford, with the promise of a place on his coaching staff as well as a playing role. It was an ideal opportunity for me. Coaching was something I was looking to get into after my playing career finished, and I'd already taken a number of badges during my time at Leeds. I knew I didn't have many games left in me at that stage in my career because I was 37 years old. Learning the managerial ropes with Lennie sounded like a dream job.

I had to wait a while before I could officially sign, because the Bradford chairman, Geoffrey Richmond, kept delaying on the contract. He didn't want to pay my wages during the close season, but I eventually signed a playing contract in the pre-season of the 1994–95 campaign, though I was just as excited at the prospect of cutting my teeth with the coaching department. I liked Lennie Lawrence – one of the best man-managers

I ever worked under, by the way – but the team struggled. Bradford were in the Second Division at the time and we never gathered any momentum as we attempted to climb the table. Rather unexpectedly, we had a difficult fight against relegation.

In April, Lennie reshaped his backroom staff, appointing me as his assistant manager. I was excited. After running more than a few training sessions at my previous club Sheffield United for Harry Bassett, I was ready to take on a full-time coaching role. It was also a fantastic experience to work alongside one of the most experienced managers in the game. We worked up a good-cop, bad-cop partnership. I was the wind-up merchant on the touchline and he was the thinker. It worked pretty well. Lennie was a man with a terrific knowledge of the game. He also remained very calm on match days, and I had to envy him for that. His relaxed demeanour and laid-back body language left me to get on with motivating the players. Sometimes I looked like a lunatic on the touchline.

The pair of us had interests away from football, too. We shared a love for horse-racing, but weirdly we never really talked about it. I first caught wind of his love for the nags when I bumped into him at a meeting at York racecourse one afternoon. He was wandering around the Knavesmire racecourse on his own. From then on, if there was a good meeting in Yorkshire, I'd see him there. He'd briefly say hello before going off to do his own thing. Lennie just seemed to love soaking up the atmosphere.

Some days in the office were tough for him. He didn't exactly see eye to eye with Geoffrey Richmond. In fact, I don't think Lennie had experienced a chairman like him in his long and distinguished career, which was saying something. The long and the short of it was that Geoffrey wanted to know every single thing that was going on at the club. You were never allowed to run the team without his interference. Because of that, the manager was never out of his office. Each meeting would last for a minimum of two hours unless there was a game to go to. Lennie couldn't stand it and I could see it was bringing him down. Neither of us could have envisaged what Geoffrey Richmond had in store after a run of two wins in 13 games.

By December 1995 Lennie had been sacked, but in reality I think he was relieved to get out of Bradford and away from Richmond. He was a good manager and he knew he could find another club without such an overbearing presence in the boardroom. It was sad to see him go.

I'd also played my last game of professional football. It was my choice. Lennie had asked me to play on numerous occasions, but I told him I wanted to concentrate on the coaching side of things. I had loved playing football so much that now I look back and wonder how I gave it up so easily. At the time it seemed the natural thing to do. I had abused my body to some extent, playing through injuries, etc, and was now feeling all the aches and pains on a daily basis, not helped by the lack of rest as I travelled the country watching match after match in my new role as assistant manager.

Even though I'd kicked my last ball in anger, football hadn't really ended for me. If anything, my life in the game had only just started.

Mr Unbelievable

Within minutes of letting Lennie go, Geoffrey Richmond rang me and appointed me as the new manager of Bradford City. His instructions were clear: I had five months to turn the club around and save the team from relegation. I was shocked, but excited. It was a role I hadn't dared dream of when I began coaching the Bradford players. I knew I could handle the pressure and the challenges of running a big club on a day-to-day basis. I also reckoned I could handle Geoffrey.

I called Lennie and told him the news. I wasn't sure what to expect, but typically he was great about it. He wished me all the best – and he didn't just mean with fortunes of the team. Geoffrey's hands-on approach at Valley Parade meant that my managerial seat was hotter than most.

CHAPTER TWENTY-ONE
LIFE IN THE DUGOUT

Being successful as a manager overshadows everything you do as a player. Life as a footballer is great, but to be in charge of a football team when you're winning games is something else. To have the whole city behind you is a fantastic feeling – there's nothing like it. Sure, there's plenty of pressure. When things go wrong the mood in the city can weigh down on you like a ton of bricks. But when things are going well, you can feel the fans pushing you forward. It was like that from day one at Bradford.

Looking back, moving into management immediately was a great move, because it stopped me from hankering after my playing days. To this day I will be eternally grateful to Geoffrey Richmond for appointing me as Bradford City manager. It meant I didn't experience the depression that some players suffer when they retire from the game. I was too busy working out how I was going to keep the chairman happy and build a successful football team.

I signed as manager with Bradford City and made big promises straightaway. Geoffrey Richmond asked me for a realistic target for the remainder of the 1995–96 season. I told him we'd avoid dropping into the Third Division, no problem. Then, like some sort of big shot, I boasted to the media that we'd get promoted into the First. Richmond lapped it up while everyone else was laughing at me. A lot of critics expected us to fall flat, but they stopped smirking when Bradford went on a hot streak and lost only three games in the last 13 fixtures to sneak into the play-offs on the final day of the season.

It felt like retribution in a way. When I first started my managerial shift, one or two managers in the division had cracked jokes at my expense. My bold predictions hadn't helped; and there were gags in the media over a pre-match routine I'd introduced to Valley Parade. I'd seen it used abroad, where many coaching teams got their boys working in small-sided games and 'keep-ball' sessions 30 minutes before kick-off. It was tightly organised and the manager oversaw every drill. I figured if it was good enough for the likes of Ajax, then it was good enough for me. But being a manager in the cynical Second Division, I took some stick.

I didn't care. At that time English clubs often overlooked the importance of tempo and touch in their build-up to 90 minutes of football. You'd watch players spray the ball around the centre circle or fire a few pot shots at the keeper during their pre-match warm-up. One wise guy would always attempt to hit the crossbar from the halfway line. After a ten-minute kickaround, everyone would head back to the dressing-rooms to change. Not on my watch. We were playing a six-a-side competitive game and working on sprints; there were shuttle runs and stretches. The fans were pointing fingers and scratching their heads, but I reckon a lot of the critics would have to admit that we were ahead of our time. These preparations quickly paid dividends in the league. In games, Bradford players seemed to have an extra yard on opposing teams from the kick-off.

We slowly but surely worked our way up the table, but our form wasn't totally unexpected. On paper, I had a good squad to pick from. Lenny Lawrence had bought well on limited funds at Bradford. Money was tight - I felt like I was forever asking for a new set of portable goalposts - but the technical quality was there for everyone to see. The players were just short on confidence. I had to build them up mentally rather than physically. I had some really good characters. Eddie Youds was my skipper; I bought Mark Stallard from Derby, while Lee Duxbury, Ian Ormondroyd, Des Hamilton and Andy Kiwomya were all local lads with the club in their veins.

Typically, Bradford's fight for a place in the play-offs went down to the wire. Our final league game was against Hull at Boothferry Park. Three teams were in the running for sixth spot in the table - us, Chesterfield and Stockport. As Bradford was placed higher than our chasing rivals we knew a win was enough to grab a shot at promotion and we would progress regardless of how the others had done. Interest was at fever pitch in the city, and Hull made the unbelievable decision to move the home supporters from their usual end of the ground. Just imagine trying that one on in Liverpool, telling the Kop to clear off up the other end. It would be like writing a suicide note without having to jump off the cliff. They wanted to accommodate the large number of travelling Bradford fans who had paid top dollar for tickets. It was a nice touch, but this had understandably annoyed the home crowd. We really didn't appreciate just how miffed they were until the team bus arrived at the ground under police escort. A mini riot had broken out and the kick-off was postponed by 15 minutes while they scraped up the broken limbs off the road and put the windows back in the away supporters' coaches. This was actually a result for us. I knew a delay would work in our favour because at 4.45 our promotion rivals would have finished playing and we'd still have a quarter of an hour to fashion the right result.

As it was, we were drawing 2–2 with Hull after 75 minutes, but scores elsewhere meant we needed a late goal to snatch the final play-off spot. We pushed on for a winner and eventually striker Carl Shutt got us there, though I can't say my nerves weren't jangling.

My boast that we'd avoid the drop and get into the First Division was still alive but it was a mixed mood on the pitch afterwards. The result didn't affect Hull in any way, as they were already down, but the coaching staff were hardly pleased for us. Tigers boss Terry Dolan was a former Bradford manager, and his assistant, Jeff Lee, had also worked at Valley Parade. Afterwards, both of them seemed gutted that we'd grabbed a shot at promotion. It was probably the quickest can of lager I ever drank in a manager's office after a game.

To get to Wembley we now had to beat Sam Allardyce's Blackpool in a two-leg semi-final. I was confident we would get through, but we got off to the worst possible start, losing 2–0 at home. It meant we had to win the second leg by three goals.

Life in the Dugout

After the home game on the Sunday I was suicidal. I just couldn't understand how and why it had gone so wrong. Mam and Dad were at the game, but afterwards I couldn't talk to them. I was inconsolable, and I knew I had made mistakes. One was to play Ian Ormondroyd, who had started up front with Carl Shutt.

Big Sam selected Andy Morrison to play just in front of the back four and cut out any service to Ormondroyd, the player we all called Sticks. I knew it was my fault and I knew early on in the game that I had got things wrong. I even tried to change things, but that made no difference. I had been out-thought, and Blackpool had our measure. Their keeper Eric Nixon made one or two excellent saves but we didn't play very well and, as the game went on, I knew we were never going to win.

Anne played her part that night. I was sitting in my own world in my office at Valley Parade after the game, even ignoring my parents as I went through the misery of the previous 90 minutes over and over again in my head. And every time I went through it, the gut-wrenching thought would come back to me that it was all my fault. Why had I chosen that team? At the time it was difficult to look forward to the second leg. I had to tell Mam and Dad to go back home because I was clearly no company, so my pal Chucky drove them back to Middlesbrough. As I said a fairly sullen farewell to my folks, Anne had a little word with my chief scout Andy Smith and suggested he took me out for a few drinks.

As it had been a Sunday afternoon kick-off, we had plenty of time and we headed to O'Donohue's, an Irish pub in Wakefield town centre, and sat in a quiet corner. Boy, did we sink a few beers, but all we could talk about was football. I dissected and analysed the entire game, but Andy and John Allott, an old pal, helpfully steered me away from the previous 90 minutes and we started to plot and plan for the next 90. Suddenly at about 9 p.m. it came to me. I told the other two: 'I know how we can beat them. I know exactly how we can win the next game.' Andy got another round in.

I was angry with myself deep down, because I should have thought more about the home game tactically. I had over-looked the fact that Big Sam might play Morrisson in front of his back four. I decided the only way to beat Blackpool and get the three goals we needed to go to Wembley was to ensure that the players only crossed the ball from the last third of the pitch. They would not be allowed to put crosses into the Blackpool area from our own half, and then only after crossing an imaginary line 20 yards away from the halfway line. We got the players into the ground first thing the next morning and immediately told them the idea. Next we went to work on it in training.

The first player I spoke to was Ian Ormondroyd, to explain why he was going to be left out of the starting line-up for the second leg. That was my main team change. 'This is nothing against you,' I told him. 'It's not your fault. It never has been your strength to win the ball in the air with your back to the opposition's goal, but because you are there and because your team-mates see you up there, they take the easy option and ping the ball forward at the first opportunity.'

Not enough players played the ball to Sticks's feet or managed to put it in the final third of the pitch where he loved it because, despite his size, he was better running on to headers and flick-ons rather than winning balls like that for others. I knew that by taking him out of the equation I was enhancing the prospects of keeping to the edict of crosses nearer Blackpool's goal. I knew Sticks would be fine with the reasoning and would want what was best for the team and, although he was naturally disappointed, he stood by my decision. It was typical of him, and I didn't really expect any other reaction, but it was important to me and the team.

We worked on it for an hour on the Monday morning and again the following morning. They responded brilliantly to the instructions and two of the three goals came that way. I thought we would need extra-time to get the third goal, I didn't expect to do it in the 90 minutes, but that night everything came to plan.

On the night I was helped by the Blackpool match programme of all things. I picked one up for a quick browse shortly after we'd arrived as the lads were checking out the pitch and having a stroll in front of the empty stands. One page in particular stood out, and I burst out laughing at the insensitivity of it all. I know it wasn't Sam Allardyce's fault. Sadly it was the last time he picked a Blackpool team because he was sacked later that week, and of course he had no idea that some genius in the club's programme-editing department had decided to publish an advert for the benefit of supporters which offered coach trips to Wembley. There was a full price list and a telephone number at the club to ring. I went out and bought 10 programmes and pinned them all over our dressing-room wall. Wherever any of my players looked, I put them – I wanted them to see the booking form. My team talk was virtually done for me.

'This lot think they've reached Wembley already,' I said.

I was feeling good about our chances. The bookies made us 33-1 to go up before the second game, but everything felt right to me. The players really looked in determined mood and we'd had a good stay at our hotel in Blackpool in the afternoon. The team was picked and we had a meeting to go through every single player's job and responsibility. The players had a sleep on the Tuesday afternoon of the match, and when they had their pre-match meal, and later when they got on the coach to head to the stadium at Bloomfield Road, they were in good humour. Every manager can tell when there is a 'buzz' about his team, and there were plenty of laughs and shouts as we made the short journey to the ground through the town centre, along the seafront and past the famous tower.

The programme content was the ideal material for my final team talk. You often hear it said that managers, and players, get results by pinning up newspaper or magazine articles in the dressing-room before a game, and this was one of those occasions. I made sure every single player read it. I really drove that message home to them and kept reminding them of the sheer bloody cheek of it all. It did the trick. They were like wild animals waiting to be unleashed on the Blackpool public. The last thing I said before they went out was, 'Don't forget, their coaches are booked.' In contrast, I don't think a bus company in Bradford had taken a phone call after the abysmal first leg, because even in Yorkshire no one really believed we would do it. No one except me and the players.

Life in the Dugout

The first call I made the following morning was to Big Sam. There had been protests from Blackpool fans in the car park as we celebrated our win, and I had to feel for Sam. He didn't deserve that. Everything just fell kindly for us that night and Blackpool really couldn't handle us. What happened on the pitch was out of our control, but of course fans don't always see it that way. Sam took the call and he was first class. He said he made his team sit in silence for 15 minutes in the dressing-room and made them listen to us celebrating the prospect of Wembley. The walls were paper thin and they could hear every word. I can't begin to imagine how agonising that must have been for Sam and his players.

✪ ✪ ✪ ✪ ✪ ✪ ✪ ✪

The scene on the pitch at Blackpool was like something out of the film *Mike Bassett: England Manager* starring Ricky Tomlinson. In the excellent comedy Ricky, who plays the unlikely England manager Bassett, is photographed dancing on the bar of a hotel in Brazil in just his underpants and vest. The poor people of Blackpool were only just spared the sight of my totally naked body – in the middle of their pitch invasion the Bradford fans de-bagged me, leaving me in my underpants.

Wembley was fantastic for everyone connected with Bradford, and every supporter worth his salt got there. Play-off fever seemed to seep into the city; I only had to pop out to get a pint of milk for someone to sing, 'There's only one Chris Kamara!'

It wasn't all plain sailing, though. In the run-up to the final I had one or two personnel problems to sort out. One was with full-back Richard Liburd, who would have been in the final 16 players for Wembley but had decided he didn't want the honour, even though we'd given him a club suit for the day. It was a shame, but that was his decision. I've no idea if he regretted it afterwards. Liburd's issue with me had started earlier in the season. He lived in Nottingham and was often late for training and first-team games. Gary Megson, the former West Brom and Bolton manager, was my first assistant at Bradford, and he often tells the story of how Liburd and I fell out. It happened before a league game. Liburd was typically late and I'd made him sub and handed in my team-sheet to the officials, even though he hadn't arrived at the ground. When he finally showed up it was 2.40 and the rest of the team were on the pitch warming up. As a manager, I didn't actually mind players being late – it happens from time to time – but Liburd's attitude really grated. He ambled into the dressing-room like he couldn't have cared less.

'Where have you been?' I said.

He shrugged. 'I was stuck in traffic.'

There was a silence.

'Is that it?' I asked.

Liburd stood there. He stared at the floor. When he finally spoke, it wasn't the reaction I'd been expecting. 'Yeah,' he shrugged.

I lost it. 'Do us a favour, will you?' I shouted. 'Bugger off!'

I motioned with my thumb to the dressing-room door. I couldn't believe it. All he had to do was apologise, or maybe ask if he was on the bench – anything to appear interested. But no, his attitude left so much to be desired. He turned around and walked out of the dressing-room like a spoilt teenager. I leapt across the room and picked up a practice ball. I saw that he was halfway down the corridor with his back turned to me as he sloped away. I hit the ball on the half volley and it pinged off my foot and curled majestically through the doorway. Within an instant it had smacked him on the back of the head with a satisfying thudding sound, rocking him forward on his toes and into a stumble. I turned back to the dressing-room, where Gary Megson was standing. 'That'll be the art of football management then,' he said, laughing.

Do you know what? I would be chuffed to bits if it was me who had inspired Sir Alex Ferguson when he famously decided to take Becks to task with a flying boot. Perhaps just once I had inspired the great man with my tactics.

⚽⚽⚽⚽⚽⚽⚽

The team stayed at the Copthorne Hotel in Slough for three days before the Wembley play-off final and every last detail had been planned. Even so, it was quite relaxed and I allowed the boys a couple of beers on our first night after we'd been to the cinema.

'Look we want to win this game,' I said on the second night. 'But if any of you feel that you want to have a drink, or you want to do something different, then do it. You have my permission.'

Not one of them did. I guess they were aware of the rewards of First Division football. They were certainly determined to make the most of their day at Wembley, and so was I.

Mr Unbelievable

On the day of the game Anne and the boys called in to pick up their buttonhole flowers in club colours which we had had delivered ready for wearing to the game. Ben, who was 11, and Jack, then 9, were the Bradford mascots that day, and we'd had kits specially made for them with their names on the back. Walking on to the hallowed turf holding their hands was unquestionably the proudest moment of my career.

They arrived in a seven-seater Ford Discovery with Linda Smith, wife of my chief scout Andy. Ben and Jack were in the back with their two sons David and James. All the boys had been singing 'Wembley, Wembley' as they'd headed to the team hotel to meet us. As the car pulled up, I came out of the hotel, and heard the M-People song 'Search for the Hero' on the radio. It had always been an inspirational signature tune for me, and to this day Linda is convinced it was an omen. It was great to see them, and hearing that song increased my belief that our victory was meant to be.

It was important to me that we arrived at Wembley after Notts County, and as I embraced Anne and the boys, the police escort arrived. It was time to put my plan into action. I knew the team arriving first had to go on to the pitch first, and I didn't want it to be us. I wanted us to have an edge on our opponents, and I knew one way to ensure that was to make sure Notts County's bus arrived before us. The club estimated we were taking at least 30,000 supporters while Notts County were expecting 12,000, so I knew that even at that stage of the afternoon, our fans would outnumber theirs, and I wanted the County players to hear the cheers from our crowd and the buzz among them when we emerged from the tunnel for the first time in our smart club suits. I wanted them to know we had arrived. I knew if it had been the other way round, instead of hearing the resounding cheers, they would just have heard boos echoing round the stadium and that might inspire them rather than terrify them. The Football League had given the police our allotted arrival time, but I had a quiet word with the main escort cop and pleaded with him to make an excuse to delay our departure so we would arrive second at the stadium.

'Leave it to me,' he said.

At the same time, Anne asked if he could give her directions for the quickest route to Wembley. His advice was simple.

'Put the flags in the car, fasten your seatbelts, stick close to the back of the bus and hang on.'

Like Thelma and Louise, Anne and Linda did just that, keeping the players at the back of the coach amused as they tried desperately to hang on to its tail-lights through north London. 'They're still with us, gaffer,' was the cry from the back of the bus as the police escort flew across the lanes and through red lights without stopping.

We were kitted out in club suits. It was another little touch I'd asked Geoffrey Richmond to fund, and I made sure that every single player in the squad, even those without a chance of playing, and every member of the staff, wore the dark-blue outfit, complete with a striped tie in our traditional claret and amber, with the distinctive badge on the left breast pocket and flowers in club colours on the lapel. We looked the business, and the added bonus for me was that all the Notts County players were in their own individual suits rather than all in the same colours, with just a token black and white carnation arrangement on the lapel. By comparison with us I knew they looked and felt like Raggy Arse Rovers. That kind of planning was instilled in me at Leeds, because as a footballer I loved the way the club had gone that extra yard to really look after us.

The game began, and we were never in any danger of losing. On the day, we were just too strong for Notts County. Midfielder Des Hamilton scored early on and their defenders couldn't handle us. We dominated the midfield. It was one of those rare games when we had very few problems with the opposition. I was confident enough to bring on Ian Ormandroyd. He'd been dropped to the bench at Blackpool and I wanted him to enjoy Wembley. With 20 minutes to go, I brought off Andy Kiwomya, and replaced him with Ian. A minute later, he had flicked on a cross with his head and Mark Stallard made it 2-0 and game over. It was one of the proudest moments of my career.

When the final whistle went, I was in pieces. The players stayed on the pitch and milked every moment with the Bradford fans. We seemed to be out there for hours. After the champagne had been drained in the dressing-room, I went into the bar and saw Dad and Mam. Dad was chuffed to bits. Apparently, tears had rolled down his cheeks. He just stood there and hugged our mam.

It was party time. The club quickly arranged to call in at a hotel near Leicester on the way back to Yorkshire for a cele-bration, but as soon as we arrived we were mobbed by City fans who had somehow got wind of our destination, so after a couple of drinks everyone headed back to Bradford. I invited family and a few friends to the house to enjoy some more champagne.

On the way home, we heard that the city had organised a civic reception for us the following day, but the lads were drinking out of the trophy and it had taken a bit of a battering. It certainly needed a good polish before an open-top bus journey through Bradford. For insurance reasons (honestly, dear people from the Football League) I kept it with me for safekeeping. But when I was dropped off at junction 41 of the M1 at the Wakefield turn-off for home, I realised my error. There I was, standing by the busiest motorway in the country, waiting for Anne to pick me up for the final leg home, holding Bradford's first major honour in years.

Phil Thompson tells a story of how he ended up taking the European Cup to his local pub one evening. Liverpool had beaten Real Madrid in the 1981 final and Thommo had been holding the trophy as the team travelled home. When the bus arrived in Liverpool, Thommo put the trophy into his bag and escorted it to The Falcon in Kirby. This was in no way as glamorous. I looked like a prize wally standing on the grass verge of a motorway junction, my suit soaked with champagne and a play-off trophy under my arm.

There was a party that night, and a memorable afternoon on the open-top bus the next day. Geoffrey Richmond even organised – and funded – a holiday for all the players and staff in Magaluf. He was different class after Wembley. I could have asked for anything and he would have paid for it. The honeymoon period didn't last for long, though, as I would soon discover to my cost.

Mr Unbelievable

I was at a dinner recently at Blackpool and somebody came up to me and told me that he had heard that the play-off semi-final between Bradford and Blackpool was fixed. I couldn't believe it. He reckoned the fans there had been convinced of it for years. Apparently, the conspiracy theory was mentioned every day by at least someone in the town.

To recap on the background of the game, we were 2–0 down from the first leg. First, rumours started flying around that one of the Blackpool players had placed a 33–1 bet that Bradford would win the play-offs, even though we were going into the second leg with a 2–0 deficit. Thinking about it, this was a pretty shrewd move (if it was true). Bradford and Blackpool were the form sides in the semis. Chances were, whichever team made it through our game would go on to secure promotion.

The fans also got it into their heads that because Blackpool weren't financially prepared to make a decent fist of it in the old First Division, they decided to throw the game and take their chances the following year. But of course it was all a load of old nonsense. There was no way on earth that the game was thrown.

I had absolutely no idea that there had even been a conspiracy theory flying around until I went to that dinner, which coincidentally was being held at Blackpool Football Club. When I mentioned Bradford City in a speech after the meal, the whole room started booing and shouting 'Fix!' It blew me away.

It just goes to show that football fans never forget. Every Saturday I stand there doing my piece to camera, and I now realise there's a few supporters dotted here and there who are shouting abuse at their screens. Fair enough, I do the same when the wrong horse comes in when I watch the racing. I forgive the horse that lets me down, and in the same way I hope all those fans accept that we've all moved on. But there's not much chance of me holidaying in Blackpool, or West Ham for that matter. Neither will I be spending the last week of July and the first week of August in Oxford or Port Vale either. I reckon I'd be safer in Baghdad than wearing a kiss-me-quick hat in any of those four places.

CHAPTER TWENTY-TWO
UNBELIEVABLE, GEOFFREY!

In TV they say never work with children or animals. On *Soccer Saturday*, the panel has a similar code, though we usually say to football people never work with club mascots or chairmen. This isn't a sweeping generalisation, more a warning from history. Club mascots – Gunnersaurus, Chirpy the Cockerel, all of them – have always been a royal pain in the bum to live broadcasters. They just don't see it, do they? It's OK walking around like that to be cheered at your own ground by your own fans, but do they really think anyone watching at home finds the weird cross-dressers the slightest bit funny when they get in the way of us lot trying to do our jobs?

Jeff Stelling has been harangued by enough chairmen over the years for his satirical 'jokes', while Phil Thompson has recently seen his beloved Liverpool demoralised by crippling debts brought on at boardroom level. I have a more hands-on experience with football dictatorship: I once worked with Geoffrey Richmond at Bradford City.

242

Unbelievable, Geoffrey!

It's fair to say that the best chairmen are the ones you've never heard of, mainly because they hide away from the limelight. Not all of them like to bring in goalscoring buddies from the Ukraine or shadowy directors of football to keep an eye on managerial affairs. Some chairmen like to leave the first-team gaffer to get on with the job of managing the players. Sadly, Geoffrey wasn't one of them.

I was warned that he could be difficult when I took over the job of manager; I'd seen Lennie Lawrence suffer those daily two-hour meetings during his time in charge. Thankfully, Geoffrey was never going to have a say when it came to picking the team – I wouldn't have stood for it – but he did want to voice his opinions when it came to buying and selling players, which caused some friction.

The club wasn't the richest in the world and we had to be prudent with cash. Selling players was important for the survival of Bradford City. I soon learnt that buying on the cheap and selling big was an art that had to be mastered pretty quickly if I was to be successful at Valley Parade. At times, though, it could be tough work keeping the players happy if the money was in short supply. Geoffrey could be frugal when it came to providing the basics, such as new training bibs, balls and goalposts for training – the day-to-day stuff that was necessary in our preparation for match days.

Then, during the run-up to the play-off final at Wembley, the team felt that the promotion bonuses on offer were quite low. They wanted more appearance money. I agreed they should talk to the chairman, my only stipulation being that the players had to do the negotiating, not me. I needed to appear impartial, even if I understood their concerns and demands. They deserved the money for sure. I also knew that giving them what they wanted would keep their minds on the game against Notts County.

Three players – Eddie Youds, Paul Jewell and Wayne Jacobs – acted as spokesmen for the whole squad. They had drawn up a list of financial demands to be put forward to Geoffrey at a meeting in the club restaurant at Valley Parade. The chairman and I sat on the top table, with the first-team players gathered around. Their demands made for uncomfortable listening.

After five months in charge, I'd learnt how to read Geoffrey and understand his moods. This was often easy, because he couldn't hide his emotions. If he was happy, the eyes would twinkle and he'd have a beaming smile plastered across his face. If he was angry, he'd be straining at the leash. As the three lads went through their notes, I watched him slowly change colour, from pale to red, from red to scarlet. They wanted appearance money for just turning up at Wembley. They had noticed that the club shop was doing a roaring trade on the back of 30,000 Bradford fans wanting and buying anything in the club colours, and they figured they should get a cut of that. By the time they got to the issue of money for the promotion bonus, he was ready to blow.

'Forget it, I'll play a youth team at Wembley,' he said, rising from his chair.

Geoffrey was out, but he wasn't down. As he left the room, he raised two fingers to the entire squad, triumphantly taking his right hand from behind his back and brandishing it to all of them. I was trying to hold a poker face, but it was hilarious. The team had never seen him in this mood before. Panic broke out. The moment Geoffrey stormed out, the senior players started to talk about the possibility of missing out on Wembley. I knew I had to act quickly to calm them down.

I reassured them that this was just his way of doing business, and it was true. Geoffrey succeeded in getting deals done as a businessman because he would make ridiculous demands or offers in meetings. When he was turned down he would storm off, but he was never ashamed to return and compromise minutes, hours or even days later. He had probably forgotten that he had told me about this negotiating technique, or just hoped I wouldn't tell the lads. Losing face didn't seem to bother him. It often worked for him too. This time, Geoffrey was outside in the corridor, still seething. He insisted the players had been out of order. I turned him around.

'They're decent fellas who want to play at Wembley,' I said. 'They want to be prepared and win promotion. Just go three-quarters of the way with them and we'll get a result.'

He nodded.

The lads fell silent when Geoffrey returned to his chair. He gave them his typically forthright views on their demands, but he also agreed to compromise. The players got two of their three demands, but he drew the line at profits from the merchandise. He also promised to do everything in his power to make sure they were properly looked after in the run-up to Wembley, and he didn't disappoint. It was one of Geoffrey's strengths: he could see the benefits of pampering the players in this way. It would get the best out of them at Wembley.

Getting the cash for bibs, balls or goalposts at any other time of the season seemed impossible. This time, he was happy to splash out because he knew he would be paid back on the road to Wembley and beyond. Literally. On the morning of the play-off final, the M1 was lined with Bradford City merchandise stalls. The motorway service stations on the way to Wembley were doing a roaring trade. Geoffrey owned most of the club merchandise, in one way or another, so he must have made a bob to two that day.

We were always hamstrung by cash problems at Bradford. I found myself working under strict financial restrictions from the moment I took over from Lennie Lawrence as manager in 1995–96. In my first season, the chairman ploughed cash to the tune of £1.5 million into the Midland Road stand rather than the squad. I had to push for promotion with next to no money. At first, this wasn't a problem, but when it looked like we might not make the play-offs (a needless panic as it turned out), I was under some serious pressure to bring extra cash into the club. On transfer deadline day in March, I sold goalkeeper Gavin Ward to Bolton Wanderers for £300,000 – which left me with a pretty big headache. I didn't have a goalkeeper.

That's not strictly true. I had one goalkeeper, a Norwegian lad called Glenn Hansen, but he was struggling with a hernia problem and even when he was fully fit he wasn't the best. I'm not entirely sure how the then Coventry City manager, Ron Atkinson, knew that I needed a goalkeeper, but out of the blue he called to offer me Jonathan Gould (son of former Wimbledon and Wales manager, Bobby) on loan.

Big Ron couldn't have called at a better time. It was 4.40 p.m. on transfer deadline day, which in those days took place in March. The window shut at five o'clock. I spoke quickly to Jonathan on the phone.

Unbelievable, Geoffrey!

'Gouldy, do you fancy Bradford?' I asked.

He was in. 'I just want to play first-team football,' he said.

With five minutes to spare, we faxed the relevant papers over to Highfield Road, the old Coventry stadium, and signed a handy goalkeeper by the skin of our teeth. It was a good deal: he was absolutely brilliant for us in the closing weeks of the season and helped our push to the play-offs. He stayed for the following year, but by his own admission Jonathan had a nightmare once we'd been promoted into the First Division. He was sent off twice for rushing out of his box unnecessarily to bring down oncoming strikers. He also made a series of costly errors. I knew he was a competent keeper, but I just didn't trust him any more. Besides, in 1996 I signed the Aussie goalie Mark Schwarzer (who went on to play for Boro and Fulham), and he turned out to be one of the best keepers in the Premiership. Agent Barry Silkman got me big Mark from Kaiserslauten in Germany for £150,000. We sold him three months later for £1.25 million.

When I was interviewed by the *Sun* a few years back, I mentioned a conversation I once had with Ron Atkinson about Jonathan Gould. Ron had called me before the end of the 1995–96 promotion season to ask me for a fee, because Jonathan was doing quite well and we'd made the play-offs. I had the upper hand; when he signed, Jonathan mentioned that his contract was up at the end of the season and he'd be leaving Coventry anyway. I flippantly told Ron I wouldn't be buying Jonathan because he'd caught a virus.

'He's got line-itis,' I said. 'He just won't come off his line.'

'Blimey,' Ron said. 'You must have improved him, then, because he couldn't catch naff all when he was here.'

Mr Unbelievable

It was Big Ron at his best, and I couldn't see the harm in using it in print in the *Sun*. By all accounts, Jonathan didn't mind it either, but his dad, Bobby – a fellow member of the League Managers' Association – took offence and complained to the chief executive, John Barnwell. John rather embarrassingly rang to say he didn't know what action Bobby wanted him to take, but to save any future aggravation, I shouldn't do it again. I felt like a naughty schoolboy being ticked off. It all seemed a bit silly really.

At the end of the 1996–97 season, I told Jonathan he could leave on a free transfer. By this time, Mark Schwarzer had been signed by Boro in February and his replacement, Gary Walsh from Boro, had fitted in nicely. I couldn't see Jonathan getting another game. I certainly wasn't going to stand in his way if another team came in for him. He didn't manage to get one immediately, but a month into the new season he asked if the free-transfer offer still stood. I told him it did.

'Where are you going?' I asked.

'Celtic,' he said.

I couldn't believe it. 'Crikey, Jonathan, you don't want to go down to Farsley Celtic, you're too good for that level.'

He thought I was taking the mickey. 'No, the other Celtic,' he said. 'In Glasgow.' He was not amused. He stormed off, kicking out at the boot-room door as he left. I really couldn't believe it – he was good, but not that good. Still, getting rid of players was never really a problem, especially if the price was right. This time, Geoffrey was annoyed because I'd allowed Jonathan to leave on a free transfer to a wealthy club at the time, Glasgow Celtic. Gouldy went up to Scotland and did brilliantly. He was a really good lad and I was made up for him.

Unbelievable, Geoffrey!

Buying new players was a completely different ball game, however. After the play-off final, Geoffrey and I drew up the dreaded five-year plan – it's dreaded because so few managers make it to the third year, let alone the fifth. Geoffrey was particularly excited because the Bosman ruling had just come into effect. This allowed out-of-contract players to sign for anyone they liked, without a transfer fee passing between clubs. He became convinced that the market would become flooded with quality – and free – players. Geoffrey also reckoned that Bradford would never have to spend another penny on transfers.

This never transpired, but the wheeling and dealing with Geoffrey in the transfer market did my head in. I suffered months and months of journeys to Scandinavia, Holland, Portugal, anywhere with a football league. We signed several players to strengthen the squad. Some worked, some were bloody awful. What we didn't fully realise at first was that the big clubs had taken all the best footballers. We'd been left with some average players and a lot of donkeys. We ended up with a few OK signings and a few bargain-basement mules.

We also picked up a Brazilian striker called Edhino. Apart from Mark Schwarzer and, wait for it, Chris Waddle, he was probably the best free transfer I ever signed. The fans loved him. They probably would have loved Gordon Watson too. Gordon, the club's record signing at £550,000 (although in truth we did not pay anywhere near that price), scored on his debut against Port Vale, but his second game, on 1 February 1997 against Huddersfield, was his last game for two years, as he was stretchered off after only four minutes. 'Flash', as he was unsurprisingly nicknamed, had caught Huddersfield's

Kevin Gray with his elbow as he went up for a header. Gray was furious, and his retaliatory tackle fractured Gordon's leg in two places. Pundit Jimmy Hill described it as the worst tackle he had seen in 50 years. It was horrendous, but referee Eddie Lomas just gave Gray a booking, so in fact everyone in the game saw red except Kevin Gray, who only saw yellow. Gordon was in agony. He needed emergency surgery that day. Surgeons later inserted a six-inch plate and seven screws into his leg over five operations. He didn't play again for Bradford until the 1997–98 season, when he made a few appearances before his contract ended. He eventually moved to Bournemouth. It was a miracle he could actually walk.

It wasn't finished, though. Geoffrey Richmond was determined that the club sued for damages, and the case went to a football tribunal at The Vermont, a hotel in Newcastle. I was called in as a witness. I didn't go in with a preconceived idea to help any party, I just recalled the incident as I saw it. I said I didn't believe Kevin Gray, or any footballer for that matter, would want to break the leg of a fellow pro. I didn't believe a player like that existed. Thankfully I still don't.

Flash won his case and I was delighted for him. He later made £900,000 in damages. Afterwards I decided to avoid the television and radio crews as I left the building. I felt it was the right thing to do. On reflection, the decision to attempt a secret exit from the makeshift court on Newcastle's Quayside was not one of my better moves. I came out with my face hidden by my coat and caused even more interest for the cameramen. I resembled the accused in a murder trial rather than a witness in a football tribunal.

Unbelievable, Geoffrey!

The 1996–97 season was a turbulent one, but we stayed up by the skin of our teeth after beating QPR, managed by Bruce Rioch, with two goals from Nigel Pepper, on the final day of the season. Survival was fair reward for some hard work in the transfer market. Geoffrey had opened his wallet and helped me to grab some bargains: I got centre-back Darren Moore and Robbie Blake for a pittance, and Jamie Lawrence came from Leicester for £50,000. He was a passionate player with a colourful past. Jamie had spent two years in Parkhurst jail for his part in an armed robbery. To be fair to Geoffrey, he backed my judgement and we gave the lad a second chance. The last I heard of Jamie, he was helping rehabilitated kids with troubled pasts to further their football careers.

Winger Peter Beagrie was a lively addition to the club. I signed Beags for just £50,000 from Manchester City. The biggest bargain of the lot, though, was Chris Waddle. What a player he had been throughout his career for Newcastle, Spurs, Olympique Marseille, Sheffield Wednesday and England. He was still a great footballer when I signed him, but unbelievably he was playing for Falkirk in Scotland. I asked my chief scout, Andy Smith, to head off north to watch him. When he returned I asked how he had done.

'Decent, Kammy,' he said. 'He can still play.' It wasn't the most incisive of scouting reports.

'Nothing gets past you, pal,' I laughed. 'I know he can still play. Everyone knows he can still play, but how fit is he? Can he run around?'

Andy reckoned he was fit enough to handle the game in England, and he was certainly technically gifted enough to have a go for us in the First Division. I was chuffed when we convinced him to sign for us on a six-month deal for free. My only problem was that everyone knew of his ambition to be a manager. The papers and fans assumed that, from day one, he wanted my job. Or else Geoffrey Richmond would wake up one morning, sack me and make Chris my replacement. After a defeat against Crystal Palace, I even heard that radio commentator Jonathan Pearce had been bellowing: 'That's 4-0 to Palace, so that's Kamara out and Waddle in!'

I can honestly say that Chris's managerial ambitions never worried me one bit. I know that other managers were running scared from him, because they were frightened for their jobs, but my main concern was keeping him with us as long as he was able. He was a great player for Bradford and he had plenty of time to try management.

The highlight of his brief Bradford career was undoubtedly the day he inspired us to victory in an FA Cup tie at Everton. Chris was back in the big time, and he relished the limelight, as everyone at Everton knew. Before the game, their keeper, Neville Southall, walked past me in the tunnel at Goodison Park. He asked if Chris was fit, because he knew he'd been struggling with a minor injury.

'He is indeed,' I said. 'Better stay on your line, Nev.'

Southall was then coming towards the end of his time with Everton, but he was still an excellent goalkeeper. I had been doing my homework and Neville was beginning to play more like a sweeper, joining in the play, and could control and ping a ball like an accomplished outfield player, so I had said to Chris, 'If the ball falls to your feet anywhere around the halfway line, just whack it.' But by saying to Neville 'stay on your line' I thought I had given the game away.

Nev just sneered,'Yeah, right, good luck,' and headed out on to the pitch. When I saw Chris I made sure to tell him what had been said. I'm sure he had a cheeky twinkle in his eyes when he trotted out. Sure enough, when big Nev did come off his line, Chris chipped him on the turn from the halfway line. Nev turned from halfway inside his box and tried to make it back to goal, but the ball sailed over his head and dropped into the back of the net.

I lost it. I went bonkers on the touchline. I was totally out of order, but I couldn't help myself. I leapt from my spot by the dugout where I always stood during games, ran on to the pitch and did a somersault – sorry, a forward roll – in my suit! It was a fantastic moment in Bradford City's history and I was doing cartwheels. Not literally, I might add, as the forward roll is about all I have in my gymnastic locker. Everton manager Joe Royle was less than impressed. We fell out that day over my exuberant celebration. One paper absolutely slaughtered me the next day, and rightly so. I was young and naive, and I still regret reacting the way I did. Mind you, it was the most nimble move I'd made on a football pitch for five years, so although I felt a pillock on the outside, I have to say I was as proud as you like on the inside. My only regret was that I ruined my suit.

Later that season, I was back at Portsmouth for the first time as a manager. Typically, it was another memorable return. Our midfielder Nigel Pepper – a player who could be described as 'combative' – made a clumsy challenge on Pompey's Fitzroy Simpson. He was sent off. Moments later, Pompey's physio, Neil Sillett, son of former Coventry manager John, appeared to deliberately barge my defender Darren Moore as he ran on to the pitch with his first-aid bag. It knocked Darren, a very substantial lad, to the ground. I immediately ran on to the pitch to remonstrate with Sillett and had to be restrained by Pompey officials and stewards. I was reported by referee Steve Bennett and faced an FA disciplinary hearing and a charge of misconduct.

Every time I stepped into a dugout, mayhem seemed to break out. In December my assistant, Paul Jewell, ran on to the pitch to break up a brawl between Edinho and Bury's Tony Ellis. Bury manager Stan Tennent and his assistant Sam Ellis had to sprint after Jewell to grab him. In November 1996 I was sent off for protesting to a linesman in a home draw with Ipswich. He'd failed to see a foul on Nicky Mohan in the build-up to Ipswich's equaliser. I was sent to the stands by the ref and later forced to apologise. I reckon I had a better disciplinary record as a player than I did as a manager, and that's saying something. I'm surprised I haven't been sent off as a commentator, to tell you the truth. I can't think how many times I must have come close for shouting 'Unbelievable, Jeff!'

I eventually lost Chris Waddle. He left in March 1997, just before the end of the season and was snapped up by Sunderland boss Peter Reid for a fee of £100,000. He wanted to help the club he and his late father had supported. As it worked out, Sunderland went down from the Premier League in their last season at Roker Park, but it was the right time for Chris to leave Bradford. I was gutted, but the flipside was that the wagging tongues stopped debating his managerial role at the club. Not that it did my career prospects at Bradford any favours. My own wagging tongue had got me into enough trouble, and I was to pay the biggest price.

CHAPTER TWENTY-THREE
THE SACK RACE

I left Bradford on 7 January 1998. A Wednesday, if I remember rightly. Geoffrey Richmond, like me, wanted Premiership football and Premiership money. He also wanted it immediately. Actually, make that a day earlier than immediately. I'd taken Bradford into the First Division, and the team was doing OK. We topped the table at the end of September and were now just four points off the play-off places. The thing with football management is that you're in the coffin from the minute you sign on for the job and the lid's already on. Unless you're very lucky – like Arsène Wenger, or Sir Alex Ferguson – it's only a matter of time before the first nail gets hammered in. Regardless of the recent run of bad results at the tail end of 1997, my nails had been coming thick and fast for the best part of 18 months, mainly because of my actions away from the dugout. Annoyingly, I was just about the only person at the club who didn't know it.

Mr Unbelievable

NAIL ONE: The Wembley Play-Off Parade, 1996

Funny how the smallest incident can kick-start a chain reaction of events, good or bad. Having won the play-off final against Notts County, I admit I got a bit funny about the trophy presentation afterwards. At the time I personally didn't think you should get a medal for winning the play-offs. We'd finished sixth that season. Blackpool finished third, 10 points ahead of us, but got nothing. Oxford United finished second and made automatic promotion, but their players hadn't walked up the Wembley steps to receive a cup. I felt like a bit of a fraud. When somebody handed me a medal, I wouldn't even let them place it over my head, and I certainly didn't want to parade the trophy around the pitch. Sure, a lap of honour to thank the fans was fine, but this wasn't a real cup final. As a manager, I wanted to win a proper trophy, the League Championship or the FA Cup, not a play-off, even though promotion was a great achievement. I thought I would wait until Bradford beat Real Madrid to win the European Cup before I went bananas, and guess what?

Geoffrey Richmond didn't see it the same way. He wanted me to pose with him for a photo, complete with the cup, in the middle of the Wembley pitch. When I explained why I wasn't so enthusiastic, he put his arm around me and held up my arm, complete with the cup.

'Just enjoy it,' he said, talking through a smile as a photographer circled us. 'This is the feeling.'

Viewing the pictures now, I look awkward and uncomfortable. I know Geoffrey was unhappy with my reaction, and I have to say, he was probably right. I should have got on with it and made the most of a fantastic day. Up until that point, we had got on really well. I was in my strongest position as manager because of Bradford's incredible run of results, and he had told me long before the final that I'd still be his manager, whatever the result at Wembley. My reaction that day changed things, ever so slightly, but it was already the beginning of the end.

NAIL TWO: Kammyoke

At the end of my first full season at Valley Parade a party at the Kamara household was arranged to celebrate staying in the First Division. It was typically chaotic.

It was supposed to have been a way to let off steam, to let the hair down after a tough year. It had been a traumatic first season in the First Division. After winning in the play-offs at Wembley the previous year, we struggled to stay up. Everyone had worked hard to keep us in the division, so it made sense to invite the players, Geoffrey and his wife and most of the club staff.

We invited 60 to 70 guests. We had caterers, booze coming out of every room in the house and a jazz band playing outside in the warm evening. After a few (dozen!) beers I even took the microphone for a singalong with the band. Wrong decision. This time I didn't run through my usual routine ('Brown Eyed Girl', 'Your Song', 'Born To Be Wild', remember?). Instead, I decided to make up my own words as I sang along to a jazz number, and my off-the-cuff lyrics took the mickey out of the chairman.

I remember the words. To the tune of George Gershwin's 'Summertime', it went something like this: 'Summertime working for Geoffrey ain't easy, he wants to pick the team and sign the players as well, but until that morning when he comes in and sacks me, all I can say is Geoffrey, please don't pry.' I warbled on like a prize idiot, believing that this was all a big laugh. I was so engrossed that I failed to notice my guests flinching uncomfortably – or Anne glaring at me from behind the shrubs! Least of all was I aware of Geoffrey, with a grin fixed on his face, appearing to the assembled guests to be the perfect good sport. Looking back, it wasn't the shrewdest move. I was struggling to get the words out through my own laughter, and I presumed that he was laughing as well. He may well have been at the time, but apparently inside he was hurting.

'Summertime, and Geoffrey Richmond weren't laughing, but I kept on singing and making a din, what a way to hand your notice in.' The new words made more sense, and there was also a new end line to the Gershwin classic: 'So hush, little Kammy, don't you cry.'

I was oblivious to causing him any offence, although I guess on reflection it was a bit strange that Geoffrey and his wife left so soon after my performance. I was used to people walking out halfway through one of my singing attempts – thousands still do – but not the chairman of the club I managed. My friend Alan Ross said the Bradford chairman had a smile on his face when I first started. As the words echoed round the room and the rest of our guests stood around laughing, the smile became increasingly strained. He was squirming by the end of it. Rossy, who couldn't take his eyes off the chairman, was squirming with him, as no doubt were many of the guests that night. The 1997–98 season hadn't even started, but I was well and truly done for.

NAIL THREE: Not signing John Hendrie from Barnsley

John Hendrie was a good player and a former team-mate of mine at Leeds United and Middlesbrough. The chairman, Geoffrey Richmond, had done a deal with Barnsley chairman John Dennis. The only reason I didn't want to bring John Hendrie into the team, I admit, was that Geoffrey had sorted the deal and I didn't need the chairman sticking his beak into the business of transfers.

It was a point of principle and I dug my heels in – looking back, I was also cutting off my nose to spite my face. We had made a fabulous start to the season and were four points clear at the top of the table, with our first game in September being live on Sky Sports on the Friday night, though Sunderland ruined that party by beating us 4–0 at home, with Kevin Phillips scoring two.

That morning the *Daily Mail* carried an exclusive that John Hendrie was about to sign for Bradford, complete with quotes from Geoffrey and the Barnsley chairman, John Dennis. I could not believe what I was reading, as I knew nothing about it. I immediately got on the phone to Barnsley manager Danny Wilson. He knew nothing about the proposed move either and promised to 'have a word' at his end. I did likewise, though I never got round to it, which was a mistake. I should have called Richmond and told him that if he was going to sign a player he should do it in conjunction with me. I shouldn't have to read it in the papers.

I was still fuming after the Sunderland game (more so, having seen us humiliated at home) when I bumped into Alan Biggs, the *Mail* journalist who had written the John Hendrie story.

'There's no point going into that press conference,' I told him. 'You're barred.'

He played dumb.

'You know what the problem is,' I continued. 'If you want to know what's going on at this football club, you can ring that interfering busybody in there.' I pointed to Geoffrey's office – with spectacular timing. His wife was coming in the opposite direction. She had heard every word.

I still went to the press conference, but as it drew to a close, I saw Biggs standing outside the door with Geoffrey. 'I want you to apologise to Alan,' he said as I left for my office.

'I'm not apologising,' I said.

'You are.'

It was like a scene from panto. I was Aladdin, Geoffrey was Widow Twankey.

'I'm not.'

'You are ...'

You get the picture. Alan piped up, saying it didn't matter, and he was sorry for any trouble, which angered me even more.

'You're not sorry – all you had to do was ring me to confirm the story.'

I could see Geoffrey turning purple.

'You apologise to Alan right now or you're sacked.'

And that's when I delivered my riposte. 'You're not sacking me, Geoffrey,' I told him, 'because I bloody well resign!'

Flustered, Geoffrey trotted off to the boardroom without another word. Alan Biggs was beside himself with guilt. 'Kammy,' he said, 'it's like a striker having an open goal – you either tap it in or miss it, and this was too good to miss. And besides, Geoffrey gave me the story.'

'Did you or did you not ring me before the season started?' I asked. 'I gave you chapter and verse on the team's new sign-ings and a list of players we might sell.'

He nodded as I went on, 'So even though I could not have done anything about you writing the story, you could have rung me to tip me off.'

'Sorry, Kammy,' said Biggsy, 'I see where you are coming from.'

I went downstairs and told Paul Jewell and Martin Hunter what had happened, and they could hardly believe it. I don't think I could either.

When I got home I related the story to Anne, who immedi-ately went into panic mode. 'What about the mortgage? What about our future? What have you done ...?' she said. 'It's all very well having principles, but they won't pay the bills, will they?'

'Don't worry, I will get another job somewhere,' was my reply, but I did not sleep that Friday night, and by Saturday evening I was feeling nervy. But we were still top of the table, so I hoped that would be keeping Geoffrey in a good mood.

Yet again, I had been a prize idiot, I realised. Anne's words about my stubborn principles not keeping the roof over our heads rang in my ears. I would go in on Monday and apologise, and maybe that would be the end of it.

But on the Sunday, club secretary Shaun Harvey contacted me at home. He told me to get to the club for 9 a.m. Monday morning as the chairman wanted to see me. This wasn't unusual, because Geoffrey would frequently call me into his office for a little chat, but under the circumstances it seemed more sinister this time. I must admit I feared the worst as I made the short journey from Wakefield to Valley Parade. I knocked on the door of his office.

'Come!' he boomed.

I popped my head round the door.

'Oh, it's you,' he said. 'I thought you'd resigned.'

'No,' I sheepishly replied, testing him, 'you sacked me first and I have a journalist to prove it!'

Thankfully, he smiled, and that was good enough for me.

I backed down. 'Yeah, sorry about that,' I said. 'It was all heat of the moment stuff.'

He smiled again and told me to sit down. Everything seemed fine, but I knew something had changed. My hunch was right. Weeks later he wanted to sign striker Wayne Allison. I'd actually tried to sign him a season or two earlier, but I knew Geoffrey's motives were different from mine. His interference was becoming unbearable to me. Our rivals Huddersfield were in the running for signing Wayne, and he wanted to upset them by bringing him to Bradford City. It was a move that was all to do with petty rivalry.

I dug my heels in. 'If you're going to give me the money for Allison, give it to me for John McGinlay instead.'

McGinlay had been prolific the season before at Bolton. He'd even been the top goalscorer in the First Division, so I was convinced I was backing a winner. On this occasion the chairman relented. But, sadly, when John joined us it all went wrong - he couldn't hit a barn door with a banjo. Bradford never saw the true John McGinlay. Meanwhile, Wayne Allison was proving to be quite a player for Huddersfield. And, boy, was I reminded of that fact every day.

NAIL FOUR: My Last Game in Charge

We lost to Manchester City in the FA Cup on 3 January 1998. I got a call from Richmond on the team bus back to Bradford that evening. 'That's our season over,' he said. 'We need to cut costs. I want you to get rid of one of your staff,' he said. 'Who do you want to get rid of?'

When I put the phone down I spoke to my two assistants, Paul Jewell and Martin Hunter. I told them straight, 'The chairman has told me to sack one of you.' He had never been a fan of Paul Jewell's, and Paul was looking the most worried.

'Don't worry, Jags,' I said. 'I need you. And I need Martin, too. It will blow over.'

I popped into to see the chairman on the Monday morning before training.

'Who is it to be, then?' asked Richmond.

'You make the decision if there has to be one,' I said, 'I need them both, there are 25 league games left.'

'OK,' he said simply, and he pulled a list of players towards himself on the desk.

'Now I'm looking at the team and I can't see anyone good enough to play in the Premiership.' Now he was really taking the mickey.

Mr Unbelievable

'They will all play in the Premiership,' I told him. 'Peter Beagrie will play in the Premiership, Jamie Lawrence, John Dreyer will play in the Premiership, Darren Moore will play in the Premiership, Gary Walsh will play in the Premiership, Wayne Jacobs will play in the Premiership, Robbie Blake will play in the Premiership. Do you want me to go on?'

He disagreed. 'No, Chris,' he said. 'I've looked at the team and the only one I can see who's good enough for the Premiership is Darren Moore.'

He was talking out of his big backside. We had a meeting in his office the following day and he delivered a brutal ultimatum: 'I've had a think about it. If you insist that you don't want to get rid of one of your staff, we're going to get rid of you instead.'

He was so quirky. Only a week earlier, he'd taken Anne and me out to celebrate the anniversary of my appointment. He hired a limo to pick us up. We even had champagne in the back when we watched the 1996 play-off final win. He knew how to do things in style.

'There will be many more nights like this to come,' he said.

Clearly, I wasn't going to be around to see them. I'd had enough of his messing around. 'OK, Geoffrey, fine,' I said.

I don't think he had been listening to me properly. 'I know you'll be distraught and upset ... what did you say?' he said, looking shocked.

I told him I was fine with his decision, I wasn't upset and I was happy to leave. 'Just do the necessary: inform the press, pay me up, and I'll be out of your hair,' I said coolly.

He began to backtrack immediately. He reckoned the pair of us were being hasty and that we should have a cooling-off period. I stood up and said, 'No, you can't change your mind. You've made your decision. How do you think I can work with you now?'

I really wasn't bothered. I was 100 per cent convinced I would get another job. I'd left the club in a good state and brought some fantastic players to the team. Bradford were also £2 million better off because of my wheeling and dealing in the transfer market.

Before I left, I recommended Paul Jewell for the job. I didn't want any of the staff to lose their jobs and Paul deserved a chance. He was installed as caretaker boss for six months before being permanently appointed. He took them into the Premiership. It was quite a success story and I was chuffed for him.

⚽ ⚽ ⚽ ⚽ ⚽ ⚽ ⚽

There was a predictably controversial twist to my exit from Valley Parade. When I was booted out, the former MP David Mellor was looking to make a name for himself in football above and beyond wearing a Chelsea football shirt while he had his toes licked. Now then, are we talking the same David Mellor here? He said he loved to make love in a Chelsea shirt. Oh my God, I could offer some England international parallels here, but I'm not going there. But it's strange how these stories come round again and again and only the cast changes. Mellor's political career was a mess after his private life was exposed in the press. By 1998 he was well and truly on the football bandwagon, writing columns, hosting radio chat shows and chairing the Football Task Force, an organisation which, among other things, was tackling racism. There was a problem, though. David was upsetting people all over the place by acting as judge and jury on a number of issues going on in football clubs around the country. After my sacking he ruffled a few feathers by claiming I could have been sacked for racial reasons.

I'd like to set the record straight on this idea: David was wrong. But to his credit there had been no satisfactory explanation for my dismissal, so he decided to offer a theory of his own. He later told me that he'd received numerous phone calls to his radio programme. Fans wanted to know why I had been sacked by Bradford. This provoked him to raise the question over race. The controversial programme was broadcast on the first Saturday following my sacking.

Even without Mellor's opinions, that day was a nightmare for me. It was the first (and hopefully last) league weekend in my career when I hadn't been involved in the game in some way. I hated it. By the time three o'clock came around I was fed up. Games were kicking off around the country, everyone in the football world was getting their fix, and all I could do was stretch out on the sofa and watch the results come through on *Soccer Saturday*. I remember thinking, 'That Jeff Stelling talks some rubbish!' Ha!

After the final whistle, I tuned into 606 to listen to Mellor's show. It hardly delivered controversy on the level of the Russell Brand/Jonathan Ross/Andrew Sachs scandal, but it still gives me the shivers.

Mellor told how he felt depressed at my 'unceremonious dumping' by Bradford City, before the caller, Andrew in Grantham, disagreed by suggesting I'd taken the club as far as it could go. All well and good so far, but then Mellor started talking about how it had left an 'uncomfortable taste' in his mouth, with Bradford still in the top half of the division, and that, as one of the few black managers in the league, he had to worry and ask, Did my colour have anything to do with it?

The caller sounded shocked, but Mellor still persisted, saying that he couldn't understand why anyone would really want to get rid of me.

Now I was under pressure. Suddenly, thanks to a few speculative comments, there was plenty of fuss surrounding my departure, and I knew that Geoffrey wouldn't like any of it. This wasn't the first incident, either. I'd been a studio guest at Sky's headquarters in Isleworth, west London, for their live Nationwide Football League game the night before. The fixture was Tranmere versus West Bromwich Albion. Denis Smith was West Brom's manager at the time and he was interviewed after the game.

'I just want to offer my best wishes to Chris Kamara,' he told the Sky reporter. 'What chance do I and all other managers have when you consider the job Chris did at Bradford in the two years he was there?'

I was touched that he felt strongly enough to speak out for me on live television, though privately I had received countless calls from other managers. This public rant had not gone unnoticed by Geoffrey, though. He rang me first thing the following morning (Denis told me that my ex-chairman also collared him at a later date, saying that he was not impressed with his public show of support for me). Geoffrey should have been worried about Bradford City's visit to Stockport County that day. Instead he was chewing my ear off.

'Things are not going the way I expected,' he said.

'All I've done is accept the situation, and I've stressed that on the TV and radio and in the press. What more can I do?'

Clearly, Geoffrey didn't see it that way. 'You're taking the mickey,' he said. 'You and all your mates are making me look a fool.'

Anne was in the room and she could hear the conversation was getting heated. She pressed her ear to the phone and caught the threat creeping into Geoffrey's voice. It was made clear to us that if I didn't play ball with him I could kiss any chance of compensation goodbye. I knew the man I was dealing with. Believe me, if he could get out of a deal, he would, if the mood took him. Mellor's rant gave him even more ammo to pull the plug on my severance pay. Apparently he later instructed his solicitor to demand an apology and a retraction from Mellor, who refused. Mellor claimed he had only voiced a question. As a compromise, he invited Geoffrey on to the show the following week. The whole episode was moving away from me. I was merely the subject of the debate, but the two of them were like a pair of Rottweilers fighting over a bone. Beforehand Richmond rang me out of the blue and asked for my full support. I hadn't received a penny in compensation at that point, and we were still negotiating a severance package. I was backed into a corner.

Like thousands of other football fans, I tuned in to hear the much-publicised debate. If the world and his wife were listening, I felt I had to as well, and it was always going to be a lively one. Over the years, Geoffrey had grown to believe that there was only one opinion worth listening to – his. Meanwhile, David Mellor was a barrister and politician who was more than able to handle himself verbally in a scrap. Weirdly, after half an hour of ranting and raving, shouting and spluttering, the debate settled nothing.

I guess it all added to the mystery of why I was sacked and why Geoffrey wanted to offload a member of staff at Bradford that day. A lot of people were genuinely surprised that I was sacked, but it had nothing to do with the colour of my skin. I was black when Richmond hired me and black when he sacked me. In some ways, the Mellor issue suited Geoffrey, because it meant he never really had to explain why the hell he did sack me. He kept saying, 'He had taken Bradford as far as he could,' but it was wearing thin. It glossed over the real issue and that was a shame. I had to laugh the whole thing off and support Geoffrey, which was something I could have done without, but I knew more than anyone that the wrong move could prove very costly to me and my family – and I mean financially for once.

Geoffrey Richmond was digging his heels in. He was not happy and was not going to simply do the decent thing: pay me what was due under my contract and enable both himself and me to get on with our lives. He informed me that we should both attend a meeting at his solicitors in Manchester.

John Barnwell put me in touch with the League Managers' Association solicitor Mike Morrison, and he arranged to meet me at the venue over the Pennines to negotiate the deal. Richmond rang me the day before and asked how I was getting there, and when I said I was intending to drive across he offered me a lift. I didn't have a problem with that and I didn't have a problem with Geoffrey Richmond. I was disappointed to lose my job, but we had had some good times together and we would continue to be friends if he treated me in the right way financially. I thought we were travelling over together to do the decent thing.

I told Mike I was meeting Richmond at Hartshead Services on the M62 near Bradford and that we would travel together. He advised me to make sure that at no point during the journey did we discuss the compensation or anything legal – we would sort that out in the office. Geoffrey must have been under instructions as well because he also failed to broach the subject and it was a perfectly pleasant trip in his treasured Bentley.

Then we sat down in a conference room in the solicitors' offices and Richmond's solicitor told us: 'We will honour every penny of Chris's contract ... until he gets another job. So we pay his wages for the next 18 months, and if he does get another job we pay him a severance fee of £30,000.'

Mike Morrison disappointed me then. When Richmond said, 'How many chairmen do you know who offer their former managers that sort of security?' Morrison said, 'No, I agree it's very generous.' I couldn't believe what I was hearing.

I was absolutely stunned. I was looking at this grandiose legal document in my hand and the words just merged together and melted into the page. My immediate thought was, 'Well, that might be all right for a bloke of 65 who doesn't want or need to work any more, but I'm young and I want to get straight back into management. I needed a severance payment.' Having made the club a small fortune of £2 million in the transfer market and having taken them to a higher division, I had hoped he would do the honourable thing and offer me a decent pay-off. But no, this offer was taking the mickey.

The Sack Race

I said, 'That's no good to me. I want to work in the next 18 months, I don't want to be sat on my backside. Just pay me some proper compensation.'

'No, no, no,' said Richmond, 'hang on. As your solicitor has just said over there, there are not many chairmen who make an offer like that.'

So I said (and this is the censored version), 'Well you can stick your flaming money where the sun don't shine. I don't want a flipping penny off you.'

He was flummoxed then. He said, 'Now, now, come on, Chris, calm down.'

Calm down? As I went in for the kill, Mike Morrison bundled me out of the room. Outside he waited whilst I attempted to compose myself, and then he said, 'Right now they don't have to give you a single penny if they don't want to. They can do you for some breach or other.'

I couldn't understand how they could do me for another breach when I'd already been sacked, but he said, 'He has now got two witnesses who can relate that you just told him to stick his money - he may well do that now.'

So he told me to keep my cool, go back in the room and allow him to sort it out. Before we got to our seats, the other two suggested we arrange another meeting, and Mike agreed that was probably the wisest course of action.

Richmond looked across at me, smiled and said, 'So you and me can jostle on the way back home' - and winked.

I replied, 'If you think I'm getting in the effing car with you, you've got another thing coming.'

Mike Morrison reached across and put his hand over my

mouth, saying, 'Be careful. Watch what you say.' But I brushed him off and said, 'You can get lost, I am not getting in the car with him. He's the last person in the world I'm getting in a car with.'

We left the offices and I rang Anne and asked her to meet me at Huddersfield station. I got the next train across from Manchester Piccadilly, staring out of the window at the glory of the Pennines in disbelief. As we went from Huddersfield to Hartshead Services to pick up my car, I filled Anne in on all the gory details. To say she was not best pleased is putting it rather mildly.

As we pulled into the services car park, it immediately became apparent that my car was blocked in by a rather large, shiny Bentley. Its owner opened the car door and stepped out. Not in a million years did I expect to see Geoffrey Richmond there, but what was even more strange was that apparently he didn't expect to see me either. 'Fancy seeing you here,' he exclaimed, as if it was just a chance meeting!

When I thought about it later, seeing him there did make a lot of sense. He was a clever man when it came to forward thinking, and he had obviously thought ahead to block me in so I couldn't escape! He was clearly worried that I might go to the papers and tell them that he was refusing to pay my money. And he just might have been right. There was no gagging order in place at that point.

Anne was desperate to come in with me and help me sort it out, but I told her I wanted to deal with it. She knew how weak I was with negotiations, but she also knew my pride wouldn't let him get the better of me. Geoffrey and I went into the restaurant and bought tea, whilst Anne remained in the car.

The Sack Race

He spoke first. 'It's Chris Kamara this, Chris Kamara that, Chris Kamara runs this club, Chris Kamara won us promotion.' It was obviously a sore point with him.

Knowing I had to soothe the situation, I said, 'No, it isn't. We did it together, but now you've ended it.'

He said, 'Well, I'm sick of hearing it, same old story.'

Tired of his sorrowful tale, I said, 'Look, just get me out of your hair and give me what I am owed.'

I know that to this day Anne wishes she had insisted on coming into that café with me. She is a better negotiator than I am, but this was something I wanted to resolve myself.

As it was, I came out of the negotiations with only about a third of what should really have been paid to me. I still had 18 months of the contract to run, but there was no compensation clause for most managers in those days.

'I didn't get all that was due to me, but I don't care. I just want rid of him,' I told John Barnwell from the LMA.

'You've done OK,' he said.

And so ended my first managerial post, although by then I could well have been onto my second job in the hot seat - at Leeds United. Geoffrey Richmond had had a chance to buy Leeds about halfway through our partnership at Bradford. He told me that if he could raise the necessary funds he would be taking me with him as the manager. Geoffrey couldn't raise the dough, and shortly afterwards Peter Ridsdale became the chairman as Leeds United became a plc.

Little did I know at the time that taking Bradford from League One to the Championship would make me the most successful English black manager in terms of achievement.

Mr Unbelievable

What is so amazing is that that statistic has stood for fourteen years. I believe that goes to show that not enough black managers have been given the chance. Here's hoping that by the end of the 2009-10 season Chris Hughton will have gone one better and taken Newcastle into the Premier League.

❂ ❂ ❂ ❂ ❂ ❂ ❂ ❂

One of the early highlights of my time on *Soccer Saturday* was a long chat with Geoffrey Richmond for the show. It happened two years after he'd sacked me, so the wounds had healed. There was no hidden agenda for the interview. It was meant to be a tongue-in-cheek chat about my time at the club and how things were going without me. Bradford were doing well at the time under Paul Jewell, and Geoffrey enjoyed having a laugh on camera. He soon stopped laughing when I pulled a gun on him.

Well, it wasn't really a gun, just a replica lighter, but it looked pretty convincing. I'd already warned our cameraman that I was going to wave it at him unexpectedly. The idea was for me to say, 'Now here's something I should have done years ago,' before pointing it at Geoffrey. It was all a bit of fun, nothing malicious.

It worked. For an instant Geoffrey was taken aback by the move, though he quickly recognised it as a replica from his time with Ronson Lighters, one of his more successful businesses. It was all taken in good spirit and it looked great on the telly. Nobody complained either, which was a miracle. These days I'd probably get arrested if I pulled a stunt like that.

CHAPTER TWENTY-FOUR
THE FAX ABOUT STOKE

I loved my time as a Stoke City player and could not believe my luck when I heard they were on the lookout for a new manager. The fact that I was unemployed, and keen to stick it to Geoffrey Richmond for dispensing with my services at Bradford, was the icing on the cake. The offer came only days after I'd emptied my Valley Parade office, so I thought it was made for me – perhaps even fate.

When I met chairman Peter Coates and vice-chairman Keith Humphreys I could not have been happier. Stoke City is a big club, not just because of the history books and Sir Stanley Matthews but in real terms as well. They're up where they belong again now, and there's more to them than long throws and route one football. Most of the people in the city love the club and I was disappointed I hadn't managed to help them get into the Premier League as a player. They were struggling when I signed as their manager, but I still felt the dream of Premiership football would be possible in my tenure.

Mr Unbelievable

Bradford City had found it hard to fill the Valley Parade stadium at times, but Stoke was a hotbed and, even though I had had a great time at Bradford, in a way I now felt as if I'd died and gone to heaven. Stoke, by now at their fabulous new Britannia Stadium, would always be a big club. Although their current league position didn't reflect this, they were a sleeping giant in my book.

As one of the conditions for taking the job I agreed with Coates and Humphreys that I would keep the previous managerial team, Chic Bates and his assistant Alan Durban. I figured that they wouldn't want to hang around for too long and that they would do the honourable thing and resign once I'd settled in. I was young, ambitious and determined to do things my way, but this also made me naive. Alan was a useful resource, and I should have tapped into his know-how rather than alienating him; Peter Reid and Adrian Heath have since vouched for him as a great coach and a nice bloke. Maybe I'd already cocked things up?

It didn't help that the club had changed dramatically since I'd been there as a player. It used to be a friendly club. The office cleaner was our babysitter when I played there, and she loved the football team. But when I arrived as manager I felt it had become a poisonous place to work; it ran on gossip and tittle tattle. It seemed like everyone was at it.

When I was managing Bradford, I'd watched Stoke play a few times. I always thought the pitch at the Britannia was too big – it gave visiting teams a chance to play good football, especially if they were technically superior. I reckoned it would give us an advantage if we reduced the size of the pitch, especially when we were playing teams who liked to spray the ball around. I wanted to pen teams in and give them a rough ride, a bit like the way the team operated under Tony Pulis.

On my first day in the job I asked Derek, the club groundsman, to shrink the pitch by a yard at either end and a yard on either side in time for my first home game, which was 10 days away. He had concerns about doing that, but I told him I would take full responsibility. Within half an hour the club chief executive, Jez Moxey, was banging on my door and waving a Football League rulebook under my nose. He warned me that the rules clearly stated that you cannot change the dimensions of your pitch once you have announced them at the start of the season. Fair enough, but secretly I was pretty annoyed. When I'd asked the groundsman I thought he'd keep the changes under wraps.

It was par for the course really; nobody was doing me any favours. The week of my first game, I'd sold my best player, full-back Andy Griffin, to Newcastle United manager Kenny Dalglish, even though I didn't really want to. Kenny and I had already done business when I was at Bradford and my midfielder Des Hamilton had joined his ever-expanding squad at St James's Park. Kenny had the bravery to follow his belief in young English talent. He often backed this belief with hard cash, even though both players I sold to him ultimately struggled to make an impact in the first team.

The Griffin transfer was a complicated affair, though. He refused to play for me in my first game at Swindon, afraid that an injury might jeopardise the move to a big club. I understood his fears, but as far as I was concerned Griffin was still a Stoke player and I told him to get on with it and play. So away at Swindon Griffin was in the squad and selected to play. He stayed at the hotel with the rest of the team, had a kip on the afternoon of the game and then refused to start the match. I was livid. I rang Peter Coates and told him that we should force him to play. He turned me down flat.

'What if he gets injured, Chris?'

It all seemed pretty weak-minded to me. I pulled Griff to one side and told him to go home. I wondered what the hell I'd let myself in for. The team hadn't kicked a ball for me at this point and, to be honest, they hardly did afterwards.

I was told that Newcastle had offered £850,000 for Griffin, with an additional £350,000 sell-on fee. I reckoned I could get more and told Stoke chief executive Jez Moxey so.

'Leave it to me I can get at least £1.5 million.'

I'd arranged an identical deal for Bradford when Newcastle signed Des Hamilton from me, but Moxey was not impressed when I told him that I would take over the transfer. I knew I could bring in the best deal for the club. I also felt I should be in charge of the transfers at the club. I wouldn't let Geoffrey Richmond organise transfers at Bradford, so why should it be any different at Stoke? My attitude ruffled a few feathers. Today, chief executives like Moxey are in vogue, but back then, in my eyes, Stoke City didn't need one.

What Moxey also didn't know was that on the day I took the Stoke job, Leicester City boss Martin O'Neill contacted me to wish me all the best. He also registered an interest in Griffin. I wanted to create an auction environment, and it worked, even though my move would eventually damage my relationship with Martin. With Kenny Dalglish involved, I contacted Martin the following day to say Newcastle United had made a £1 million offer up front, with £250,000 added on for appearances. Martin more than matched that with a firm offer of £1.25 million with an additional £250,000. I had triggered the bidding war I'd hoped for.

My only major headache was Griffin's determination to sign for Newcastle. He'd made it clear to everyone at the club, too. I contacted Kenny Dalglish, told him of Leicester's offer and he agreed to match it, with more cash thrown in for Griffin's future first-team appearances.

Even interest from Arsenal failed to turn Griffin's head from the direction of Tyneside. The Gunners' chief scout, Don Mackay, contacted me to register Arsenal's interest, but no offer from Highbury could change Griffin's mind. I couldn't believe he didn't even want to talk to Arsenal, where he could have been Lee Dixon's understudy and eventual successor in a terrific Arsenal side managed by Arsène Wenger. I called him into the office and told him of Arsenal's interest.

'I don't want to go there,' said Griff.

'Are you sure?' I asked him.

Judging by Griffin's vacant expression, his mind was made up and he wanted to go to Tyneside.

I updated Martin on Newcastle's latest offer and he made a final bid of £1.75 million. Newcastle refused to go any higher and were sticking at £1.25 million and £250,000 on appearances, but by that stage they knew that Griffin would not talk to another club. He had no intention of talking to Leicester or Arsenal, and when Martin O'Neill found this out, he was furious. He figured that I'd used him to up the money, and he was partially right, but I genuinely had no idea that Griffin's head wouldn't be turned from Newcastle. In fact Leicester would have suited me and Stoke better, because we would have made more money.

Martin understands all that today, though he was very unhappy with me at the time. Before Villa and Celtic, he had worked at Wycombe Wanderers and Norwich City. He knows what it's like to fight on the breadline and survive on a pittance. Even at Leicester he had to live hand to mouth. When you're a manager in that situation, you'll do anything to get the best deal for your club, especially when faced with selling one of your best players.

⚽ ⚽ ⚽ ⚽ ⚽ ⚽ ⚽ ⚽

My time at Stoke was a disaster. Under my charge, the team won once in 13 League games. It's a hopeless statistic, and it still haunts me today, but it's also identical to the record that Bates and Durban had before I arrived. The club was in freefall and it couldn't be turned around.

At the same time, Joe Royle had taken over at Manchester City and he also faced a near-impossible task. City were relegated to League Division Two in May, despite a last-day win at Stoke of all places. Joe stayed at Maine Road, and within four seasons he got them back into the Premiership. I wasn't given the same chance. It didn't help that I'd opened my mouth and gobbed off when I started at the club. I told the fans we'd get promotion to the Premiership in two years and I fell flat on my face.

The Fax about Stoke

It had all been my own fault. I squandered what little money I was given from the proceeds of the Griffin sale. We needed a striker and I was very close to getting Gareth Taylor from Sheffield United, who I knew, deep down, would get us the goals. The deal fell through because we couldn't agree personal terms. I also, through sheer stubbornness, turned down the chance to sign proven goal machine Marco Gabbiadini. Jez Moxey set up the deal, which put me off immediately. I told him I'd rather buy my own players, and Moxey pulled the deal, telling Marco that he should blame me. What I hadn't been told at the time was that he'd given up a contract in Cyprus because he believed the move to Stoke would go through. He even wanted compensation from us at one point. Marco signed for Darlington instead. They couldn't match the money Stoke had offered, but he was on a healthy goal bonus. Thankfully Marco scored goals every week and made a few bob.

I bumped into Marco at the Sunderland Stadium of Light in 2008. When we first met, he wasn't exactly chuffed to see me. I told him I regretted snubbing him. It was true. My decision had back-fired on me. I also admitted to him if I'd been made aware of his contract situation it might have made me change my mind. I honestly thought he was a free transfer. Of course, it is easy for me to say that now, but if I had been aware of all the facts, it might have made a difference. Marco is now running a guest-house in York and doing very well for himself, I'm happy to report. If I ever stay there he'd have every right to poison my eggs and bacon or do something nasty in my coffee, so I think I'm better off just wishing him luck and keeping my distance.

Mr Unbelievable

Someone once suggested I didn't sign Marco Gabbiadini because my spelling wasn't good enough to sort out the contract. Gabbiadini was a tried and tested goalscorer and would have been good for the club on reflection, but I still ain't staying at your gaff, Marco!

I tried everything to steer the ship away from trouble, but it wasn't working, no matter who I signed. I've learnt that Captain Smith, who commanded the *Titanic*, was born in Stoke. I think I had the same feeling that he must have had that night.

I bought Kyle Lightbourne for £350,000 from Coventry, but he picked up a virus almost immediately and never showed anything decent, apart from a bit of a rash if I remember. I nearly signed man-mountain Emerson Thome from Benfica after he impressed in training. We gave him a run-out in one reserves game and he mopped up strikers like a sponge. We were even told his name was really 'Paradou', which I later found out was Portuguese for The Wall. I should have signed him there and then, but instead I invited Moxey and one of the directors to another reserves game on a miserable, wet and windy night and Emerson had a nightmare in the gale. I watched the deal fall through before my eyes – I knew they wouldn't back me. Big Ron Atkinson signed him for Sheffield Wednesday a fortnight later. He later played for Chelsea, Sunderland and Bolton. At one point he was Sunderland's record signing and commanded fees in excess of £10 million. He was only with me for seven days, and yet he still calls me Gaffer to this day whenever I see him.

From day one it was obvious we needed a goalkeeper. Harry Redknapp, who was then at West Ham, agreed to let us have

The Fax about Stoke

former French international stopper Bernard Lama, which would have been a real coup for us. Predictably it fell through over money, because Bernard wanted a £15,000 lump sum on top of his high wages. Jim Smith agreed to sell Russell Hoult from Derby County before getting cold feet and changing his mind. My chairman Peter Coates then told me that Neville Southall was available. This time I was happy with the chairman's interference, because I needed the help. I was struggling big-time, so I snapped him up.

Neville trained like a demon on his first day and looked ready for first-team action. I'll never forget the moment I saw him walking over to me in the middle of the training pitch, ball under his arm, heading slowly but very deliberately towards me.

'This is a poisonous football club,' he whispered.

It had only taken him about an hour to work it out. It had taken me just over three months. I signed for the club in late January; I was out in early April. I should have listened to Neville Southall and got out, because the ex-bin-man knew all about rubbish and he was absolutely right. At the time the fans of Stoke deserved more, and it's great to see them doing so well nowadays.

✿ ✿ ✿ ✿ ✿ ✿ ✿

Want to know what a football manager's resignation letter looks like? Well here you go:

STOKE CITY FOOTBALL CLUB
Chairman and directors,
With much regret I have to announce my resignation from Stoke City FC.

The reasons are as follows:

1: I came to the job full of hope and with my eyes open to the full extent of the task. I also knew that I was expected to work with the existing management structure, but the backing I have had from most of the existing staff has been non-existent and I have been unable to maximise the full potential of Stoke City through the club not allowing me to hire and fire the people I believed were right or wrong for the club, both the playing side and the backroom staff.

2: I have had a very poor response from several of the players, who appear to have their own idea on who they want as manager and it does not appear to be me.

3. There appears to be some sort of hidden agenda going on at the club and there are several outside influences that seem intent on causing unrest. This makes it impossible for me to make Stoke City the successful club I know they can be.

I wish Stoke City all the best for the future.

Chris Kamara

It's not that spectacular, is it? Sadly, the circumstances surrounding it were. I had tried everything to get the right formula, but it wasn't working. I was also hurting because my

The Fax about Stoke

dad was dying from cancer. Nobody at the club knew about this apart from my secretary, Liz. Throughout my entire spell at Stoke I was travelling backwards and forwards between Staffordshire and Teesside (and also trying to see the family in Yorkshire in between), while he was wasting away. I would never use his illness as an excuse, which is why I didn't tell anyone at the time, but my mind was not fully on my job at Stoke.

A board meeting was planned on the Monday evening of my ninth week at the club, and for the first time I seriously considered getting out. Chic Bates and Alan Durban were still hanging around, and I felt their presence wasn't doing me any good, particularly with the directors and the players who were not in the team. I was losing face among the Stoke supporters. The reputation I had worked so hard to establish as Bradford manager was being ruined.

So I penned my resignation letter ready for the board meeting. That morning I used the club fax machine to send a copy to Andy Smith, an old pal I trusted and my former chief scout at Bradford. I just wanted to run the wording by him.

Andy rang and advised me to think very carefully about what I was doing. For a while he even tried to talk me out of it. He planted the first seeds of doubt in my mind, and I began to reconsider my decision. I wondered whether I should hold on and attempt to improve the team. In addition, Andy pointed out that in the resignation letter I had attacked the directors over the continued presence of Bates and Durban. He felt that was wrong, because I had agreed to take the job with them still installed at the club. It wasn't the fault of Coates and

Humphreys that we weren't getting on, and he was right, the board had always been supportive.

Andy added his amendments to the letter and faxed it from his Yorkshire office back to Stoke. Nothing came through. I stood next to the club's main fax machine outside Moxey's office, but there was no activity. After 10 minutes I started to sweat. This letter was dynamite. I knew if it fell into the wrong hands it might be presented to Stoke City or the media, and with me now having second thoughts about it I definitely didn't want that to happen. If it did, the job would blow up in my face and I would be out of there pronto, desk cleared, no future wages, no compensation, nothing.

I rang Andy. He said it had definitely gone through. I raced through to my secretary, Liz. I asked her how many fax machines there were at the club. 'Including the one out there?' she asked. 'There's one in the club shop, one in the commercial office and one in the Football in the Community office.'

Anyone who has walked round behind the scenes at the Britannia Stadium will appreciate the formidable magical mystery tour I now had to embark on. I casually closed Liz's door and set off like the wind. I pressed the button for the lift, but I was so desperate to start the hunt that I flew off down three flights of stairs without even waiting for it to arrive. Tell you what, I'd never run that bloody fast ever before in that stadium, even as a player. First stop was the club shop – it wasn't exactly busy that day as the club hadn't yet got to the point of selling small Kammy dolls for the fans to stick needles into. I steadied myself before walking in, calmly, then I speed-walked past the shop assistant with his feet on the table and examined the fax machine. Nothing.

The Fax about Stoke

'Any faxes?' I asked casually. He recognised me and quickly moved his feet from the table.

'Er, no, nothing, Gaffer,' he stammered. 'What are you looking for?'

I hadn't time to answer. I was hastily walking out of the shop doors ... before sprinting back up the three flights of stairs to the commercial department, very reminiscent of John Cleese in *Fawlty Towers*. The office was packed, the staff all busy at work. So busy they barely noticed me walk in, breathless, panting and panicking. I sauntered over to look at the fax machine. Commercial officer Tony Tams and his secretary Lorraine caught me looking at the faxes in the tray.

'Can we help?' said Tony as I checked the dozen or so sheets accumulated. I was now in a daze, I couldn't believe it – it wasn't there! I was sweating, angry and couldn't believe what Andy was putting me through. Help! I had found nothing!

'Anything I should be looking out for?' shouted Tony Tams as I bolted back out through the door.

'Where did Liz say the next fax machine was?' I whispered to myself. I remembered, in the Football in the Community office. Bugger! That was the other side of the ground, so it was back off down the stairs again. I was now mentally running faster than Linford Christie could ever dream of, even though in real life he probably would have beaten me if he'd walked. Down the stairs, on to the pitch and, after a run round the perimeter, I was there.

My next move was straight out of the eighties cop show *Miami Vice*. Detective Tubbs would have been proud of me. First I banged on the Football in the Community door. I didn't get an answer. What was I going to do? I had to get that fax. I had never broken into anywhere in my life, Dad would never have allowed that, but needs must. Sorry, Dad.

I took a short run and, slamming into the door with my shoulder, I pushed the bolt through the splintered wood. I gave a little victory salute to myself, a rarity during my time at Stoke, certain the hunt was now over. Surely this was where the resignation letter had been sent? My heart fluttered as I saw a sheet of A4 sitting on the purring machine. My heart sank when I read the contents of the fax: it was a birthday request for a young fan to be a Stoke City mascot. There was no way Andy wanted to be a Stoke City mascot, so it could never have come from him.

I sprinted back to my office, wringing with sweat and my head totally gone. I rang Andy back. No time for any pleasantries.

'Where the effing hell have you sent it?' I shouted.

Andy began to retrace his steps. He had done me a favour the week before, checking out Port Vale for me ahead of the Potteries derby. In the build-up to that game I and the team had stayed at Lilleshall Hall, the FA's coaching headquarters. Andy had faxed the details of Port Vale's free-kicks and corners to the office there, so I could use them as vital preparation in training. The idiot had pressed last number redial on his fax and the elusive resignation letter, it seemed, could now be sitting somewhere in the wrong hands, along with my fate. I needed to think and act quickly, before some bright spark efficiently phoned the Britannia Stadium to inform us that they had received the fax by mistake.

The Fax about Stoke

I called Lilleshall immediately, not knowing exactly where the fax had gone. Thankfully it turned out that it had gone to the FA's technical director, and a former gaffer of mine, Howard Wilkinson. He wasn't in the office that day and luckily his secretary, Mandy, hadn't seen the offending article yet, but she soon found it in the in-tray.

'Shred it,' I said. She did, and I lived to fight another day. I headed back to my office, relieved but thoroughly exhausted.

That evening in the board meeting the directors told me they were disappointed with the results and performances, but still wanted to give me the chance to turn it around. In my mind I wasn't convinced any more, but after the day I had had I was keeping quiet. But I did ask the board whether, if I could create any interest in any of my players in terms of sales, I could then bring in one or two fresh faces. They agreed.

The following night, Andy and I set out to watch Stockport at Edgeley Park. The pair of us had just been laughing about the whole missing fax episode when my phone rang. It was the reporter from the *Evening Sentinel*.

'I've got some bad news,' he said. 'We've received a fax.' My heart fell to my shoes and I looked across to Andy. If looks could kill I would have had a corpse beside me. My anger turned to despair as we both resignedly braced ourselves. Our secret was out after all.

'Oh, yeah. What fax is that then?' I bluffed.

In my head I could see the front page of the *Evening Sentinel* the next evening: 'Kamara Resigns.'

'You're not going to like this,' said the journalist, clearly enjoying what he was about to tell me, whether I wanted to hear it or not. 'It's the fax which says you will listen to offers for any of the players at the football club.'

I could hardly believe my ears. We were still in the clear. The reporter must have wondered why I sounded so delighted that he had uncovered this potentially devastating exclusive, but I knew it could have been a million times worse.

'Oh, that one,' I said. 'Yes, that's right, everyone is on the list, we need to listen to offers for them all.'

This was typical of what I had to deal with behind the scenes at Stoke. Some kind soul at the club had decided to feed confidential information to the local press for publication even before it managed to land in the hands of any other club's manager.

So, hey ho, the *Sentinel* got their back-page story. But it wasn't as explosive as Andy and I had feared. When he put the phone down we burst out laughing again. Speaking of confused and mixed-up faxes, I even offered Andy the chance to be Stoke mascot at the next home match, but he declined.

⚽ ⚽ ⚽ ⚽ ⚽ ⚽ ⚽

The laughter didn't last long. We beat QPR, which lifted us off the foot of the table, but it was our only win in three months. Dad was getting worse, and I wanted to spend my time with him. A week later, with Dad losing his fight for life, I called Jez Moxey and mentioned the possibility of me getting out. I was somewhat surprised to hear he was planning to go away in the middle of the season. Given that we were a team struggling against relegation and there was in-fighting at the club, I couldn't believe that the club's chief executive was planning to go abroad. I agreed to put the move on hold and wait until he got back.

True to his word, the day he got back Mr Moxey told me he had spoken to the board and they would agree to part company. I eventually called an end on Wednesday, 8 April 1998. We said it was by mutual consent, but I'd had enough and I quit. Stoke vice-chairman Keith Humphries claimed it was 'a nightmare for all concerned', but I couldn't be bothered to fight him or anyone else by then. Alan Durban was given the caretaker job for the remaining games, so he had the job he wanted so desperately. In a bizarre role reversal, Chic Bates took over as his assistant.

The day I packed it in was the same day I had received the keys for my new rented house in Stoke. It was right next door to my old pal Adrian Heath. I collected the keys in the morning, left my unpacked suitcases there and headed to work. Three hours later, I was out of a job and using the keys for the very first time, simply to empty the place. I didn't spend a single night there. I stayed for half an hour. I made a cup of tea and sat in absolute silence in the cold, furnished flat, just me and my thoughts. I am not a quitter but, just as I had after my final meeting with Geoffrey Richmond, I felt nothing but absolute relief that the nightmare was over. My number one concern as I left the flat for the last time was Dad.

My Stoke dream had died, and I knew that the Sierra Leone warrior who'd stood up for himself so many times when I was a kid was finally losing his last fight. Eleven days later he died. And so ends a horrible chapter.

CHAPTER TWENTY-FIVE
THE LAST WORD

A lot of people have asked me whether I'd fancy another shot at football management and the truth is, no. I love my role at Sky, where I get to be involved in the game every weekend. It's a pretty relaxed environment. I've got it easy if I'm being honest.

There have been some interesting offers, though. Gordon Gibb, Geoffrey Richmond's successor at Bradford, offered me the chance to manage the club again. They were in a financial muddle at the time, and although some rumours went around that I'd be taking the job and leaving Sky, my heart was never really in it.

Elsewhere, David Sullivan (who later became the owner of West Ham) asked me to take over at Birmingham City on a temporary basis in 2001. In fact it was more of a precautionary offer: their latest manager, Steve Bruce, had left Crystal Palace to move to City. Palace's chairman, Simon Jordan, was pretty unhappy about it and threatened legal action. David was concerned that this might lead to Bruce's suspension and was looking for a temp to stand in, just in case.

The Last Word

I decided it was only right to meet the Birmingham chairman, especially when he suggested we rendezvous at Spearmint Rhino in London for a chat. For those unfamiliar with the club, it's a salubrious spot in the West End where the surroundings are glamorous, the drinks are expensive and the girls take all their kit off.

Now, before you start raising your eyebrows, I was on my best behaviour, as ever. I reckoned my prospective employer might not have been too chuffed if I'd asked for a lap dance halfway through our discussion (from one of the girls, not David). At the end of it all I lost on both counts: I didn't get a dance and I didn't get the job. Birmingham and Simon Jordan sorted out their differences and Steve was allowed to embark on the difficult but ultimately pretty successful task of rebuilding Birmingham City.

I have had a few conversations with Fulham FC owner Mohamed Al Fayed over the years, and he always makes me feel very welcome at Craven Cottage. We have often discussed players, new signings or potential targets, and he is not afraid to throw a name at me and ask my opinion. I'll give my honest opinion, as I always do – I think people in the game appreciate my neutrality in these things.

When covering the West London derby game between Chelsea and Fulham for Sky at Stamford Bridge, I bumped into Mr Al Fayed in the tunnel before the game. We had one of our usual highly animated greetings, with hugs all around, big smiles and plenty of compliments coming my way about how much he enjoys both the funny side of my involvement on *Soccer AM* and the analysis on the Sunday morning show. I thought he was joking when he said, 'I like what you do on the television, why don't you come and work for me?' I laughed it off, thinking I hadn't come this far in my life to work in a corner shop, albeit the biggest in the world, but he was insistent and requested I meet him at Harrods the following week to discuss it further.

I was, understandably, both excited and intrigued as to what exactly his offer might be. I made my way to the store, nodding to the uniformed doorman as I entered – probably a Chelsea fan when he was wearing his civvies at the weekend. Inside I made my way through the hundreds of shoppers and tourists and carried on up the escalator, at the foot of which is the humbling shrine to Mr Al Fayed's son Dodi and Princess Diana. I then faced a door marked PRIVATE which I had been told to make for. After knocking on the door and giving security the clearance they required, I was taken into a waiting room, a room full of store nostalgia including historic photos of the shop, ornately flamboyant models of the store layout as it was at that time and collectables of brands the store has stocked. As I sat in one of the four grand thrones, Mr Al Fayed came in, at exactly five o'clock, as arranged. 'I am normally late, but today I made an exception,' he quipped. 'I wouldn't want to be late.' I wasn't sure if it was tongue-in-cheek or not, but none the less I was impressed.

He had done his best to make sure I understood that this part of West London revolved around him. His personality and his aura had certainly made a big impression on me, and he had me waiting all agog as to what he had to say. What I found out when we finally settled down to talk business was that he wanted me to become his new press secretary, which meant I would be the media face of the Harrods business empire, and also director of football at Fulham FC! The meeting lasted only an hour, after which I said goodbye to my new best mate, 'Big Al', and boarded the train back to Yorkshire. I had so much to think over on the journey.

When I got home, Anne was waiting. She quickly made us a cuppa and sat me down, excited at the prospect of being set free with her new Harrods Gold Card. She said 'Come on then tell me, what has Mr Al Fayed got in mind for you? Is it sales assistant? Is it doorman? Come on, I can't stand the suspense. Is it loo attendant? – well, they are rather posh, them loos! Or was he just wondering how fast you could do the Supermarket Sweep?'

'You may well scoff,' I replied, 'o ye of little faith! He would like me to be the new press secretary of Harrods.'

Anne began rolling around laughing. 'Never!' she squealed. 'You're pulling my leg! Did Jeremy Beadle pop out of the cupboard as well!' she chortled. 'Press secretary?!'

'Yes, and director of football,' I said sternly. My bottom lip had gone – Anne was killing me!

I swear to this day that the Fulham chairman had been genuine in his offer, and not just on the football side of it. I was genuinely hurt that Anne could not take the proposal seriously. But then again she is one of the few people who knows that I failed my eleven plus, and that I have yet to finish the crossword in the *Sun*.

Mr Unbelievable

The next day my first call was to Chris Coleman, who was Fulham manager at the time, and he was all for it. Chris really believed it would work and that we would get on.

'It's a fantastic idea,' he said. 'We'll have a great time.'

I agreed with him and was encouraged that it was something he wanted. I knew we could have worked together, no problem. It was the 'press secretary' role that was troubling me most of all. I was told by Mr Al Fayed to contact his former press secretary Michael Cole, and arrange to meet him to get an insight into what would be involved in being press secretary of a company like Harrods. When we spoke Michael suggested we go for lunch.

'Let's go and spend some of the chairman's money,' he said. I wouldn't be in it for the money, even though Mr Al Fayed had talked about paying me extremely well to take on the role, not to mention 'all expenses paid'.

With the Diana inquest due to start the following year, I wondered what role I would be expected to play alongside the Harrods chairman. That was a daunting prospect, which I thought about long and hard, and I took plenty of advice along the way before I eventually turned it down.

I was enjoying my work with Sky more than ever, which is where my heart was, no matter if the offer had had the power to turn my head. I had found a place at Sky that not only pushed me to learn and grow with each and every show, but that I genuinely loved being a part of. Let's be honest, I'm just Chris Kamara from Middlesbrough. Can you imagine watching a breaking news bulletin on Sky News and Eamonn Holmes saying, 'And now we go over live to the Harrods store in Knightsbridge for a company statement from spokesman Chris Kamara'? People would be sitting there thinking, 'What the hell does he know?' I am sure many people would still expect me to open with 'Unbelievable, Eamonn ...'

That was certainly on my boss Vic Wakeling's mind when I told him of the offer. I felt I owed it to Vic to speak to him about the proposal before I had made a decision, as he had been very good to me in my television career, and my television career was really the only reason Mr Al Fayed had made me this offer in the first place. Vic was one of the main reasons I turned it down. I didn't go in looking to get a new deal from Sky, the way most players do at the first sign of interest from another club. It wasn't about that.

Vic warned me I might be out of my depth acting as a press secretary to the store and Mr Al Fayed. Could I handle reading out carefully prepared statements, the contents of which are going to be reflected in share prices, and making sure that every word I said was in line with company policy? He said it just wouldn't be me. I think he was right; there would be no adlibbing, no giggling, and certainly no mention of beavers, even though I wouldn't be at all surprised if they sold them in the Harrods pets department.

I can't tell you how flattered I was by Mr Al Fayed's amazing offer – well, I can because I just did. I can't help thinking what Mam and Dad would have made of it. It would have been my dear old dad's turn to say 'Unbelievable!' As for my mam, long after the days of having to beg down the street for bread and milk from the neighbours, she would have been able to boast that her son worked in the most famous corner shop in the world.

☻ ☻ ☻ ☻ ☻ ☻ ☻ ☻

Anne and I had taken possession of our own corner shop, 'Kamara's Off Licence', only three weeks before my family and many friends travelled to Swindon on 29 May 1982 for the wedding of the decade. We were forfeiting the traditional honeymoon holiday to stay at home and get the business up and running in the close season. Mam and Dad made the journey, of course, along with a couple of Mam's sisters, Auntie Gwenny and Auntie Joan, and my sister, Maria, and her son, Jonathan. My pals from back home in Middlesbrough – Bernie, Skipper, Ricky, Tommo and Dowlo, to name but a few – made their maiden voyage to Swindon to attend. How I convinced Anne that they didn't need to book a hotel, that they could stay with us, I don't know! And 'Chuckie', Peter Conley, who was my best man, arrived a week ahead of the rest, having made it clear that he was going to take his job seriously and stay with me in the run-up to my special day.

I thought I had been clever, insisting the wedding date came immediately at the end of the season, so all my pals from the footballing world could attend before they scattered for their well-earned family holidays. I had overlooked one very impor- tant thing – England were playing Scotland the afternoon of our wedding day in a Home International fixture. This was a very important annual event back then, and a rare live tele- vised football match.

The Last Word

Given that we had to say ours vows at three o'clock – kick-off time – I agreed with Anne that I would not watch the game live! Which I thought was very good of me, but there was no way I could totally miss it, of course. One of the best man's duties that day was to make sure, whatever happened, that the video recorder was set and the game was taped.

It was a lovely day all round. The weather was glorious, and it was fantastic to see friends past and present from the footballing world representing my time at Portsmouth, Swindon and Brentford. Fred Callaghan, manager of Brentford, even laid on a minibus to make the 160-mile round journey, bringing players and staff for the celebrations. Ron 'Chopper' Harris, famous ex-Chelsea hardman, was Fred's assistant at Brentford, and he piled into the minibus with the others, including a great friend of ours, Christine Mathews, who was club secretary at Griffin Park. Director Gerry Potter and the groundsman, Alex, also tumbled out of the bus when it pulled up – I started wondering who else was going to pop out of the back doors!

Alan Ingledew and his wife Carolyn came, and I was so pleased to see him there, the man who had helped me so much in my early days of football. Hazel, my first landlady from Portsmouth, and her husband Keith came, as did another two of my lifelong friends from my Pompey days, Jack and Nellie Holmes.

Anne's friends and relatives were there in force, and I reckon her younger brother Mike, who was to become such a good pal of mine, had his first hangover the next day, he had enjoyed it so much.

Mr Unbelievable

Both sets of parents loved the day, Anne's mum and dad, Sylv and Roy, and my own mam and dad, Irene and Albert. Dad insisted the DJ played 'The Rivers of Babylon' (quite a few times, actually) so he could boogie away into his own little world – that's when we knew he was at his happiest. There's a fantastic picture of me and Dad beaming like Cheshire cats and looking very dapper in our wedding suits, each with a cigar in hand.

Anne and I were so pleased that everything had gone off well, and she was still looking forward to a wedding night to remember. And she did get one – though not quite what she was hoping for, I guess.

During the day I had given strict instructions to all and sundry not to let on to me the score of the England match. As we prepared to leave the reception for home that night, I pulled Chuckie aside and I asked if he was certain he had definitely recorded the game, and he assured me he had.

'Good,' I said. 'We'll watch that later.'

'Later?' he asked incredulously. 'On your wedding night?'

'Don't worry,' I said, ever the optimist. 'Anne won't mind. We'll just skip through it and then you go off and meet up with the lads out on the town in Swindon for some more partying. Just don't let on to Anne at the moment ...'

As soon as we got back to the off-licence that night, the best man was in tow, helping to carry our wedding gifts. Anne went off through to the shop to check all was OK and that it was locked up properly. That was the cue for me and Chuckie to race through into the lounge and flick the video on, and we started to watch the game, which England won 1-0 (a Paul

Mariner goal), but were not even conscious when a rather disgruntled Anne disappeared upstairs for the night.

As she passed through the lounge she glanced lovingly at her knight in shining armour – sorry, her comatose slob of a 'husband' – who just a few hours before had pledged to love, honour and obey her. I was slumped there, snoring, mouth open, in front of the television, but it is a sight she has grown used to. She was later to discover that the TV remote control is my best friend. Best man Chuckie was in a similar pose. No wonder she thought, 'Is this as good as it gets?' as she headed up to the master bedroom alone.

To make matters worse, Chuckie was supposed to either meet our mates in the Brunel Rooms nightclub or at least wait up to let them in when they returned from their long day and night on the razzle. I couldn't believe it when I was told the next morning that poor Anne had been woken by their frantic knocking, when they failed to rouse Chuckie from his slumber, and she had to let them in. They'd been singing and dancing round the streets and only managed to keep the volume down when the blushing bride opened the door to greet them.

Fancy putting a bride through that on her wedding night – Chuckie was well out of order!

I am sure all you guys out there understand my passion for football, and for all you ladies who think I am scandalous, please remember that football is my life and I love it. And to my wife Anne, sorry. I hope I have made up for our disastrous wedding night along the way.

I can't live without football, but my home life with Anne and our boys Ben and Jack means everything to me. Following my humble upbringing I could never have imagined having two such wonderful sons. I am so proud of them, and not only are they my sons, they are my two best pals.

I know my place is in the football world. I can't think of anywhere else I'd like to be on a Saturday, other than in a precarious gantry in the roof of a Premiership stadium, with some rain, a mob of football supporters banging drums behind me, a blundered goal-line clearance, a wonder strike from a Ukrainian kid with an unpronounceable name, and lots and lots of football.

In a word, my life so far has been Unbelievable!